An Introduction to the History of the Assyrian Church

or the Early Christians of the Sassanid Persian Empire, 100-640 A. D.

By W. A. Wigram

Published by Pantianos Classics

ISBN-13: 978-1-78987-110-4

First published in 1909

Contents

Dedication v
Preface v
Synchronistic Table vii
List of Authorities ix

Chapter One 11
   1. The Sassanid Empire 11
   2. The Foundation of the Church 13

Chapter Two - The Church Under Arsacid Kings 17

Chapter Three - The Episcopate of Papa 21

Chapter Four - The Great Persecution of Sapor II 29

Chapter Five - Reorganization of the Church - Council of Mar Isaac (410) 39

Chapter Six - The Councils of Yahb-Alaha and Dad-Ishu 52
   I. The Council of Yahb-Alaha 52
   II. The Persecution of Bahram V 57
   III. The Council of Dad-Ishu 61

Chapter Seven - The Patriarchate of Dad-Ishu--Persecution of Yezdegerd II 64

Chapter Eight - Bar-Soma and Acacius 72

Chapter Nine - Disorder and Reform - Patriarchates of Babai, Silas, Mar Aba 88

Chapter Ten - The Patriarchates of Joseph, Ezekiel, Ishu-Yahb I, Sabr-Ishu (552-604) 107

Chapter Eleven - The State of the Church in the Sixth Century. 115

Chapter Twelve - The Vacancy in the Patriarchate--Struggle with Monophysitism--608-628 126

Chapter Thirteen - Official Christology of the Assyrian Church 136

    Note II - The Assyrian Church and the Council of Chalcedon 154

Chapter Fourteen - Last Efforts at Reconciliation--Embassy of Ishl-Yahb and the Sahdona Episode 157

Footnotes 164

Dedication

TO BENYAMIN MAR SHIMUN,

PRESENT "HOLDER OF THE THRONE OF MAR ADAI"

AND

PATRIARCH OF THE "ASSYRIAN" CHURCH

I DEDICATE THIS

RECORD OF THE WORK OF HIS SPIRITUAL ANCESTORS

Preface

This essay is an attempt at the filling of what appeared to the writer to be a distinct void in English ecclesiastical histories; and to give some account of a branch of the Church unknown to all except a very few students, during the most critical and important period of its history.

No one can be more conscious than the writer how much his work has suffered and been handicapped from the circumstances of its composition. The book was necessarily written away from any libraries except what was contained in the author's study; at a place where the procuring of any pamphlet required might take any time from six to twelve weeks; and where on one occasion the consultation of an authority implied waiting till a chance offered of making a laborious and dangerous journey of fourteen days' duration.

If it gains anything in vividness, and in grasp of the difficulties of those of whom it treats, from the fact that it was written among their modern descendants, whose circumstances have changed but little during the course of ages--this may be one compensation among many disadvantages.

The writer has throughout used for the Church in question the name "Assyrian." There is no historical authority for this name; but the various appellations given to the body by various writers ("Easterns," Persians, Syrians, Chaldeans, Nestorians) are all, for various reasons, misleading to the English reader.

To the ordinary English Churchman of today "the Eastern Church" is the Church to the east of him-viz. the Greek Orthodox; the Church of the old "Eastern Roman Empire," of Constantinople, with her great daughter, the Russian Church. The name "Eastern," however, as applied by those Greeks, meant the Church to the east of them-beyond the oriental frontier of the Roman Empire.

To speak of "the Persian Church" is to do as much violence to ancient facts, as to speak to-day of "the Turkish Church" (meaning thereby some one Christian *melet* in the Ottoman Empire) is to disregard modern facts.

"Syrian," to an Englishman, does not mean "a Syriac-speaking man"; but a man of that district between Antioch and the Euphrates where Syriac was the vernacular once, but which is Arabic speaking to-day, and which was never the country of the "Assyrian" Church. "Chaldaean" would suit admirably; but it is put out of court by the fact that in modern use it means only those members of the Church in question who have abandoned their old fold for the Roman obedience: and "Nestorian" has a theological significance which is not justified. Thus it seemed better to discard all these, and to adopt a name which has at least the merit of familiarity to most friends of the Church to-day.

The representation of the Syriac problem of men and places in English, presents a problem almost as incapable of ideal solution as that of finding a name for the Church; and we make no claim to consistency in our practice. As a rule we have transliterated; marking compounds by a hyphen which has no existence in Syriac (e.g. Ishu-yahb). But where the name has a western version (Greek or biblical), which for any reason is familiar to the western reader, we have employed it.[1] Few English readers would recognize in "Khizgi'il" the familiar "Ezekiel"; and though most students of Church history have a bowing acquaintance with Ibas of Edessa, how many would understand who was meant by "Yahba"? Greek versions are usually barbarous etymologically; and their historians are not even consistent-who without special study can recognize Cyrus and Chosroes as the same name? But at least they are familiar and are more euphonious than most Syriac names in English letters.

Van,
Turkey in Asia, 1909.

Synchronistic Table

Date	Assyrian Patriarch	Persian King	Roman Emperor
309	Papa	Sapor II	Constantine
328	Shimun bar Saba'i		
337			Constantius
340	Shah-dolt		
346	Bar B'ashmin		
347	(vacancy)		
361			Julian
363			Jovian
364			Valens
379		Ardashir II	Theodosius 1
383	Tamuza	Sapor II	
388		Bahram IV	
395	Qaiuma		Arcadius
399	Isaac	Yezdegerd I	
408			Theodosius II
411	Akha		
415	Yahb-Alaha I		
420	M'ana	Bahram V	
421	Dad-Ishu		
438		Yezdegerd II	
451			Marcian
457	Babowai	Piroz	Leo
474			Zeno
485	Acacius	Balas	
488		Kubad (1st reign)	

491			Anastasius
496	Babai	Zamasp	
498		Kobad (2nd reign)	
505	Silas		
518			Justin I
523	("duality")		
527			Justinian
531		Chosroes I	
539	Paul		
540	Mar Aba		
552	Joseph		
565			Justin II
570	Ezekiel		
578		Hormizd IV	Tiberius
582	Ishu-yahb I		Maurice
590		Chosroes II	
596	Sabr-Ishu		
602			Phocas
604	Gregory		
608	(vacancy)		
610			Heraclius
628	Ishu-yahb II	(anarchy)	
632		Yezdegerd III	
640		Khalifate	Constantine III
644	Mar Imeh		

List of Authorities

TITLE OF BOOK	REFERENCE IN FOOTNOTES
History of Mshikha-Zca (Sources syriaques, vol. i., ed. Mingana).	M.-Z.
Acta Sanctorum, 6 vols., ed. Bedjan.	Bedj.
Histoire de Jabalaha et de trois autres palriarches, etc., Bedjan.	IV Catholici.
Synodicon Orientale, ed. Chabot.	S. O.
Greg, Bar-Hebraei Chronicon Eccles. III. Primates Orientis, ed. Abbeloos and Lamy.	B.-H.
John of Ephesus, Ecclesiastical Hist., ed. Cureton.	John of Ephesus.
Amir et Sliba De Patriarchus Nestorianorum.	Liber Turris.
Die von Guidi hurausgegebene syrische Chronik, ed. Noldeke.	Guidi
Chronicle of Zachariah of Mitylene, ed. Hamilton and Brooks.	Zach., Mit.
Ecclesiastical Histories of Socrates.	
" " Sozomen.	
" " Theodoret.	
" " Evagarius.	
Book of Governors (Thomas of Marga), ed. Budge.	T. of M.
Mar Babai, "De unione" (MS. consulted).	Babai
Ishu-yahb, "Letters" (ed. Duval, *Corpus scriptorum syrorum*).	Ishu-yahb, Letters.
Tabari, *Gesch. der Sassaniden* (ed. Noldeke).	Tabari.
Assemani, *Bibliotheca Orientalis,* 4 vols.	Ass., B. O.

Among other books consulted, the following are the most important:

Labourt, *Christianisme dans l'empire perse.*
Chabot, *kole de Nisibe, son hisloire et ses statuts.*
Duval, *Histoire d'Edesse.*
Coussen, *Martyrius-Sahdona: Leben and Werke.*
Chabot, *De S. Isaaco Ninevita.*
Hoffmann, *Syrische Martyrer.*

Hefele, *Councils.*
Bethune-Baker, *Nestorius and his Teaching.*
Rawlinson, *Seventh Oriental Monarchy.*
Christiensen, *L'Empire des Sassanides.*
Bury, *Later Roman Empire.*
Ceiseler, *Ecclesiastical Hist.*

Chapter One

1. The Sassanid Empire

IN the year A.D. 225, when a revolution in Mesopotamia substituted the Sassanids of Persia for the Arsacids of Parthia as the rulers of what Roman writers called "the East" (meaning thereby all the countries of which they had practical knowledge to the east of their own border), dwellers in the country concerned regarded it as simply the rise of one more in the series of empires that rose and passed away in those lands. All the difference that it made to them, at the moment, was that the local governor was called "Marzban" or Marquis, instead of "King." From long usage, they were accustomed to be regarded by their rulers much in the same light as they themselves regarded their bees; and they took so little interest in the matter that the wise men of the countryside could see in the same event a warning of the downfall of a kingdom, and of the production of a good crop of honey.

As a matter of fact, the revolution of 225 was not merely the exchange of one loose federation of kings, for another a little better organized; it was the revival of a nation that had a great history behind it, and the aspiration to make that history live again. The Persian Empire had indeed fallen before Alexander in 300 B.C., and had remained in more or less uneasy subjection to his Seleucid successors, or to the semi-Hellenized Arsacids, who took their place. Still, the national life of Persia had not passed away; and after 500 years the opportunity came, and it rose again. Its ambition, however, was not to form a new empire, but to revive an old one; and it claimed to be the lawful heir, not of the Arsacid kingdom of modern Mesopotamia and Persia, but of the Achaemenid Empire of Xerxes and Darius, stretching from the Hindu-Kush to the Mediterranean. It was the dream of the Sassanids to revive this empire; and the dream was so far a national aspiration also, that a warlike king could always rouse the enthusiasm of the nation by a challenge to the Roman Emperor to "withdraw from the inheritance of the ancestors of the King of kings."

The greatest of the Sassanid house, Chosroes II, actually realized that dream for a moment, when in his great war against Phocas and Heraclius he pushed back the limits of the Roman Empire till it hardly extended beyond the walls of Constantinople; and the ruins of the palace at Mashita,[2] in the land of Moab, are a testimony that this king did not intend his occupation of Roman territory to be, as was the case on some other occasions, a mere raid. During the years that the watchers at Constantinople saw the lights of the Persian camp at Chalcedon, practically the whole of the elder Persian Empire was actually subject to the ruler of the newer one.

We are completely accustomed to look at this period from the Roman standpoint, and to think of these wars as unimportant episodes in a history of which the main interest lies elsewhere. But it may be useful to remember for a moment how they appeared to an empire which was by no means the barbarous power that we are accustomed to conceive.

It is obvious that, when such aspirations were entertained, the relations between the Empire of Rome and that of the East must have been normally hostile; and that only truces of more or less uncertainty could break a perennial state of war. Lest, however, the imperial aspirations of one of the two powers should be insufficient to provide a proper amount of fighting, fate had also seen to it that there should be two perpetually open questions, either of which could afford at any time a decent *casus belli*. These were, the control of Armenia, and the question of the frontier provinces. Armenia-that unhappy territory whose office in history it has been to be "a strife unto her neighbours" during such periods as she could claim some shadow of independence, and a problem to her rulers during the periods when she was avowedly subject to somebody--formed a "buffer state" between the Romans and Persians for most of their joint frontiers. The question, who was to control this kingdom, was one that constantly gave rise to friction; and the Armenians, as a general rule, seem to have employed themselves in intriguing against the suzerain of the moment with the emissaries of the rival power.

Where the two empires "marched," which was the case only in the northwest of Mesopotamia, another question was open. Here, a comparatively narrow belt of fertile territory intervenes between the mountains of modern Kurdistan and the desert of Arabia, The power that held this district, and with it the great fortress of Nisibis, was somewhat in the position of the holder of Alsace-Lorraine. It had control of a gate which might admit its armies into the territory of the enemy, or which might be effectively shut in the face of an invader. Hence both, parties claimed the five small, and otherwise not very important, provinces into which this country was divided, and neither could be content to see them in the hands of the other.

With all these causes for war ready to hand, it is not surprising that only unusual combinations of circumstances, like the simultaneous accession of two peace-loving monarchs, or simultaneous invasion of both empires by the barbarians who threatened the northern frontiers of either, could keep their relations friendly.

It was not only as an empire that Persia thus rose from the dead in the third century; it rose also as a religion, of a definite and militant type. The Persia of Achaemenid days had accepted Zoroaster's reforms of the ancient fire-worship as a national faith; and that religion had been preserved by the nation as its heritage, and treasured as only a subject nation can treasure its national faith (if, indeed, it had not been, as is possible, the force that had kept the nation alive) during the 5oo years of dependence. Now, when Persia rose to power once more, their religion rose with them; and the Sassanian

Empire had a definitely established Magian Church, loyal membership of which was the test and condition of loyalty to the empire.

This religion had its system of theology and its sacred books. It had its priestly caste, the Magians; who were at once one of the seven great clans of the nation, and an organized hierarchy under their "Mobeds" or prelates, with the "Mobed Mobedan" at the head of all. The fire-temple stood in every village; the shrine in every orthodox house. Education was in the hands of the priests, and considerable temporal power and large endowments. The Shah-in-Shah himself dared not offend them, lest mischief should befall him.

The Sassanian kingdom, then, was no mushroom growth, with much magnificence but no strength. It was an empire, organized in an efficient way; whose provincial governors (though, when of royal blood, they might bear the honorary title of King) were kept well under the control of the Shah-in-Shah.

The empire was inhabited by a tolerably homogeneous nation, as far as its central provinces went; though a fringe of sub-kings (Armenian, Arab, Turk) ruled districts round its borders. It had a national religion, with an organized hierarchy, and it could fight at least on even terms with the whole power of Rome. One Roman Emperor, Valerian, died a captive at the Persian Court. Another, Julian, fell in battle against it; and his successor could only purchase his release by an ignominious peace. It endured for 400 years, and when it fell, its organization and machinery were simply taken over by its successor, the Khalifate of Baghdad.

In the following pages we propose to trace, not the history of the kingdom, but the story of the Church of Christ within its borders; the Church of Assyria, of the "Chaldaean Patriarchate," or, as it was usually called by Greek, or even by Syriac writers, "The Church of the East." Broadly speaking, the Christian Church, as it existed to the east of the Eastern border of the Roman Empire.

2. The Foundation of the Church

The Christian Church was a thing that the Sassanids found existing-when they established themselves in the country, and one that was already widely spread, and organized on apostolic lines. This fact was of considerable importance for the future relations of the two, for the struggle would have been very hard before the Church could have established herself, *de novo,* in a Zoroastrian kingdom. The difficulty would have been comparable to that found in the spreading of Christianity in Fez or Morocco at the present time. As it existed, however, prior to the rise of the dynasty, it was, so to speak, taken over by it, as a part of the new empire; and when the relations between the two came to be formalized, it was on the assumption that Christianity had as much a legal right to exist in the Sassanid Empire, as it has in a Moslem kingdom like the Ottoman Empire of to-day. In each case, this qualified toleration was accorded to it on the same ground, viz. that the Christian religion was one that the dominant faith found existing at the time when it conquered the country.

The Church was widely spread; it extended from the Mountains of Kurdistan (for this last refuge of the descendants of these Christians was apparently not then evangelized) to the Persian Gulf, and was governed by "more than twenty bishops,"[3] whose sees were distributed over all the country named. It is to be noted., however, that though the bishoprics were thus widely scattered, there was as yet no bishop in the capital city, Seleucia-Ctesiphon, a fact that was to have some importance in the history of the body. Nisibis, too (at this time a Roman city still), had no bishop, a fact due probably to the circumstance that it was a purely military station. It is, however, a curious coincidence that the two most important thrones in the later history of "the East" should both have been founded late in its development.

The question now arises, how and when did this Church come into being?

It has long been an admitted fact that the lands of Mesopotamia and Adiabene, and in fact the whole of what we may call by anticipation the Sassanid Persian Empire, received the gospel from teachers whose head-quarters were at Edessa. The little kingdom of Osrhoene had but a precarious independence during the brief period of its existence; still that independence was sufficient to give, for as long as it lasted, a distinctive character to the Christianity that existed in its capital, and made it an appropriate "nursing mother" to the two national Churches founded by teachers who came from thence, those, namely, of Armenia and Persia.[4] When the Edessene Church vas merged in that ecclesiastical circle that developed into the Patriarchate of Antioch, one at least of these "daughters" was strong enough to stand alone; and the circumstances of its infancy probably contributed to give it that instinct of independence that was always so marked a feature of its life.

The "Church of the Easterns" was the daughter, not of Antioch, but of Edessa, and was never included in the Patriarchate of the former city.

While, however, the Edessene origin of the Church of the East is admitted (and indeed the laws of geography postulate it, for it is hard to get from Antioch to Mesopotamia without passing through Edessa), the date is a matter more open to dispute. Syriac tradition is clear enough on the point, of course. According to this, Mar Adai (who is variously described as either the Apostle Thaddeus, or as one of "the seventy") came during the first century to Edessa and planted Christianity there. His disciple, Mari, starting from thence, became the true evangelist of Persia; descending even into Fars, until he "smelt the smell of the Apostle Thomas,"[5] the traditional evangelist of India. Modern writers, and particularly Westphai and M. Labourt (to whom all students of Persian Church history owe much for his painstaking work), treat these traditions very cavalierly. While admitting the possibility of the real existence of Adai and Mari, as evangelists of wholly uncertain date, they refuse to admit the presence of any organized Christianity in Persia before Sassanid days.

They sweep out of existence the older Catholici (whose names and biographies occur in the Chronicles of Bar-Hebraeus and Mari Ibn Sulieman, of the thirteenth and twelfth centuries respectively), and date the origin of the Church in the latter half of the third century; making Papa,. Bishop of Seleucia about the year 3oo, its first figure of any reality and weight.

With much of this criticism the writer fully agrees; the episcopate of Papa is a definite and important turning-point in the history of the Church, though not the starting-point which they incline to make it. The portentous length of Episcopate assigned to him by both medieval historians[6] is a sign of confusion only, and most of his predecessors are as apocryphal as the copes with which Mari Ibn Sulieman carefully endues each one. Moreover such of them as had some real existence were not, as we shall see, Catholici (i.e. archbishops) of Seleucia. Still, tradition in the East has a way of justifying itself, at least as regards the main facts which it asserts, as evidence accumulates; and a work has recently come to light that goes far to *combler la lacune* between Mari and Papa, which Al. Labourt laments. This is the *History of the Bishops of Adiabene* (Khaydab), a work composed in the sixth century by one Mshikha-Zca (Christ conquers), a scholar of the great college of Nisibis and a native of the province whose history he writes. The author frankly declares himself to be only a compiler, and refers to earlier and now lost authorities.[7]

Mshikha-Zca plainly acknowledges Adai as the apostle of Adiabene and Assyria, and states that he ordained his disciple, Pqida, as first bishop of that district, in the year A.D. 104.[8] Pqida was by birth the slave of a Magian, and was of that faith. He had apparently gained his personal freedom; and he had been converted by the sight of a miracle wrought by Mar Adai, who was then travelling and teaching in the land. He had to undergo some persecution from the family (not from his owner), for his "apostasy"; but escaping from them, remained the personal disciple of his master for five years; at the end of which time he was consecrated as stated, apparently just before the death of Ajar Adai.

In the face of this record, there seems no reasonable ground for refusing to admit the absolutely historical character of Adai; or the rank which ancient tradition accords to him of founder of the "Church of the East," and possibly of that of Edessa and Armenia also. If, however, our author establishes the existence of Mar Adai as a real fact and not as a figment only, he at the same time makes it almost impossible to identify him with Thaddeus, the Apostle of Christ. Traditionally, we regard the Twelve as all adult men, with one possible exception, during the period of their association with the Redeemer. A man full grown in the year, 30 could hardly have travelled about, as Adai is represented as doing, in the years 100-104. That he should have been one of the "seventy" is less impossible; and a tradition that has justified itself in much has a right to a respectful hearing in its other statements. If we may regard Mar Adai as a youth of sixteen or seventeen when "sent out" as one of the seventy disciples, he would have been hard on ninety (no impossible age) when called to his rest in 104.

In the case of Mari the supposed disciple of Adai, and the evangelist, not so much of Adiabene as of Khuzistan, and in a less degree of Seleucia and the "Aramaean province," we are at present on less certain ground. The *Acta S. Maris* which we have to-day is certainly not the contemporary document it professes to be; it is not earlier than the sixth century, and possibly later still. Even if contemporary with the *History of the Bishops of Adiabene*, it is far inferior to it as an authority, the one being a history, and the other a piece of hagiography.

Mshikha-Zca makes no reference whatever to Mari in his work, and his editor is inclined, on that ground, to regard the saint as purely legendary. This we consider too stern a judgment. Even if the Acta be ruled out of court altogether as an authority, we have to account for the fact that from the fifth century and before it (i. e. from before the time of the composition of the Acta) this Church has looked back to Adai and Atari as its founders.[9]

How came they, on the legendary hypothesis, to select an absolutely unknown name as that of their founder, when such an one as St. Thomas, who traditionally passed through the country on his way to India, was ready to their hands?[10] That the life contains much legend (even apart from some of the miraculous episodes) need not be doubted. But it also contains matter that a mere hagiographer would scarcely ascribe to his hero, unless he were following some older tradition or authority. The saint's discouragement, and request to his Edessene senders for his recall; his finding Christian traders in Khuzistan; his comparative failure in Seleucia itself, where, as we now know, Christianity gained no strength till late in the third century; and his peaceful death at the obscure shrine of Dor Koni;--all these have the ring of truth rather than of invention; and the most conspicuous "blunder" in the book, namely, the fact that Papa, the fourth-century bishop, is declared to have been the immediate successor of Mari as Bishop of Seleucia and Catholicos of the Church of the Persian Empire,[11] admits, as we shall see, of a natural explanation.

We incline then to admit, not only the traditional founding of this Church by Mar Adai at the close of the first century, but also its extension from Adiabene southwards by the teaching of Mari and his companions, as well founded in fact, though embroidered by later traditions.

It remains to sketch the history of this Church as far as our authorities admit, for the first 200 years of its existence, until it emerges into clearer light at the beginning of the fourth century.

Chapter Two - The Church Under Arsacid Kings

THE history of the Church from the time of Adai to that of Papa, or, roughly, from the year 100 to 300, is, on the whole, one of quiet progress, unmarked either by the quarrels or organized persecutions that were to chequer its later history; and unmarked, too, by the rise of any such striking personalities as we find, for instance, to the story of the African' Church, or, in a less degree, in our own. Adai is too shadowy a person to have, for us at any rate, the charm of an Aidan; and not even the inventiveness of his chronicler can give to Mari's life the romance that encircles Columba's. The conditions of the life of a subject *melet*[12] in an oriental empire do not tend to produce very striking characters in normal times.

At first, at any rate, the body was not formidable enough to excite the State to persecute; and the rule of the Parthian kings was always tolerant. They appear to have favoured a sort of religious eclecticism themselves, and to have recognized all creeds among their subjects; though there is some evidence that the political power of the Magian clan won for their religion a favoured position. Still, the Government was so far indifferent that about the year 160 Abraham, then Bishop of Adiabene, had good hopes of procuring a formal edict of toleration from the then King, Valges III; and apparently only failed in his object because the outbreak of war with the Romans put such a trifling circumstance out of the King's mind. As things turned out, the Church had much to suffer before obtaining her "Edict of Milan" from the Shah-in-Shah 250 years later.

The faith of the people which the Christian teaching had to combat (as far as it is shown by the chronicles of Syriac writers, and by the collections of magical formulae and invocations which still survive) seems to have been the old idolatry of Assyria and Babylon, "run to seed" in a strange fashion, and sunk into the worship of sacred trees, and a star worship which was no higher than a very debased astrology.[13]

Both in Mesopotamia and in Asia Minor, as probably in Egypt (thou h not in Persia), the old faiths were outworn. Fence it was that nations who, whatever their faults, do not lack the religious instinct, turned so readily to the new light that came to them from. Judaea; and embraced it with a readiness that makes the progress of Christianity in these lands at once so startlingly rapid, and so undeniably sound.

Among the Zoroastrian fire-worshippers the advance of the Faith was far less rapid than among the pagans, and it was here that the Church found its most formidable opponents. Still, it could win converts here also; and (as is often the case) men won from this most obstinate of foes were the best worth winning, and included some of the Church's greatest and most saintly bishops and martyrs. In these early days, however, at least in the north, this Zoroastrian hostility was that of a powerful corporation, rather than of a national faith. Its stronghold was in Persia proper, not in Mesopotamia, and there it was not, as yet, directly attacked by Christianity. In its native land it has left abundant traces of its former supremacy, and has not even yet wholly passed away.

As a corporation, and one enjoying apparently a measure of royal favour, it had enough power to persecute; and was, of course, specially ready to seek as victims men who were converts from it to any other faith, Thus Samson,[14] the successor of Pqida as Bishop of Arbela, died a martyr at the hands of Magians in 123-the first man to die for the Christian faith in a land that has supplied, probably, more members of *candidatus exercitus* than any other country. A little later, Isaac,[15] his successor, converted a Zoroastrian of the name of Raqbokt, who was an "Agha" of some importance in Adiabene. The Mobeds at once sought to kill the "apostate," but when the men dispatched for the purpose of assassinating him arrived at the house of their victim they found him away from home, and had to turn their wrath on the bishop, whom they captured and confined for some time "in a dark pit." It would seem that this was a usual way of punishing apostates from the worship of the sun, for it was also employed in the case of Pqida by the family of that convert.

It is specially stated,[16] too, that during the episcopate of Noah (163-179) many Christians fell away from the faith under pressure of a persecution of a singularly dastardly kind--the kidnapping or "capture" of their daughters. This consisted (and consists still in the same lands) in the carrying off of Christian girls from their families as either concubines or slaves. Then, once let some sort of confession of Zoroastrianism--or of Islam--be procured from the victim, and how can the "convert" be thereafter abandoned to "a false faith"? Few of such captives can find the strength for a life-long confession of their Lord--a confession none the less meritorious for being absolutely unknown. But some such hidden saints have existed, and do still exist.

This, however, was not a State persecution, such as the Church in the West had to endure repeatedly during the same period; it arose from the weakness, not from the malevolence, of the Government, which would not take trouble or run a risk for the sake of doing right by so unimportant a person as a mere *rayat*. When the agent of persecution is specified at all, it is always the Mobeds, or members of the Magian clan.[17] Persecution ordered by the Government, and carried out by its agents, is not encountered till the days of the Sassanids; and even then, not until the conversion of Constantine-and the adoption of Christianity as the official faith of the Roman Empire-had made all Christians in the rival kingdom politically suspect. Syrian historians state emphatically that there was no formal persecution in the East until its day was over in the West.[18]

Thus Adiabene became a haven of comparative safety for Christians during persecutions over the border, and many took refuge there and made it their home. The presence of these immigrants, and in later days of large "captivities" brought from Western Syria by the Sassanid kings, formed an important element in the life of the Church, breaking its isolation, and keeping its thought more or less in touch with the growth of theology in the West; though, as we shall see, this touch was by no means always a close one.

Easterns, too, went westwards at times, for there was, of course, a good deal of commercial intercourse between the two empires. One man in particular, Noah, by birth a Jew of Anbar [1](Piroz-Sapor), was converted to Christianity while on a pilgrimage to Jerusalem with his parents, and became the disciple and successor of the Bishop Abraham. Abd-Mshikha,[19] too (Bishop of Arbela 190-225), embraced Christianity when at Antioch for purposes of education; and came back a Christian to his own country, where his new faith apparently roused no resentment among his own family.

Persecution being thus local and sporadic, and partly personal at times in its origin (arising out of such incidents as Magian resentment at the "apostasy" of the Agha Raqbokt), it could often be checked by personal influence. In at least one instance the reverence felt by all creeds for the personality of the Bishop Abraham brought about a cessation of persecution locally about the year 160; and another bishop, Abel, was particularly famous as a reconciler of disputes between heathens and Christians.

Occasionally Christians had to suffer, in common with all inhabitants of the country, from wars and tumults. The Arsacid Empire had never, it would seem, the strength and organization of the Sassanid, and a weak central power meant, of course, a disturbed kingdom. Roman invasions made apparently little mark, or perhaps are regarded by our historians as part of the course of nature, like an occasional flood; and are therefore received as signposts by which to date a chronicle, rather than as causes for astonishment or complaint. Less regular invasions, however, are noted. Thus, during the second century, the descent of hordes of robbers "from the mountains of Kardu"[20] is recorded, as if to show us that the Kurd of the period was still the turbulent fellow that Xenophon found him to be, and that he is today. A royal army had to be sent to put a stop to the inroad; and it was the good service rendered during the campaign by the Christian, Agha Raqbokt, that rendered it impossible for the Magians to proceed against him at the moment. It was his local knowledge that enabled the royalist general to extricate his army with credit from an awkward situation. Possibly the Magi might not have forgotten their quarrel, but the Agha was killed in action before the conclusion of the campaign.

A little later, about 190,[21] a rebellion of Persians in Khorassan foreshadowed their return to power a generation later. The rebellion was put down by Valges IV, not without difficulty; and Narses, King of Adiabene, who was apparently a Persian sympathizer, paid the penalty of his treason by being drowned in the Zab. His country was plundered as punishment for the crime of its king, and all creeds suffered alike.

These, however, are but the ordinary troubles of an oriental kingdom; and on the whole it will be seen that under the Arsacids Christianity had a fair field, and came as near to complete toleration as was possible at the time. Hence it spread rapidly; particularly during the long and peaceful episcopate of Abd-Mshikha (190-225). Many churches were then built; and even we are told-monasteries founded, though this must surely be an anticipation of later events.[22] Bishoprics must certainly have multiplied steadily, though Mshikha-Zca, our sole reliable authority for this period, gives only the history of Adiabene, and the succession only of the Bishops of Arbela. The date of the foundation of other sees outside the province does not concern him; and it is only when he reaches the year 225 that he informs us that the Church, after a century and a quarter of existence, had more than twenty bishops, and gives us a list of eighteen sees. As none of these are bishoprics which were afterwards included in the jurisdiction of Arbela, when the bishop of that see was recognized as Metropolitan at a council held in 410,[23] it is probable that Arbela was for these early centuries the only episcopal seat in Adiabene.

Thus the Church continued in peace, till, in the year 225, the rule of the Parthians gave way to that of the Persians; a fact that Mshikha-Zca mentions with somewhat less of interest than that shown by the ordinary English writer in a general election.

The advent of the Sassanians produced no very conspicuous change, at first, in the attitude of the governing body towards the Church. or local appeared by the side of the governors, and these might, on emergency, show themselves almost equal to the civil authority in power. Fire-temples sprang up generally,[24] perhaps in the place of idol fanes; but the fact that in Persia, for instance, the "Zoroastrian mounds" which marls the sites of fire-temples are conspicuous local features, while in Assyria they are unknown,[25] shows plainly enough where the cult was national, and where it was exotic.

These were the only formal changes; but in spirit things were considerably altered, though this would, of course, only show after the lapse of some years. Magianism, as a religion, now received all the prestige that "establishment" could give it; and while Christianity and paganism continued to be tolerated, proselytism from them to the State faith was encouraged and facilitated, while then, or soon after, it became recognized as a law of the State that to win a convert from Zoroastrianism to Christianity was a crime punishable with death for both teacher and disciple. Further, a Christian, though his right to continue in the faith of his fathers was recognized, took, as Christian, an inferior position; and every one knew that, under ordinary circumstances, the abandonment of his religion meant the greatest possible improvement in his worldly prospects. Christianity, in short, was made to take the position which it occupies still in those lands. It was recognized, but as the religion of an inferior race: and that influence was set to work which has ever since continued to act, in spite of many changes of rulers and of ruling faiths; and which has always tended to draw, not indeed the highest or the lowest, but, in a worldly sense, the most manly souls from the Church to another faith.

A saintly soul's service to his Master may be only the higher and purer for the humiliation that the service imposes on him. A man of inferior type may accept the position into which he has been born; and by striving "to do the best for himself" in it, may develop in a few generations into the supple and often cringing and deceitful person, whom we know as the Levantine of to-day-an instrument, that is, whom his soldier master of the ruling race uses for his convenience, and whom he despises. a youth of fire and ambition, with no more than the average young man's realization of things unseen and spiritual, is always tempted, under these circumstances, to find a career for himself where he will not be exposed to the constant fret of knowing himself undeservedly despised; and to find it either by abandoning the faith which for him spells humiliation, or the land whose laws impose it on the faith. Apostasy, indeed, except under actual stress of persecution, was and is a great rarity. Hereditary attachment to the faith of his fathers is an instinct rather than a habit with the oriental. And it is no mean testimony to her power that the Christian Church should, on the whole, be able to hold her own children under this constant temptation to leave her. All the same, through the ages the tendency of the dominant faith has been to draw away from Christianity, or from service to their own Church, those best worth perfecting. Islam has in this been only the heir of Zoroastrianism: both have taken throughout the centuries a "Janissary-tribute," not from the lives only, but also from the souls and characters of the Christian races subject to them.

Chapter Three - The Episcopate of Papa

RAPID and strong. though the growth of the Church had been elsewhere, there was one conspicuous exception to the rule of progress. The capital city, Seleucia-Ctesiphon, for some reason difficult to explain, was a spot where Christianity did not take root in early centuries. The author of the *Acta S. Maris* shows that he was aware of this, by his declaration that his hero was so discouraged by the incurably vicious and frivolous character of the inhabitants of the place, that he actually demanded his recall from his superiors at Edessa; a statement that shows the saint as somewhat easily cast down by one check following on a series of magnificent successes, and which is probably more true to historic fact than the said successes.[26] It is true that he covers up Mari's defeat by assigning a whole series of miracles to the saint's later ministry in the neighbourhood; but in spite of this his account gives a general impression of agreement with the express statement of hlshikha-Zca,[27] that Christianity could not establish itself in any strength at the capital for some considerable time.

As late as 270 Shakhlupa of Arbela, visiting the place, found only "a few Christians" there, worshipping probably in the Church which Mari is represented as establishing in a ruined temple; and he ordained a priest for them, staying for a year ill the city. This example was followed, a few years later, by his successor, Akha d'abuh'.[28] It was probably a vague recollection of indebtedness to these two bishops that led to the inclusion of their names in the lists made by mediaeval chroniclers in later days, when it was judged necessary to discover predecessors to Papa, who should fill the gap between him and Mari.

Later historians made Akha d'abuh' the hero of an episode of which writers nearer the time are conspicuously ignorant. Mari Ibn Sulieman, for instance (Bar-Hebraeus giving the same story in a shorter form), states that when Jacob, fourth Catholicos, was dying in the year 190, he specially ordered the sending of two of his disciples, Akha d'abuh' and Qam-Ishu, to Antioch, in order that one of them might be consecrated Catholicos by the patriarch there. On arrival, however, the unlucky Qam-Ishu was seized as a Persian spy and crucified; Sliba, Bishop of Antioch, sharing his fate. His companion was smuggled out of the city and sent to Jerusalem for consecration, whence he returned to the East with a letter from all four Western patriarchs declaring that (to avoid a recurrence of such misfortune) the Church of the East should in future elect its own patriarch without reference to Antioch, and that that prelate should take rank with the other four great sees of Christendom. Once elected, he was to be superior to all judgment of his suffragans, or of any human power except the King, when God should grant a Christian King in the East. Even if he should fall into open vice no bishops could pass sentence on him, but "differatur judicium ejus ad adventum Christi Domini nostri."[29] The story is clearly fictitious, considered as evidence of the origin of the independence of the Eastern patriarchate. The absolute ignorance of it shown not only by the biographer of Akha d'abuh' and the contemporaries of Papa, but also by the bishops assembled in council at the time of Dad-Ishu[30] (when its production would have been eminently *ad -rem),* are enough to condemn it, even if the anachronisms[31] of the Liber Turris did not betray a later hand. Of course it is possible that Akha d'abuh' may have had some personal adventures in Antioch., when he visited the place as a Persian soldier; but the whole Qam-Ishu episode belongs to the realm of romance, whither we unhesitatingly but regretfully dismiss it.

So far from Seleucia being recognized at this time as the seat of a patriarch equal in dignity to Rome or Antioch, it had not even a bishop of its own and was dependent on the ministrations of chance visitors. It was in no diocese, but was *res nullius;* and apparently any bishop available, or who happened to be in the capital on business of his own, performed any episcopal act that the small body of Christians there present required. We have record of such good offices being rendered by visiting prelates from Arbela and Susa--sees each of them at least ten days' journey away--and we may infer that similar visits were paid by bishops known to have been existing in the much nearer province of Garmistan.

Akha d'abuh' paid one of these visits during[32] his episcopate of eighteen years, but was obliged to stay considerably longer than he had intended, as he seemingly felt bound in honour to remain in what became a post of considerable danger until the excitement produced by an episcopal indiscretion had fairly subsided. The Bishop of Arbela had been accompanied to Seleucia by two colleagues, Shabta of Bait Zabdai and Zca-Ishu of Kharbeth-Gelal. During their stay in the capital the former of these preached an unfortunately vivid sermon, which being reported to the Shah-in-shall by a non-Christian auditor very nearly produced a general persecution.

The worthy bishop, falling into the preacher's error of thinking that every one must take his statements in the sense that he intends, waxed eloquent over the victories--greater than any of those won by the "Great King"--that Christians could gain; and called on his hearers not to envy the Shah-in-Shah, seeing that in days to come he would be burning for ever with Satan while good Christians would be ruling in heaven. The sermon was no doubt stimulating for the congregation, but as reported to the King (probably Bahram III) it had a very different effect. He and his took it (to quote a modern parallel from a land where little changes, except the uniforms of the soldiers) much as Ottoman officials took an unfortunately literal translation of "Onward, Christian Soldiers," while the preacher on his part was as genuinely astonished at the misunderstanding, as were the American translators of the hymn.

It was no doubt startling for the "King of kings" to hear that his subjects were preparing great victories independently of him, and that a fiery furnace was in readiness to consume his own "divine" person! The only interpretation that suggested itself to him was that of a conspiracy of all Christians. And for a time it seemed more than likely that he would anticipate its outbreak by ordering a massacre of the "conspirators." The king was fairly frightened; and an oriental in such a case is apt to "take precautions" of a grim kind, for nobody can be so utterly merciless as an Eastern ruler in a panic. The danger could not be considered over for two years, and at the end of that time Akha d'abuh', naturally anxious to return to his own diocese, joined with the Bishop of Susa in giving a responsible head to the Church in the capital.[33] They chose and consecrated a man named Papa, who thus became the first bishop of Seleucia-Ctesiphon after the legendary Mari, and began a series of prelates whose representatives to this day continue to the same land.

It was in all probability this position of his, as first bishop after the traditional founder, that made the biographer of Mari assert[34]--with a gay defiance of possible chronology-that the "Apostle" himself selected and consecrated Papa for Seleucia, and decreed that that see should ever hold the primacy in the Church of the East.

The date of the consecration of Papa was probably about 280.³⁵ Accordingly, we can hardly conclude that a picturesque incident related by Mari Ibn Sulieman actually happened in his day, though it is by no means an impossible thing in itself. The writer states that Demetrius, Bishop of Antioch, formed one of the immense horde of captives carried off by Sapor I when he raided Roman Asia in 258-259, after his capture of the Emperor Valerian. The bishop, with the other captives, was settled in Gondisapor; the great cite into which Sapor transformed the little village of Bait Lapat in Khuzistan. Here, refusing the office of Catholicos, which the chronicler declares that Papa offered to yield to him, he remained as pastor and bishop of his fellows of the captivity; and in compliment to the rank that he had held in the West, his new see was granted the position of first among the Metropolitans subject to Seleucia.

As Seleucia had no bishop at the time of the raid, and the metropolitical provinces of the East were not organized for 150 years after this date, the tradition must not be taken *au pied de la lettre*. Antioch, however, was almost depopulated by Sapor,³⁶ and thus it is likely enough that the bishop was among the captives; while the presence of many Christians among them, and the fact that they became an important element in the Church of the East, is amply attested by the *Acta Sanctorum*. Demetrius, however (if the name given in the *Liber Turris* be correct), must have been comfortably established as bishop in his new see, long before Papa was even consecrated.

One effect of the presence of this "captivity" must, of course, have been a strengthening of the bonds that united the Church of Persia to that of the Roman Empire: and some time after, and within Papa's episcopate (297), another political event repeated the process. After the defeat of parses by Galerius, the "Caesar" of the Emperor Diocletian, five "trans-Tigrene" provinces, of which Cordyene, Zabdicene and Arzenene were the chief,³⁷ were ceded to Rome by Persia; and the frontier of the empire was thus pushed forward, till it rested on both of the rivers called Khabor. These provinces contained many Christians, and at least two bishops (B. Zabdai and Arzun), who were thus made Roman subjects and brought more or less under the control of the patriarch of Antioch. On the retrocession of these provinces sixty-five years later, the returning bishops brought with them knowledge of such events as the council of Nicaea, of which (startling as the statement is) the Church of Persia seems to have been, in great measure, ignorant.

By the same peace Armenia was recognized as within the Roman "sphere of influence." This fact must have had important effects on the coming national conversion of that kingdom, which was brought about soon after the peace by that same Tiridates, King of Armenia, who had been the comrade of Galerius (afterwards the persecutor) in the war with Persia.

Papa was in many ways a remarkable character. A man of considerable learning both in Persian and Syriac literature, and of some power of statesmanship,³⁸ he was able to see that it was time for the unorganized episcopacy that had hitherto been the government of the Church of the East, to give place to an ordered subordination of all the bishops to one archbishop or catholicos; and he apparently bent all his energies to securing the acceptance of this change by his colleagues. Though temporarily defeated, he succeeded in his aim. The catholicate was established. The man who did most to hinder it in Papa's day succeeded unchallenged to the primacy whose establishment he had endeavoured to defeat; and the fact that Papa's work has existed ever since in Papa's Church, shows how thoroughly he gauged the disposition and needs of his people.

If, however, his aims were lofty and statesmanlike, it appears that he lacked tact in executing them. The facts of history show him to have been ambitious, if not personally, at least for his see; probably overbearing and oppressive as a ruler, and certainly of a passionate and hot-tempered disposition.

All the circumstances in his day, in the West as well as in the East, were promoting the growth of metropolitical and patriarchal jurisdictions. Rome, Antioch, Alexandria, were each of them drawing the provinces round them under their sway; and the "customs," growing up thus informally, were to be regularized at Nima. A little later, Constantinople was also to show that the bishop of the capital of an empire must inevitably develop into a chief of bishops, if only from his position as the standing host of a stream of episcopal visitors. No historical insignificance in his see, no memories of apostolic preaching or residence in other centres, could prevent their mutual relations becoming those of patriarch and suffragan. Ecclesiastical convenience is apt to be stronger than ecclesiastical tradition.

All the facts that produced patriarchal jurisdiction elsewhere, tended to produce it also in the Church of the East; and another important fact, peculiar to its position, probably did as much as any one cause to elevate the Bishop of Seleucia into a Catholicos.

As bishop of the capital, in touch with the King, and (an even more important thing in the East) with the King's ministers, Papa was almost bound to become chief of those bishops who came to him for assistance in their business. They "had need of him, *ad externa*" as the chronicler puts it.[39] The patriarchal jurisdiction, here as at Constantinople, was a frank development, and could never claim apostolic origin or sanction with any seriousness.[40] If thus one throne acquired supremacy over others, it was simply because that arrangement was found to work best practically.

Further, Christians in Persia were a subject *melet* in an oriental empire; and such a *melet* always develops some one head. The ruler is usually willing enough to recognize a division, or several divisions, of his subjects; but he always demands some one responsible *melet-bashi* through whom he can deal with them, and they with him. The phenomenon is universal in both the Arab and Ottoman Empires. In the Sassanian Sapor II deals with the Bishop of Seleucia as the responsible head of his *melet;* and Isaac is put by

Yezdegerd I in a position exactly parallel to that of the patriarch of any one of the many Christian Churches of today. We have no positive evidence that Papa had any dealings with the kings of his time; but it is at least probable that the influence that did so much to confirm the position of the Catholicos, helped also to establish it.[41]

Had Papa then held his hand, and allowed circumstances to work for him, it is probable that before the end of his life-especially as that life was destined to be a long one--he would have seen himself Catholicos, in fact if not in name, without friction. This, however, he could not do; on the contrary, he claimed supremacy, apparently in right of his position as bishop of the capital, and by so doing naturally roused odium.[42] Further, as Catholicos, lie claimed to use discipline on certain bishops, who may or may not have deserved it,[43] and so made them his enemies. He was also accused of oppression and tyranny in his own diocese; and the truth of this charge is rendered probable by the fact that his own clergy, under his Archdeacon Shimun bar Saba'i,[44] were among the principal opponents both of him and of his policy.[45] One suspects that there must have been good reason for opposition on their part to a line of action that tended so directly to their own exaltation in the Church. Charges of personal misconduct were also made, but these are simply "common form." One remembers how easily such charges were trumped up against an Athanastus; and in the East they are an ordinary feature of controversy. The opposition soon found episcopal leaders, and the first council in the history of the Church of the East met at Seleucia about 315[46] to investigate the matter.

The two leaders of the accusers in the council were Aqib-Alaha, Bishop of Karka d'Baith Slok, and Miles, the non-resident Bishop of Susa. Of the former we know little, save that on conversion he showed such zeal that he gave all his father's goods to feed the poor (a socialistic form of charity, of which there is more than one instance in the history of Eastern ascetics, and which always seems to have been regarded as an indubitable act of virtue); and that later he was a zealous and successful evangelist. The career of Miles is sufficiently characteristic to be worth sketching. Born in the land of Raziqai, the modern Teheran, lie was apparently a Zoroastrian by birth; but was converted while staying in Khuzistan, and was "led by the Spirit to the ascetic life." He became Bishop of Susa, and there began to show that combination of devotion, zeal, quarrelsomeness and restlessness, which make him so typical a son of his nation.

It did not take him long to quarrel with his diocese--"because they were utterly. given to idolatry and Magianism," says his biographer, though one would like to hear their side of the case also. Whatever the cause, he was stoned in the streets, and left the city in a rage, solemnly cursing it as he did so. The biographer is at some pains to tell us how destruction fell on the city, in accordance with the word of the holy man. After this, lie went wandering "to countries," much in the fashion that men of his race still do, equipped with the clothes he stood up in and a copy of the Gospels in a satchel. Neither traveller nor beggar ever starves in the East, and Miles arrived safely in Jerusalem; whence, "drawn by the fame of Ammonius,"[47] he descended to Egypt. Here a hermit, unnamed, received the wanderer; but very soon found, as his flock had done before, that the saint was no comfortable man to live with. In this case the *casus belli* was a tame snake of huge size that lived with the hermit (who apparently had not warned his guest of the fact), and that came in and disturbed the saint at prayers. Miles promptly destroyed it-miraculously, says his biographer and when the hermit not unnaturally protested at this treatment of his dumb friend, rebuked him severely for un-Christian conduct in making a pet of a creature between which and mankind Heaven had established enmity. The hermit left his rather difficult guest in sole possession of the cell, and went to seek another. Miles, however, soon abandoned it, and returned to the East by way of Nisibis; where he scented the quarrel with Papa from afar, and hastened to join in the fray. Though he had abandoned his own diocese he had this much of sympathy with it-that he would not see it made subordinate to another see that had once been more or less under its authority.

Feeling ran very high when the council met. Papa absolutely refused to submit to its authority, "exalting himself above the bishops who were assembled to judge him," though it is not clear on what he based this claim to supremacy. Perhaps he simply "would not receive" the council; much as a modern Assyrian often will declare, when angry, "I do not receive X. as my patriarch," and considers himself thereby freed from all obligation or obedience to the man named. Old Syrian writers reveal a state of mind, if not of circumstance, so exactly similar to that of their modern descendants, that one is often tempted to "fill up gaps" from modern knowledge.

Miles called the angry bishop to order. "Is it not written, lie that is chief among you, let him be a servant?" "You fool, don't I know that?" replied the Catholicos. "Then be judged by the Gospel, if you will not be judged by man," retorted Miles, and drawing his copy of the Gospel from his satchel lie placed it on a cushion in the midst. Papa, who was obviously in a furious rage, struck the book with his hand, exclaiming, "Then speak, Gospel, speak!"[48] This sacrilege roused the horror of friends and foes alike; but the fury of the old man then overcame him-struck with paralysis or apoplexy, he fell senseless in the council chamber, and we cannot wonder that all present felt that they had seen judgment fall on him from Heaven for his impiety. After such a portent the condemnation of the Catholicos followed as a matter of course. He was deposed from his rank; and his archdeacon, Shimun, consecrated in his room, unwilling though he apparently was to accept the honour. All accusations against Papa were taken as proved, and published as such. The supremacy of Seleucia over the Church of Persia seemed to have been strangled at birth. Papa, however, though defeated, was by no means a broken man. His stroke, whatever its nature, must have passed soon, at least as far as his mental powers were concerned, though apparently he never recovered the use of one arm.[49] He was resolved to recover his position, and with that object he laid his case before the "Western bishops." An Assyrian's ordinary course in such a case is to appeal to the Government, St. Paul's dictum about going to law with unbelievers being held in scant respect practically among them; and it is to Papa's credit that he refrained from this, and took a course more ecclesiastically correct. Possibly, too, the appeal to secular authority was barred to him, on account of the fact that the family interest of his archdeacon and rival, Shimun, stood very high with the guardian of the boy king, Sapor II.[50]

The appeal of the Catholicos to the Western bishops was made, not to the Patriarch of Antioch, but to the Bishop of Edessa, S'ada.[51] Neither then nor at any other time did the Church of the East regard Antioch as its mother or superior. Later tradition asserted, and in this case probably with truth, that the appeal went also to the famous James of Nisibis.[52] It appears that the matter was put before the nearest Western bishops of eminence. The answer, whoever gave it, was definite enough, at least as quoted in a council held a century later. All the proceedings against Papa were annulled, the accusers were deposed from their orders, and only such members of the council as had acted in "their simplicity" were allowed to retain their rank. Shimun, as having been consecrated against his will, was to remain as archdeacon, "cum jure successionis."

According to another historian, however, the judgment of the Western fathers was not nearly so trenchant, and simply recommended a general reconciliation, on the ground that- submission to a patriarch was for the common advantage.[53] Certainly the decision, even if given as quoted, was not carried out. The only protagonists in the dispute of whom we know anything were not degraded. Miles and Aqib-Alaha retained their rank; and the only reason why the former did not resume his see was that lie preferred the work of wandering evangelist to that of diocesan bishop. Shimun was specially marked for promotion as a result of what he had done. The most probable explanation is, that all parties were a little ashamed of themselves and their actions, and were glad of a reconciliation on any, and preferably on indefinite, terms. It is with some regret that we find that the one man who resisted the reconciliation was Shimun. He refused to accept the advice of the Western bishops; was anxious to appeal to the Regent of the kingdom; and was only withheld from doing so by the flat refusal of his father, on whom his political power depended, to stir in the matter.

Ultimately all consented to let the matter drop, without attempting to reach too formal a settlement. Possibly it was expected that tension would soon be eased automatically, by the death of Papa; though, as a matter of fact, he seems to have lived for twelve years after this time. Shimun was reconciled by the prospect of the succession, and what else we know of his story gives us ground for hoping that higher motives also may have influenced him. Practically, the victory rested with Papa, who regained his see, and whose primacy among the bishops came to be accepted as a thing too practically useful to resist. All recognized that it was useless to argue against the law of gravitation, which had decreed that Seleucia should be the primary, round which all the planets of the system must revolve. Papa's ambition, says Mshikha-Zca, worked out to the advantage of the Church.

What remained of his long episcopate was peaceful, and about 327 he died,[54] having held his office for hard on fifty years-a length sufficient to be remarkable, even if it be less than the seventy or eighty which later historians assigned him. Shimun bar Saba'i took his place peacefully. By the irony of fate the man who had strained every nerve to prevent the establishment of the Catholicate of Seleucia, was destined, by his glorious death, to establish its prestige on an unshakable foundation.

Chapter Four - The Great Persecution of Sapor II

PAPA died about 328; and Shimun bar Saba'i succeeded him peacefully, and ruled, at all events for some years, with the prosperity that came from the royal favour. He was a *persona grata* at Court, and the young King Sapor (whose coming of age had approximately coincided with the accession of Shimun) apparently had a real personal liking for the bishop.[55]

The great ecclesiastical events that were passing in the West no doubt excited interest in the Church of the East, as far as they were known; but though destined to affect its history most profoundly in time, they had little effect at the moment. The news of the conversion of the Roman Emperor, and of the Edict at Milan, would reach the East, probably, about the time of the council held against Papa. During his later years, and the earlier portion of his successor's episcopate, rumours of the gradual establishment of Christianity as the State religion, of the rise of the Arian heresy, and the assembly of the Great Council of Nicaea, must gradually have filtered through to the Christians of Persia.

That portion of the Church, however, had this piece of exceptional good fortune allowed it-that it (and it only, of all portions of the Church Catholic of the day) was absolutely untroubled by the Arian controversy. None of its bishops were present at Nicaea; and the doctrine of Arius was known to it only as an accursed thing to be repudiated.

This fact, the ignorance of a not unimportant Church of the greatest of all Church controversies, will bear some examination. First, the fact must be admitted, explain it as we may, that the "Assyrian" Church did know nothing officially of the Nicene Council at the time of its assembling. Not only is there no reference to it in any of the nearly contemporary documents that remain to us (for they, with one important exception, are *acta martyrum* where such reference might naturally not be found); but the one work of theology (properly so called) that remains to us from the period, is obviously the work of a man who had no knowledge of the council, or what was debated therein. The author in question, of course, is Afraat, the "Sage of Persia." Writing about fifteen years after the council (337-346) he uses expressions, and formulates a creed[56] in a fashion that one may fairly say would have been impossible to a man who had heard of the rights and wrongs of the great controversy that was then agitating "the West," no matter which side he took in it.

The Church of "the East" was not asked to accept Nicaea, or its doctrines, until eighty-five years later, when it frankly and fully accepted both the council and its creed. Individual bishops may have (must have)[57] known of the fact, but not the auto-cephalous Church as such.

The most probable explanation of the phenomenon is as follows. Constantine regarded the council as an "imperial affair." In the whole controversy, it was the peace of the Empire that he saw endangered, not the vital truth of Christianity; and the council was summoned to guard the first, by determining the second. Under these circumstances, it was natural that he should not summon bishops from outside the empire to settle a domestic matter. The Emperor was, of course, aware of the existence of the Church in Persia, and took an interest (too much interest, perhaps) in its fortunes; but in the matter of the council he seems to have regarded it as outside his purview. So the synod met, and the "Easterns" were not represented to it.

A few years elapsed, and the rise of the great persecution protected them (at a frightful cost) from the weary controversy that followed.

It is a fact, however, that one of the greatest of "Assyrian" saints, and the holder of one of the most important metropolitical sees of later "Assyrian" history, was undoubtedly present at Nicaea. James of Nisibis certainly, and Ephraim Syrus his deacon probably, were at the council; but they were there as representatives, not of a see in the Persian Empire, but of one in the Roman. It was not until 363 that Nisibis, hitherto the bulwark of the Roman frontier, was abandoned by Jovian to Persia, and a throne that had hitherto been (if in any patriarchate) in that of Antioch, fell naturally under that of Seleucia-Ctesiphon.[58]

Incidentally we may note that it is a matter for profound thankfulness that so obstinate a heresy as Arianism should not have been allowed to find a national *point d'appui* in such a Church as that of the Persian Empire. Had it done so, the struggle in the eastern half of the Empire might have been prolonged indefinitely, and Teutonic Arianism have found that support for lack of which it sank and passed away.

In Persia, Sapor II, who had begun his life and reign together in 309, had come to his kingdom and won his spurs in his earlier wars against the Arabs, where he had shown both the vigour and the cruelty that marked his whole career. Now, lie was preparing to renew the long quarrel with Rome, and to demand, if not the whole Achaemenid Empire, at least the retrocession of the five lost frontier provinces ceded by Narses to Diocletian. Probably, however, the Persian hesitated at the thought of challenging Constantine "the Victorious," old though he now was. He certainly waited until the great Emperor had passed away (though had his life been prolonged a few months Constantine might not have stayed to be attacked) and left a divided empire to sons weaker than himself. Then Sapor straightway attacked the weakest and nearest of the three.

During the twenty years previous to the war the fact of the definite Christianization of Rome had sunk into Persian consciousness; and this had a natural, but disastrous, "repercussion" on the position of the Church in Persia. While the Empire was pagan and persecuting, Christianity was regarded with no suspicion by the Government of the Shah-in-Shah. It was not the true faith, of course; and its adherents were regarded probably with some contempt; such. contempt as was the lot, for instance, of a Jew in Moorish Spain. Persecution existed, no doubt, but was sporadic at worst; being stirred up usually by some enthusiastic Mobed, and started by some act of "apostasy." But with the conversion of the Roman Emperor, all this was changed. Christians were thereafter -politically suspect, and from the Persian point of view naturally and properly suspect, as co-religionists and presumably sympathizers with Persia's enemy. It was inevitable that this should be so. The State establishment of Christianity was a good, if, not an unmixed good, for the Church in the empire; but the Church outside it had to pay the bill. In lands where religion and politics were, and still are, inextricably mingled, it was simply impossible that the Government official (whether Sassanid Persian or modern Ottoman) should not suspect those whose faith cut them off from the body politic, and linked them with its enemies. Whether the suspicion was just or not, is beside the point; to ask that it should not be entertained, was to ask too much of oriental human nature. In the collision of these two activities, political and religious-a disaster as inevitable and as hopeless as that brought on by "Nemesis" in a Greek tragedy-we have the key to much (perhaps one half) of the sadness of the history of Christianity in what we now call "the middle East." The natural suspicion of the governing class produces what one side calls "precautions"; and what the other calls "persecutions," if the date be 340, and "massacres" if the year be 1896. It produces, too, on the side of the Christians, constant efforts to hold fast their faith, and yet avoid persecution. The efforts may take the shape of the corporate adoption of a form of Christianity different from that in favour over the border[59] (an act which people in safety over that border complacently call "falling into heresy"); or the means of defence may be deceitfulness and slipperiness, which again those who have never been similarly tried loathe and despise. The problem has changed its form a little during the centuries, but it still remains essentially the same. Given a State professing a certain form of militant religion (it matters nothing whether its prophet be Zoroaster or Diahommed) how can loyalty to that State be reconciled with the profession of the religion of its rivals? How will those prosper, who are now making the latest, and not the least noble effort, at the solution of this secular problem?

Suspicion of the Christians who were Persian subjects was thus inevitable; and the Mobeds, at least, if no one else was available, were always ready to fan that suspicion into persecution, even if Christians on both sides of the frontier were careful to avoid giving cause for offence. Unhappily, this was not the case. Those in Persia undoubtedly gave cause for suspicion; they were restless under Magian rule when they saw Christianity triumphant in the West; and looked to the Roman Emperor as their deliverer, as naturally as, for instance, the Armenians under Turkish rule looked, at one time, to Russia.[60] Constantine, too, was no more averse to the post of general protector of all Christians than were some Czars. Theodoret quotes his letter to Sapor, and applauds him for his care for those of the true faith in Persia.[61] The good bishop, safe in Cyrrhus, saw in the proceeding only a proof of the wonderful virtue of the Emperor. Perhaps it was so, but how did it look to Sapor? The interest of their would-be friends has not always been an unmixed blessing for the Christians of the "Oriental Empire," either in politics or in religion.

Mons. Labourt, noting these facts in his book,[62] observes that "precautions" would have been justifiable enough, but "only the barbarity of the time can explain, not excuse, the pitiless repression that the King ordered." "Repressions" of the kind Sapor adopted are not of one age only; but are the "precautions" adopted by most oriental rulers under such circumstances, from Sapor's time to our own. Which side is most to blame? The writer has seen the problem from close at hand, and dare not judge the excesses of either side too harshly.

Thus, when once Sapor had started a war with Rome, it would have been almost a miracle if he had not also started a persecution of Christians; and when he returned to his palace after the first campaign, sore and angry at a humiliating repulse from Nisibis,[63] it was natural to turn furiously upon them and declare, "at least we will make these Roman sympathizers pay!" That Jews, Manichaeans, and Mobeds should have urged him to this course (as the biographer of Mar Shimun believed) is probable enough; but their influence was hardly necessary.[64]

Thus the first "Firman" of persecution was issued, ordering all Christians to pay double taxes, expressly as a contribution to the cost of a war in which they were taking no share, the Catholicos being ordered to collect the same. The special order may have been a kind of test for Afar Shimun, but there was nothing unusual in the Government thus dealing with the *melet* through its recognized head. In any case Shimun refused to obey the order, on the double ground that his people were too poor, and that tax-collecting was no part of a bishop's business. On this it was easy to raise the cry, "he is a traitor and wishes to rebel"; and a second Firman was issued, ordering his arrest and the general destruction of all the Christian churches. Shimun was arrested at Seleucia, the Court being then at Karka d'Lidan (*i.e.* Susa), and in the leisurely fashion characteristic of Eastern justice, was allowed to collect his flock and to take a last farewell of them, before being conducted, with several colleagues, to what all foresaw would be his death. All gathered to receive the solemn blessing which a contemporary writer has preserved for us: "Alay the Cross of our Lord be the protection of the people of Jesus; the peace of God be with the servants of God, and stablish your hearts in the faith of Christ, in tribulation and in ease, in life and in death, now and for evermore."[65]

The story of his martyrdom has been told by abler writers,[66] to whom we may refer for the moving tale of Shimun's interviews with the King; of the fall, penitence and triumph of Gusht-azad the eunuch; of the **offer** of freedom, both for himself and his *melet,* made to the Catholicos, if he would consent to adore the sun but once; and of the personal appeal of the King to him to yield, by the memory of their personal friendship. The last scene toot place outside Susa, on ,the morning of Good Friday, 339; when the Catholicos, five bishops, and about one hundred clergy sealed their testimony together, Shimun being the last to die. To him it AN-as given to die for both of the two noblest causes for which a man may lay down his life-for his faith in God, and for his duty to his people.

It is impossible to give any general account of the persecution which, thus inaugurated, raged over all Persia for fully forty years. The "Acts of Martyrs" indeed are abundant, and many of them are of the highest historic value, but they give on the whole a very confused impression.

Nothing, in the Last, goes in orderly legal fashion, according to Western ideas; and persecutions were not carried out in the regular Roman fashion. Further, a Firman is not so much a decree as a permission (the standing order being, "thou shalt do nothing at all"); and the result of the Firmans of persecution issued by Sapor was not the setting of the machinery of lacy in motion against a *religio illicita*, in Roman wise, but something that resembled much more closely the Armenian massacres of our own day, viz. the releasing of a race hatred and fanaticism normally held in check, to do its will upon its objects. The slaughter that followed was assisted frequently rather than regularly by the Government officials.

The grounds of this feeling are stated, and probably with fair correctness, to one of the series of Acta, as follows: "The Christians destroy our holy teaching, and teach men to serve one God, and not to honour the sun or fire. They teach them, too, to defile water by their ablutions; to refrain from marriage and the procreation of children; and to refuse to go out to war with the Shah-in-Shah. They have no scruple about the slaughter and eating of animals; they bury the corpses of men in the earth; and attribute the origin of snakes and creeping things to a good God. They despise many servants of the King, and teach witchcraft."[67]

Summed up, these causes of offence amount to this. The Christians were men of different habit to the Zoroastrian, and therefore were hateful and despicable as the foreigner is to the Chinese to-day. Some of their customs (particularly the burial of the dead, and the growing habit of thinking celibacy the higher life) were specially abhorrent to 1llagians, to whose thinking it was man's primary duty to produce fresh servants for Hormizd, and to refrain from profaning Hormizd's earth. As usual, it was the accidents of the presentation of the Faith that made it hateful to men whose religious philosophy was by no means low; and "whose views of God, of the world, and of man, approach more nearly to the fulness of truth than anything else that heathen literature can show."[68]

The correct Christian conception of celibacy, as a thing higher per se than marriage, needed correction; and Pauline theology might have taught its disciples that no one way of disposing of the bodies of the departed was in itself more reverent than another, or to be insisted on if it "made a brother to stumble."[69] Thus prejudice born of outraged habit, and prejudice born of offended religion, joined with the bitterer prejudice bred of patriotism to produce a race-hatred between the holders of the two faiths. The Christians were Roman sympathizers, and friends of the enemies of the land. As a matter of fact the last charge was only half true. Christian unwillingness to serve in the royal armies was not nearly so marked as the distrust of them which made the King unwilling to accept their service as a rule.[70] Still a consideration of that kind was not likely to do much towards abating a popular antipathy.

Thus that race-hatred, so unintelligible to us Europeans, grew up between Christians and Zoroastrians; and according to the law of the East, that religion is the determinant of nationality, they rapidly became separate nations, for all that they dwelt to the same land. Such race-hatred can, as we see in India, be kept under control for generations by a Government resolved to keep the peace; but it blazes up like the fires from a long dormant volcano if it be given opportunity or permission for its indulgence. In Europe, Highland may despise Lowland, or one nation another. But put them to live together in one country (in Canada, for instance), and to a generation or so the hatreds die out, the races mingle, and a new, possibly a finer type of humanity is produced. It is only in the East that races (Kurd and Armenian, or Kurd and Assyrian) will live side by side for generations, each in villages of their own; doing life's business together fairly amicably, and obeying the orders of the Government (if any) to keep the peace--but mixing no more than oil and water, and abating no jot of mutual and bitter hatred.

The persecution in this case began with an indiscriminate massacre of Christians round Susa,[71] continuing for about a fortnight, and reproduced, in all probability, in most of the Christian centres of the kingdom. Later, indeed, some method was introduced into the proceeding; for Sapor discovered that a favourite of his had met with a voluntary martyrdom,[72] donning the "dress of a Rabban" (monk or rather celibate) and mixing with the crowd of confessors. Then a decree was issued, to the effect that all arrested for Christianity were to be examined by some one in authority, and a register of executions kept; further, that before any person was ordered for execution, he or she was first to be put to the torture[73] (and Sassanid executioners were adepts at that art) and only executed on proving obstinate. It will be understood that this order was genuinely meant to be on the side of mercy, but how far it was carried out is doubtful. Any man of position[74] apparently-certainly any provincial governor or Mobed-could examine a Christian, and sentence him to death; or might put him to death without examination--for who was going to inquire with any strictness as to what was done by way of executing the King's decree in remoter districts? The death of a Christian 7ayat was not a more important thing in the fourth century than in the twentieth.

This looseness of organization, however, had its advantages. If any governor could persecute, any could protect. For instance, the Marquis (Marzban) of Adiabene, Pigrasp, simply refrained from persecuting,[75] during the four years for which he held office after the decree was published--"except just during vintage time," when for some obscure reason, fanaticism could not, apparently, be held in check. What one merciful man could do on a large scale, others no doubt could do on a smaller; just as in a later age, a generous Kurdish Agha could protect and shelter occasional Armenian villages. In fact, though the persecution lasted its full forty years (and indeed there were numerous isolated cases of persecution, both before and after that period), yet it was unsystematic in character, and did not and could not press on all equally for that time. Often, no doubt, when a merciful marquis or "Rad" died, the Mobeds of the district could procure the appointment of a zealot in his place. We know, for instance, that this took place on the death of Pigrasp in Adiabene.[76]

It was only to be expected that the clergy, and more specially the bishops, and also the converts from Magianism, should be specially aimed at by the persecutors. Two successors of Mar Shimun, Shah-dost and Bar-b'ashmin, followed their former chief within six years; the former of them being warned of his fate by a vision of his predecessor in glory,[77] calling on his follower (and nephew) to come up to him without fear. After the death of Bar-b'ashmin the throne remained vacant for more than twenty years, as to fill it was to secure the death of a devoted man. Other bishops, however, must have been consecrated, and the succession was secured.

Among other bishops, Miles of Karka d'Lidan, who was still alive and vigorous when the persecution began, was far too conspicuous a man to be out of danger, and was too fearless to shun it. Hence, he was soon arrested. On examination, the violence of temper that had marred a fine character blazed out once more. He taunted the Agha who was judging him, till the official cut him down with his own sabre, and this somewhat pugnacious martyr died proclaiming vengeance on his murderers, "whose bodies the fowls of the air shall eat." The doom could hardly have sounded very terrible to a Zoroastrian; but as a matter of fact, the man was soon after killed in a hunting accident.[78]

Aqib-shima, the venerable Bishop of Khanitha near Arbela-an ascetic known and revered by all for his labours in converting the heathen[79] of the hill country round the modern Rowanduz (where the Christian villages that are his monument still remain)-was one of the later victims of the time of trial. Like many of the more notable prisoners, he was finally sent for execution to the "door of the King," but an incident that occurred at one of his many examinations is worth recording.

The martyr was before his judges, when a Manichaean was brought in, and ordered to abjure his peculiar version of Christianity.[80] This he readily agreed to do (as indeed was the practice of this sect, when they were not asked to abjure the secret doctrine known to initiates alone), and lie killed an ant, which either was, or was thought to be, the sacred symbol of life according to his creed. One notes, with some regret, that the confessor had no feeling but joy and triumph at the fall of the heretic.[81]

Aqib-shima was finally executed by the personal order of Sapor; while Joseph the Qasha, who had been his companion in suffering, was stoned by renegade Christians as the price of their lives. This, it may be mentioned, was a common practice throughout the persecution; any one who fell away from the faith being compelled to earn his pardon by acting as executioner to his more staunch companions.

Monks and nuns were naturally as much the object of persecution as were the clergy-partly as Christian leaders, partly on account of the horror with which all Zoroastrians regarded the profession of the celibate life. Nuns were commonly offered their lives if they would consent to marry;[82] renunciation of Christianity not being always insisted on in that case. The frequency with which martyrdoms of these ascetics occur in the Acta, is evidence of the firm hold which the ascetic and monastic principle was taking (naturally) on the oriental mind. But less than a generation had elapsed since its first introduction; and the institution was as yet in a somewhat primitive and unorganized condition, a "Daira" being simply the gathering of a group of devotees, male or female, round some one leader.

Syriac historians, as a rule, have not much of an eye for the artistic in narrative; and are so busy in proving to us (by the recounting of miracles generally) the surpassing sanctity of their hero, that they leave little room for the personal touches which, to us, are much more illuminating. The author of the earlier Acta of the martyrs of the persecution, is a gratifying exception to the rule; and has recorded for us, not only the moving story of the martyrdom of Mar Shimun and his companions, but several other picturesque and pathetic incidents of the time. Thus it is to him that we owe the story of Yazdundocht,[83] the noble lady who cared for the 120 confessors of Seleucia, during their imprisonment; and only revealed to them the fact that the day of their "release" had come, by the final gift of white raiment that she made to each of them, and the prayer that they would intercede for her before the Throne. The bodies of martyrs were as a rule surrendered to their friends (though in some cases attempts were made to prevent this[84]), and the lady was allowed to complete her pious task by the burial of these bodies in one great martyrium.

On another occasion, when the right of burial was refused and the bodies left by the roadside, panic was spread among the Magi, and triumph among the Christians, by a mysterious light that hovered above the corpses.[85] It was, of course, some kind of phosphorescence, but was universally regarded as a proof that these were indeed holy men that had been done to death; and the bodies were interred with all honour. It is an indication of the absolute changelessness of the East, that the phenomenon and the effect should have been exactly repeated during the Armenian massacres of 1896.

Persecution must have flagged at times, for the blood-thirst, even of an oriental fanatic, is not insatiable. It is probable, too, that the great Roman invasion of Julian gave some respite to Christians (a fact that would hardly have pleased the author of it), by giving King and nobles something else to do. This is not, however, directly referred to in the Acta. Certainly after its conclusion the storm burst out again with fresh violence, for there was fresh material to work on. Sapor, it will be remembered, insisted on a "rectification of frontier" as the price of peace; and five provinces, with six bishoprics and a population largely Christian, found themselves handed over by a Christian Emperor to Sapor. Jovian has a good name in ecclesiastical history, owing mainly to his Nicene Orthodoxy, and to the high opinion St. Athanasius entertained of him. Something, however, must be entered on the other side when we remember that, in making peace, he not only incurred the military shame of handing over to Persia the maiden fortress that his enemy had never been able to win in fight; but also made absolutely no effort, as far as we know, to secure decent treatment for the inhabitants of those provinces which he was handing over to a notorious persecutor. As a result, not only were those inhabitants deported into distant provinces of Persia (that was perhaps a necessary measure of precaution), but instructions were given to mark their leaders, and to arrest and "deal with" all who would not abandon "the religion of Caesar."[86] There was unintentional irony in the order, when the only Caesar they had known of late had been Julian; but that fact did not save the victims. The historians tell us of one of the detachments of captives (the men of B. Zabdai), among whom were found the Bishop Heliodorus, and several of the clergy. These were given the choice between apostasy and death, and were massacred to the number of nearly 300; only twenty-five of the band accepting their lives at the price offered. Other detachments suffered in the same way.

The cession of territory was important ecclesiastically, as by taking Nisibis and "the five provinces" out of the Roman into the Persian Empire, it also took them, as stated above, out of the Antiochene Patriarchate, and into that of Seleucia. When peace was restored to the Church this position was accepted without a murmur. It may seem strange to a purist, that ecclesiastical boundaries should thus, as a matter of course, follow civil; but convenience in such a matter is apt to be stronger than correctitude. No King of Persia could tolerate such an anomaly as the subjection of some of his subjects, even *quoad ecclesiastica*, to an Archbishop outside his boundary; nor would any Persian Christian, when the persecution was over, go out of his way to invite its renewal by starting such an idea.

It must be remembered, too, that in the fourth century the idea that ecclesiastical divisions followed civil was already familiar--as we see in the life of St. Basil; and that patriarchates were still inchoate. The greater sees, like Antioch, Rome and Alexandria, were gathering round them the bishoprics that lay within their sphere of attraction, just as Seleucia was doing in the Persian sphere. We shall see that (owing probably to the conditions of the life of a subject *melet*) the dependence of the metropolitan and diocesan bishops on the Catholicos was even more defined in Persia than inside the Roman Empire. Still, patriarchal boundaries were so far from being defined, that a new Patriarchate was actually in process of formation round Constantinople; and we can trace its first beginnings under Chrysostom in the next generation.

Up to the very end of his life Sapor continued to persecute relentlessly; and it is only natural that, as the persecution goes on, a bitter and resentful tone should creep into the minds of the sufferers, and should find expression in the Acta. Sayings like "Your accursed King,"[87] or "I will not worship fire, but you will be burning for ever in it some day," are to be regretted; though one cannot wonder that a generation of suffering should have produced them. Still it is saddening to note the contrast between them, and the stately dignity of Mar Shimun, the unswerving loyalty of Gushtazad, and the genuine cheerfulness and even "chaff" of Martha the nun.[88]

Even during the persecution, the Church did not lose her power of drawing men to her. More than one chronicler tells with pride of the conversion, when persecution was hottest, of men like Ait-Alaha of Arbela,[89] the priest of the goddess Sharbil. He was subject to some complaint resembling dysentery; and was told by a Christian, who succoured him in one of his paroxysms, to go to the Bishop of Arbela, who would cure him. The Magian, being cured as promised, professed himself a Christian; and the bishop, after some natural hesitation, admitted him to baptism, and subsequently to ordination.

Naturally, a price was put upon the head of the "renegade," and also on that of the Bishop Maran-zca. Ait-Alaha, though preserved for some time, was arrested at last; and as he remained steadfast tinder torture, was sent with a fellow-prisoner to the King at Bait Lapat, or Gondi-Sapor. On the journey, the two were apparently on parole, being allowed personal freedom by their guards, and even permitted to go in and out of a city (Shehrgard in B. Garmai) where they were delayed for some days. One is glad to see that the trust was not abused, and that both Christians loyally delivered themselves up to execution rather than break their plighted word.

Maran-zca--the name means "our Lord conquers" or "has conquered," and is one of many that have a curiously Puritanic ring to the English reader-- always evaded arrest; being able to retire into the mountains to the north of his diocese, where the "King's writ" does not run to this day. Though both of his predecessors, John and Abraham, were martyred, he died in peace after an episcopate of twenty-nine years.

Sapor, "the long-lived," also died, at last, in 79; and the persecution practically died with him. Not that there was safety from local outbreaks of zeal, or Mobed fanaticism; that could not be secured, till a royal Firman of toleration had been issued, and neither of Sapor's three feeble successors could take so decisive a step. The worst of the storm, however, was past; and the Church which had endured as severe a trial as ever national Church was called upon to face--and which had endured it so nobly--could rest a while, recoup her energies, and repair her organization; and count up the total of those 16,000 martyrs whose names were known and recorded,[90] who had "enriched the Church with their deaths" during those terrible forty years.

Chapter Five - Reorganization of the Church - Council of Mar Isaac (410)

THREE great conflicts, or rather a stage in each of three great conflicts, came to an end when Sapor the long-lived died, and one of the lengthiest reigns in history was closed. In Persia the first great attempt of the Magian hierarchy to destroy Christianity by force lead been made, and failed.

In the Roman Empire paganism had practically passed away as a religion; and the victory of Christianity over it had been proclaimed by the removal of the altar of Victory from the Senate House at Rome, and the destruction of the Serapeum at Alexandria. Furthermore, Arianism had been definitely conquered as an official creed. For some time past it had been beaten in the Church; but yet, while it was supported by imperial patronage it had remained formidable--at least in Asia Minor, and the other parts of the Empire which had found their natural centre in Constantinople. Now that support was withdrawn by Theodosius, and the faith passed out of practical importance within Roman territory. The Emperor held a council of the bishops of the Eastern Empire, to solemnly proclaim its burial, so to speak; and this gathering, almost accidentally, took rank as "oecumenical" in later years, though at the moment it passed almost unnoticed. One incident in the course of it, however, has some importance for our main subject, viz., that this council saw the commencement of that rivalry between Alexandria and Constantinople (the throne of the Evangelist, and the upstart city of yesterday) which was to cost three bishops of the capital their lives, and one his see. Now, Gregory Nazianzen, the duly appointed bishop[91] of the capital, was practically cast Out of his diocese by the protest of the Egyptian bishops against the translated "intruder"; and the feud, for it was nothing less, between the two sees was to continue till communion between them had been finally broken off. In the course of it three bishops of Constantinople (Chrysostom, Nestorius and Flavian) were hounded to death by as many patriarchs of Alexandria, assisted by the emperors; and at least one patriarch of Alexandria, Proterius, was murdered to his own cathedral. This quarrel is an important factor in the ecclesiastical history of the next seventy years; for it was destined to y have considerable influence in embittering the Christological controversy, and to have a "repercussion," of which the effects are felt to-day, on the history of the Persian Church.[92]

Politically the question of the day for the Empire was the defence of the State against the barbarians. Theodosius was to effect this during his life; and thanks to his genius, the eastern portion of the empire, though raided from end to end, was destined ultimately to survive the flood before which the western half of it went down. This, however, was not so clear at the moment; and while the Ostro-Goths were riding at will over Asia Minor, and Athens and Antioch were in the act of being plundered by Visi-Goths and Huns respectively, it must have been difficult to believe that so overwhelming an attach was destined to pass away.

In Persia, as is often the case, a series of nonentities followed the death of a great king. Neither Ardashir II, Sapor III, nor Bahram IV made any impression on their contemporaries; and the only important event of the twenty years that covered their three reigns was the practical extinction of the kingdom of Armenia.[93]

During the Romo-Persian War, Arsaces, the ruler of that country, had endeavoured to keep himself safe by impartially betraying both sides, and then executing his own agents. There was this much of excuse for him-that he, like the dukes of Savoy, was forbidden by his geographical position to indulge in the luxury of a conscience. Naturally, when peace was made, his convenience was consulted by neither party, and Armenia was handed over to the mercies of Persia. Sapor requited treachery with treachery; and having secured the person of Arsaces by a safe-conduct, blinded him, and consigned him to the "Castle of Oblivion," the ominously-named "Loches" of the Sassanid kings.

The Shah-in-Shah then attempted to govern the turbulent province by the appointment of Armenian nobles as Persian satraps, or Marzbans; but the effort failed. This Poland of the East showed itself in the character it has borne ever since-a land that can neither govern itself, nor submit peaceably to the government of any foreigner.[94] As it is in the twentieth century, so it was in the fourth. A patriotic party existed which united a real care for their country with a good deal of personal ambition, and an absolute lack of scruple in their methods. They intrigued with Rome or Persia, and betrayed each to the other. They invited in a foreign garrison; and then,_ in panic at their own act, butchered them in a sort of "Sicilian vespers." None of these "patriots" would be loyal to the foreigner; though at any time any of them would betray his fellows and his country to whatever power was the enemy at the moment. But he would act thus, be it understood, to gain neither money nor power (though he would take both, if they came his way as reward), but the gratification of some petty personal spite. Probably, too, all were genuinely convinced that Armenia-civilized and Christian Armenia-was the true salt of the earth; and that these regrettable incidents were purely the result of oppression, and the fault of her oppressors.

Was it wonderful that the two great powers whose peace was endangered by such a neighbour should agree to partition the country; and resolve to govern somehow-however badly-those who were unable to govern themselves? Thus the Armenian kingdom ended, and the Armenian question began. It is a proof of the continuity of history, and the permanence of national characteristics, that this problem, started in the early fifth century, should still remain unsolved. During the persecution, the Christians of Armenia (that is to say, the nation, which Tiridates had brought to confess Christianity *en masse* by the most drastic of methods) were left undisturbed. Their independence protected them; and while their coreligionists to the south were undergoing their great trial, the Armenians--under their Catholicos Narses[95]--were peaceably organizing their hierarchy, after the most approved Western model, that of Caesarea. Of course the Church had its troubles; but these arose either from the royal contempt of Church discipline, as not made for kings; or from the attempt of Narses to force all the ecclesiastical machinery of civilized Cappadocia on semi-barbarous Armenia-a blunder which the rulers of infant Churches have repeated more than once since. Once the Catholicos was exiled, only to return with fresh zeal from the mother-Church to carry out the precepts of St. Basil. The cause of this quarrel was the establishment by the King of a "city of refuge"-an institution in which Arsaces (probably gauging the needs of his people much more accurately than Narses) saw a means of abating the blood-feuds that devastated the country but which the archbishop called "a licensed Sodom." On his return from banishment, Narses was poisoned by the then King, Para or Bab; and the crime caused a breach with Caesarea, and the proclamation of Armenian ecclesiastical independence. This policy was no doubt welcome to the Persian King when in 3S4 he became the avowed suzerain of the bulk of the country; and a few generations later the Christological quarrel was destined-both in Armenia and Persia-to make a temporary breach permanent. Up to the close of the fourth century, however, there was no religious persecution in Armenia; or rather, all persecution had been of pagans by Christians, when the nation was forcibly converted. Massacres, and extensive ones, had taken place when the Persians occupied the country on the deposition of Arsaces; and here the sufferers were Christians, and the inflictors Zoroastrians; but these were acts of war, not of religion. The Church of Armenia, however, -%s*as to have her full share of persecution, properly so called, during future centuries.

In Persia, as the long persecution gradually flickered out (and there is evidence that it was not fully over till thirty years after the death of Sapor), it is not wonderful that the Church should be left in a most shattered and disorganized condition. The marvel is, indeed, that life remained in the body at all; and it is doubtful whether a Western Church would have survived such an ordeal. An Eastern *melet*, however, if it has not the vigorous and energetic (perhaps interfering) vitality of its Western counterpart; and if, like certain animals, it maintains itself by an external armour of custom and inherited habit, rather than by a strong principle of internal life; has this in common also with the crustacean--that it can endure an amount of cutting and slashing that would be fatal to a more highly organized body.

Thus, though crushed and maimed--with probably hardly any bishops remaining, and certainly a very scanty supply of priests--the Church began its reparative process almost as soon as the persecution was staved. Naturally it is difficult to trace the stages, for the confusion of the time is repeated in the confused and fragmentary statements of the historians.

It appears, however, from the statements of both the later writers who give us an account of this period[96] that a Catholicos, or, at all events, a bishop of Seleucia, was chosen soon after the death of Sapor; and probably in the time of his son, though not immediate successor, Sapor III. Bar-Hebraeus, indeed, declares that permission was given for the election by Sapor II, after the death of Julian had convinced him of the iniquity and folly of persecuting Christians.[97] As, however, we know from other sources that the event had no such effect, the statement of other writers that it was Sapor III who gave the necessary leave seems much more probable. We know from Persian history[98] that this King had the reputation of being "a just and merciful man"; and it was also during his reign that the Bishop of Arbela, Shubkha I'Ishu, ventured on what he had feared to do before, and commenced the ordination of clergy for his diocese.[99]

Of the bishop chosen, whose name was Tamuza,[100] or Tumarsa, we know little; except that he was assisted in his organizing work by "Bokht-Ishu the martyr"[101] (of whom nothing else is known), and by Mar Abda.

The name of Bokht-Ishu suggests the continuance of persecution in some cases; and Abda we know as a famous ascetic who founded a monastery in the little Arab state of Khirta or Kufa, whence came more than one Catholicos in later days.

As a rule, however, Tamuza was no great advocate of asceticism. Death and apostasy had so diminished the *melet* that he urged all young people to marry, and produce children to recoup its numbers.[102] The advice was sound, under the circumstances; but it shows how thoroughly the *"melet* conception" was getting into the minds of the people. It was far more natural, in their eyes, that the Church should extend by growth rather than by conversions. The thought was taking root that a man born in the Church naturally belonged to it; but that it was out of the common for folk to join it from outside, or for men to work with the object of winning them.[103]

In recommending marriage, however, Tamuza had to guard his people against marriages condemned by the Christian conscience, though ever. applauded by the Magian code. This was one of the standing temptations of all Persian Christians; and their obedience to their stricter law was one of the standing provocations that their existence offered to Zoroastrians. That the incestuous unions of Magianism should be unknown now thanks to the influence of a faith that borrowed this point of its morality at least from Christianity -is not the least of the triumphs (albeit an indirect one) of the faith.

Tamuza died a natural death-a thing sufficiently unusual among bishops of the period for Bar-Hebraeus to note the fact specially-but in spite of this encouraging event it was hard to find any one who, at the time of his departure, would accept the dangerous post. After a considerable interval, one Qaiuma (Cajumas) volunteered for the perilous honour; on the ground that he, being already an old man, had little to lose by a speedy death, and that such service as his age could render was at the disposal of the Church. The date of his consecration is both uncertain and unimportant. For a few years (five, according to Bar-Hebraeus) he acted as an avowed stop-gap to the see; and then the accession of Yezdegerd and the commencement of friendly relations with the Christian Empire of Rome offered a prospect of definite peace for the Church. The Catholicos at once offered to lay clown an office which he had only accepted when it was dangerous, and whose duties he could not efficiently discharge. A gathering of bishops, however, unanimously refused the resignation; though they appointed as his coadjutor a man named Isaac, of ancient and honourable house, and of kin to the late Catholicos, Tamuza. This man acted as son to Qaiuma during the brief remainder of the old man's honourable life, and succeeded to his throne at his decease.

Such is the story given to us, with no important variations,[104] by both the Monophysite and Nestorian writers. Both are certainly late in date, but there seems no solid reason for doubting the substantial truth of that which both affirm.

In 399 Yezdegerd I became King of Persia. Magian historians are hard put to it to find epithets adequate to express their detestation of this prince -- "the apostate," "the wicked," the friend of Rome and of Christians, and the persecutor of Magi. As a matter of fact, this much-abused man appears from his acts to have been a strong and able king of peaceful disposition; who refrained from making war on the Roman Empire when it was hardly in a state to resist him, and who was uniformly friendly to the two emperors of his day.

The statement made by Procopius[105] that Yezdegerd actually acted as guardian of the infant Theodosius II has been naturally questioned; but even its startling character makes it credible when given us by an historian who, when not blinded by prejudice, is usually painstaking and accurate. In his home policy Yezdegerd set himself steadily to oppose the nobles, and specially the Magi whose great corporation was powerful enough to be formidable to the King. Hence he appears to Alagian writers as a tyrant; so suspicious of everybody that if ever A. came to him to ask a favour for B., he would at once ask A. what payment he was to receive as his share.[106]

This philo-Roman and anti-Alagian policy naturally led him to show favour to the Christians of his land; though there was probably never any ground for the hope entertained by them that this Shah-in-Shah would declare himself a Christian, and be the Persian Constantine. When Christians threatened to be dangerous, he could repress them as sternly as he disciplined Magi; and while good folk in Constantinople were hoping to hear of his conversion, he was actually issuing a Firman of persecution.[107]

Still, for all the early part of his reign Yezdegerd was distinctly a pro-Christian king; and was probably much influenced in this direction by a Roman subject who was a welcome guest at his court-the diplomatist-prelate, Alarutha of Maipherqat by Amida. When relations between Rome and Persia were friendly, embassies (to quote the contemporary historian) "were always being necessary"; and though the post of ambassador might be trusted only to some high dignitary of the empire sending the embassy, yet it was constantly found convenient, in both countries, to associate with him one or more episcopal assessors, who were no doubt valuable assistants, thanks to the ecclesiastical free-masonry that then prevailed from York to Seleucia-Ctesiphon.

Marutha was one of the men most frequently employed in this fashion. So frequently that one doubts whether, between the claims of embassies and of councils, his diocese had much benefit from his services! Thus, having been present, apparently, at the council of Constantinople in 381,[108] he makes his first appearance in Assyrian Church history at the somewhat informal council that elected Isaac to the Catholicate-the decision reached being much affected by his advice.[109] Next (perhaps two years later) he is at Constantinople once more; and not, it must be owned, in the best of company, as he was a member of the too notorious synod of the Oak that condemned St. Chrysostom[110] Five years elapsed, and the great opportunity of his life presented itself to the diplomatist bishop, who seems to have added the art of a physician to his other accomplishments. In 408 or 409 he was again dispatched (and this time apparently in all three of his capacities, as diplomatist, bishop and doctor) to the Persian court; and during a lengthy sojourn there he rendered to his Eastern brethren the greatest service that a "Western" bishop ever performed for them. He accomplished his work as diplomatist and doctor to the satisfaction of his employers; and displayed his versatile character in a new light, as a Church historian, or at least as a collector of material for Church history.

The diplomatic side of Marutha's work was soon accomplished, if, as is the most probable suggestion, the embassy had nothing more serious to do than to formally announce the accession of Theodosius II to his brother and guardian. Medically, he cured the King (by his prayers, says Socrates) of severe attacks of headache, which the Persian doctors had been unable to alleviate. According to one account,[111] the presence of a doctor in the embassy had been specially requested; the Persians declaring with regret that there were no physicians like the Christians, and that all the best of them had been killed or driven away during the persecution. Grateful for his cure, the King showed such honour to Marutha that Magians began to fear the conversion of one who was no strict Zoroastrian, and took measures to prevent it. When Yezdegerd was at one of the usual services in one of the fire-temples of the capital, a voice was suddenly heard proclaiming from the midst of the sacred fire, "Turn out that apostate." All applied the words to Yezdegerd, who seems to have been genuinely frightened for the moment, and to have hurried from the temple. Marutha (who, of course, was not in the building) reassured him, and advised him to make close search for evidence of fraud; which he did, and was rewarded by finding a place where a man could stand concealed and utter "supernatural" messages. Severe punishment for the Magi followed, of course (though neither this nor. the remembrance of ignominious failure prevented the repetition of the trick, with like result, on another occasion); and Marutha was emboldened to ask and obtain from the Shah-in-Shall the two great favours that he had been charged, if possible, to procure. These were, first, a firman of toleration for Christians; and second, the leave to assemble a council for the regulation of Church affairs.

There was no difficulty about the firman, which was issued some time in the year 409.[112] Permission was formally given to the Christians to worship openly, and to rebuild their churches. Confessors who were still in prison were set at liberty, and bishops were given free leave to travel in their dioceses. This decree was practically the Edict of Milan for the Assyrian Church. It was the formal recognition of the Christians as being in law what they had hitherto been in fact, viz. a *melet* with the right to exist and worship in the Persian Empire. Of course this toleration was something very far removed from liberty or equality, as we understand the words. First, the decree was valid only *durante beneplacito*--till it was the pleasure of the Shah-in-Shah to withdraw it; and next, while in existence, the toleration that it gave was limited. A Christian might exist, but not proselytize. Apostasy from Magianism was as much a capital offence as ever; and the leave to rebuild old churches did not (and does not) imply the right to build new ones. Still the grant was a long step forward for the Church; and the simultaneous recognition of the right to organize and make, laws for itself gave to it all that was necessary for its future growth.

Incidentally, we note the right given to "the chiefs" (*i.e.* the bishops) to travel and itinerate in their dioceses without being disturbed. Of course this is necessary for a bishop anywhere, and it is doubly necessary in the East; yet where the clear right to act thus is not recognized the proceeding rouses the suspicions of every oriental official, who is accustomed to the belief that those who are doing. nothing are doing right, and that inexplicable activity is either insane or treasonable. "What is the man really after that he goes round among the *rayats* in that fashion?" is the question that is always asked; so that the right to visit his diocese undisturbed by officials must have been an immense relief to any zealous Assyrian bishop.

Further (though this is assumed rather than expressed in formal documents), the Shah-in-Shah now fully accepted Isaac, Bishop of Seleucia, as head of the *melet,* and Catholicos of the Church in his dominions. Again, this was only the recognition of what was the fact previously, though hardly for long enough to make it established custom. Facts had created the presidency of the see; and though circumstances had put it, and everything else that was regular, in abeyance for about seventy years; nevertheless, as soon as peace %vas restored, and the gxistee.ee of the Church recognized by the State, it was natural that the existence and position of its chief officer should be recognized also. The Catholicate, thus established, has remained an established fact ever since; and the right of the throne of Seleucia-Ctesiphon, or its successor,[113] to the presidency of the Assyrian Church has never been challenged. There have, of course, been disputes over the succession, which has been claimed by two rival lines since the seventeenth century; and there have been occasional vacancies; but the right of this throne to the Catholicate has been axiomatic.

The title, henceforth used habitually and regularly[114] by the Bishop of Seleucia-Ctesiphon, and still employed by his successors (though in the course of the nest half-century they began to use the term Patriarch along with it, and still continue to do so), needs a word of explanation. In the Roman Empire it was the name of a civil and financial office; but previously to its use as an ecclesiastical title in Persia it had been adopted by the Armenians as the title of the principal bishop of their national Church. It was probably from them that the Bishops of Seleucia adopted the word, and they used it in the same sense.[115]

The office, as we have seen, was a natural growth from the conditions of Christian life in Persia. In later ages men felt obliged to account for the origin of the Patriarchate, as it has by that time become,[116] by the fiction of a grant made in the year 190 by the four "Western" patriarchates to an "Eastern" brother;[117] and other writers, referring back to primitive times the growths of the fourth and fifth centuries, have seen in the "Catholicos" of Seleucia the Procurator-general or legatus natus of the see of Antioch.

There is, however, so far as I am aware, no evidence in writers of the Assyrian or Persian Church that they ever regarded themselves as under Antiochene jurisdiction; or their chief as in any sense the delegate of that patriarch.[118] It is extremely improbable that any Persian king would ever have tolerated the subjection of "his rayats" to "the Roman Emperor's patriarch"; or that members of a Church liable enough to persecution in any case would have thus gone out of their way to secure a perpetuity of it! The "Patriarchates" of Seleucia and Antioch are parallel growths, and neither of them is an offshoot of the other. Just about the time that the "custom" referred to at Nicaea was bringing the sees round Antioch, Alexandria and Rome into formal dependence on those bishoprics, circumstances were bringing the sees of Persia into like dependence on the bishopric of their capital. Kings and councils recognized the facts, but did not create them.[119]

Toleration and the State recognition of the Catholicos, however, were not all that was needed. Forty years of persecution, and thirty of no-government, had naturally left a legacy of confusion behind them; and a council was necessary, both to straighten out this tangle, and to link up the Church "of the East" once more with her Western sisters. Further, the decision of some indisputable authority was needful to settle various disputes that had arisen.

Some sees had two, some three bishops contending for them; and there were other quarrels current. For instance, there was in existence a party of personal opponents of Isaac, the members of which were filing accusations against him before the King.[120] No doubt these accusations collapsed as soon as the royal favour towards Isaac was shown beyond possibility of error, and no opportunity for their revival ever occurred. This, however, did not necessarily mean that they were dead in the minds of their promoters until Isaac was dead too. It is one of the special beauties of oriental intrigue that any accusation may be dropped automatically when its object is in favour; and, after remaining dormant for half a lifetime, spring to full life again if he lose power.

Marutha, in expectation of the permission which Yezdegerd granted readily enough, had brought letters from "the Western. bishops" (or those whom Assyrians called Westerns[121]), both for the hypothetical council and for the Catholicos, recommending the action that they judged advisable. There was also a covering letter to the Shah-in-Shah, to whom Marutha discreetly showed all the documents before the council met.

The "Western" bishops thus writing were Porphyrius, "Catholicos" of Antioch, and Acacius of Beroea; both of them friends of Theophilus, and bitter foes of John Chrysostom, then quite recently dead. One of them, it must be owned, was to play a worthier part in his old age, as the peacemaker between John of Antioch and Cyril of Alexandria. Joined with them was another, Acacius of Amida, later the saintly ransomer of Persian captives, and ambassador to the Church of Assyria on a second occasion; and the Bishops of Edessa and Tella. Thus all the greater sees of the Antiochene province were represented. It is noteworthy that there is no evidence in the acts of the council of the slightest claim made by Antioch to jurisdiction in Persia. A "Catholicos," with some brother bishops, writes to a brother "Catholicos," making recommendations which the independent national Church accepts and adopts.

The recommendations were simple enough;[122] namely, (a) That in future only one bishop should be allowed in each see, and that care should be taken to have at least three consecrators. (b) That in future all should celebrate the feast of Easter, and the feast of Christmas and Epiphany (still regarded as one solemnity), on the same days; and should observe the fast of forty days[123] and Good Friday. (c) That if a council were possible, that council should solemnly declare its adherence to the decrees of Nicaea.

Yezdegerd, in giving permission for the council, gave licence also to use the royal posts for its assembly; and forty bishops were thus summoned, from Nisibis in the north to Fars by the Persian Gulf in the south, "to put a stop to all quarrels, schisms and divisions, and to establish proper canons for the regulation of the Catholic Church."

On the feast of. Epiphany, 410, the council met at Seleucia; and after a brief formal sitting under the presidency of Isaac and Marutha, adjourned for nearly a month-an interval spent probably in discussions, and in the drawing up informally of the canons which were to be passed at a later session. On February t the second session opened. The letter of the "Westerns" was read and approved; the Nicene canons, including, of course, the creed, were read, adopted and signed by the council; and either then or at the next session the twenty-one canons of the council formally passed unanimously. A second adjournment followed, during which Isaac and Marutha had an audience of Yezdegerd, probably submitting the canons for his approval, as a preliminary to their publication; and finally, two royal commissioners of high rank the (Grand Vizier and the Commander-in-chief) summoned the synod to their presence, republished the Firman of Toleration, declared that Isaac had been established by the King as "Chief of all the Christians of the East," and that the joint decisions of the Catholicos and Marutha were to be final in all existing disputes and would be enforced by royal authority.

Thus, at this council the Church was put formally and finally into the position of a recognized *melet* in the Persian kingdom. It was subject to its own ruler (who was also its religious head), whose appointment must be at the least approved by the State. It could make its own laws in its own way, subject to State approval; and disobedience to them could be punished by State authority, if the moral and temporal power of the Catholicos failed. And it could own its own buildings, endowments and institutions. Any man could leave the *melet* by either abandoning his Christianity, or (in later times, when *melets* multiplied) by leaving his original Church for some other; but while he remained in it he must obey its rules.

This precedent set by Yezdegerd has been followed so often, through so many centuries, by so many varying non-Christian rulers, and towards so many varieties of Christianity, that the first setting of it forms a really noteworthy point in oriental history. This system is essentially the one under which all Christians in "the Empire of the East" (whether the rulers of that empire are Persian, Saracen, Mongol, Seljuk, or Ottoman) have lived since, and still live to-day; and if survival can prove fitness, this fact would seem to show that it is, on the whole, well adapted for them.

Of course it has disadvantages. The appointment of all high officers of the Church by a non-Christian Government tends, in oriental circumstances, to bribery and intrigue; just as free election (supposing, *per impossibile,* that an oriental ruler would allow it) produces equally inevitably quarrels and schisms. Further, it tends, on the whole, to keep the strong and saintly characters out of the episcopate, and in obscurity. As things go in the East, it is the supple intriguer rather than the straightforward man who will get such prizes as are open to the *rayat;* and there is, further, a natural tendency to select as bishops such men as will be "safe," and give the Government no trouble. Hence., great men are rare among Eastern bishops; and respectable nonentities and followers of routine are the rule under good rulers, and self-seeking courtiers under evil. Thus it comes,. too, that when reform is needed, and a feeling in favour of it is in the air, the standing obstacle in the way is apt to be the hierarchy. It is not often that sheer force of lofty character can prevail and win high office in the Church under a Government that does not care for loftiness of character, and dreads strong men anywhere.

At first, no doubt, the fact that the secular Government was ready to support the head of the *melet* made for strong discipline in the Church. But *melets* tend to multiply; a Government that distrusts its Christian subjects is always ready to encourage them to divide, and will readily recognize a new division among them; while their ingrained quarrelsomeness always leads them to take advantage of this. Under such circumstances discipline can hardly be pressed. A bishop may threaten a rich evil-doer with excommunication; but will be met by the threat, "If you dare, I register myself as Jacobite or Romanist. They will receive me readily enough, and it will be bad for any man in my village who does not follow me."

The *melet* system guarantees the existence of, and gives some freedom to, the Church of a subject population; but it also puts a premium on that spirit of quarrel and intrigue which is the bane of Eastern Christianity.

The canons passed by the council numbered twenty-one; and are in effect an adaptation of certain Nicene rules to the circumstances of the Church, together with other rules of their own devising for its organization. It is a strong proof of the spirit of independence in the Assyrians that at this moment-when they owed so much to the West-they should have dealt thus boldly with the canons even of Nicaea. The creed, of course, they accepted; but all other rules they seem to have felt themselves free to accept, alter or neglect, according to their own judgment as an autocephalous Church.

The creed that was put before them was the original Nicene,[124] including the anathemas. But Assyrians of to-day do not use it in the precise conciliar form, any more than Westerns do; and in each case the story of the growth of the form used from the form sanctioned is an extremely difficult one to trace. Of the two crucial technical terms in the creed, is rendered by ܐܐܚܕܐ ܒܪ;[125] a different and (to the writer's thinking) much better rendering of the Greek than the ܚܕ ܒܪ[126] which is in use to-day. in the third anathema is rendered by ܩܢܘܡܐ[127], a fact which was important in future doctrinal controversy. The Greek term, as is obvious, is here equivalent to or the Syriac ܐܚܕܐ;[128] and ܩܢܘܡܐ [129] has therefore the same force. Unfortunately, under the influence of the Cappadocian fathers, was already being used in the West in the different (and very artificial) sense of Person; so that the Assyrian Church--just when effort was being made to link their thought to the West--adopted an important technical term in a sense which the Westerns were just then abandoning. This was to be fruitful of misunderstanding, and a principal cause of separation.

In the remaining canons the tone is that of the substitution of law for tolerated indiscipline; and the large majority of them concern themselves with the position and duties of the various ranks of the hierarchy, from the Catholicos and his metropolitans to the sub-deacon. Certain things are forbidden that would naturally be the custom in times of peril, such as celebration of the Eucharist in private houses, and consecration of bishops by one bishop only. We also find that which occurs in every oriental council-and was apparently equally ineffective in every one--viz., the stern prohibition of the practice of magic and the use of charms. No canons, in East or West, have prevailed against the fascination of that forbidden fruit.

Other canons (XX and XXI) regulate the position and precedence of the five metropolitans, Bait Lapat, Nisibis, Prat d'Maishan, parka d'Bait Sluk and Arbela, which owed obedience to the Catholicos. Their provinces are duly assigned to them, and the number of suffragans under each clearly laid down.[130] A special canon (XVIII) secured to each bishop the right of appeal to the Catholicos, without whose confirmation no episcopal consecration was valid. Definite rules (Canons I and XX) were laid down for the election of bishops; but not for the choice of a Catholicos, though provision was made for government during a vacancy. Later, rules were made on the point; but, as a matter of fact, he was usually nominated by the Shah-in-Shah.

Broadly (Canons 1, VI, XVIII), the council recognizes in, or confers on, the holder of the see of Seleucia a power over his suffragans that is singularly extensive and defined. He has a practical veto on their appointment; appeal from all their acts lies to him; and they are to report themselves to him personally twice a year. It may be doubted whether any patriarch to the Roman Empire (except possibly the Patriarch of Alexandria) had so unquestioned, and so clearly defined, a sway over his diocese as. the "Catholicos of the East." It is not surprising that the holder of it should soon have begun to use the term "patriarch" (though not dropping the title Catholicos), before the Christological controversy had separated him from the West, and long before it was the habitual and peculiar title of five special sees in the empire. This centralizing tendency is the fruit, as we have seen, of *melet* life, and is fostered, no doubt, by the natural Eastern attraction towards an autocracy; but it should also be noted that a force which retarded similar development in Asia Minor was absent in Persia. In the empire, if there was no provincial self-government, there was considerable municipal independence; and the tendency of the oriental to submit to authority-and of the greater sees to exalt themselves over the lesser-was counterbalanced, in a measure, by the fact that the bishop was a principal citizen of his own town as well as a subject of the Emperor, and a suffragan of Antioch or Constantinople.

One other tendency we see in the fathers of Seleucia which might well have spelt disaster for the Church had their circumstances allowed them to give way to it. This was the desire to rely on the State, the secular arm, even when that arm was non-Christian. The King decrees the supremacy of the Catholicos, the King will enforce the decrees of the council, and so on. Centuries of obstinate hostility, to their creed and to themselves, on the part of several successive rulers have not eradicated this feeling from any branch of Eastern Christianity. The fact that their rulers have never been Christian has saved them, at a terrible cost to themselves, from becoming a mere State Church of Byzantine pattern; but the fact remains that every variety of Christian Church in the Ottoman Empire (which is in this, as in much else, the heir of the Sassanid) is State established and State controlled, and that its officers, up to the date of writing, are partially State paid. It was, of course, out of policy (and admirable policy too, from their point of view) that Mahommedan rulers allowed this to continue; but the proceeding absolutely coincided with popular feeling, and it will be long before the theory that connection between Church and State is necessarily iniquitous finds acceptance in the East.

Note on the Catholici, Tamuza and Qaiuma.

Mons. Labourt *(Christianisme dans la Perse,* p. 86) doubts the existence of both these Catholici, on the double ground that (a) Elia of Damascus, whose list of the Catholici is older than any other, places both before, not after, Papa (Ass., ii. 391); and that (b) the Council of Dad-Ishu--or to be accurate, a speaker in it--speaks of a vacancy of twenty-two years before Isaac's election. The list given by Elia, however, is purely traditional, and very incorrect in other ways. The speaker in the council (Agapetus of B. Lapat, Chabot, Synod. Or., 48, 292) certainly uses language suggesting that the vacancy of twenty-two years in the Catholicate (which admittedly came somewhere) was immediately before Isaac's election; but it also could mean that such vacancy was simply "before Isaac."

If however there was no holder of the office after the death of Bar Washmin till Yezdegerd gave leave for an election, the vacancy was not for. twenty-two but for fort%_ seven years at least; and this does not agree with other information. Hence the explanation that gives least difficulty is, that Tamuza and Qaiuma were real characters, and Bishops of Seleucia during the period 380-408. It is quite probable, as Labourt suggests, that the authority of neither was recognized outside the limits of Seleucia. The Catholicate had no length of custom behind it, to give it weight; and it would be quite natural that the holder of it should be disregarded, till the firman of Yezdegerd put his position beyond challenge. To this day a patriarch may be duly elected and consecrated; he may be the lawful nephew of his predecessor, duly marked out from childhood for the post, and nominated by that predecessor before his death; but yet, lacking the firman of the Sultan, he is only half a patriarch in the eyes of half his people, and there is no getting over the fact.

You may prove to the full that he has every title--from the most admirably regular to the most scandalously uncanonical--for his office; but till he has the firman, much is lacking. It is a prejudice only, of course, and therefore argument fails. To argue away a European prejudice is not easy. But for a European to argue away the oriental variety is hopeless.

Similarly, when the firman has been granted, and in virtue of it the patriarch has been duly installed, loyal obedience will usually be rendered to him. A Western may kick at an order, but show him that obedience is for the general good, and he will often give up his own ideas. To the oriental, to give up your own ideas for the general good is impossible; but it is wonderful how often loyal obedience will be rendered to "a good large order."

Chapter Six - The Councils of Yahb-Alaha and Dad-Ishu

I. The Council of Yahb-Alaha

THE Council of Seleucia dispersed. Marutha returned home from what was, as it turned out, his last visit to the East, laden with the relics and histories of martyrs, his work well and thoroughly done. The Church of the East settled in its new security to a period of quiet and rapid growth.

As is usual in Church history, periods of peace and spiritual-work have no history; and it is only from the names in the episcopal lists of the two councils, held during the next fifteen years, that we can see how rapid that growth was. Forty bishoprics are enumerated as existing in 4Io, at Isaac's Council, and that gathering was at all events intended to be complete. But in the next two councils no fewer than twenty-six additional sees are mentioned, which do not appear in the former list. It is possible, of course, that some of those existed before Yezdegerd issued his firman, and were vacant then; but most are probably evidence of increase.

And this increase, so rapid and so sure (for most of the sees named are known to have been still existing centuries later), took place either in lands where Christian missions do not exist to-day, or where they find their work least promising and most difficult. Bishops sign for the sees of Segestan, Teheran, Ispahan, Herat, Khorassan. What would we give to have native, self-supporting bishoprics in those centres to-day? Merv, which is also in the list, has now probably a bishop once more-an official of the conquering Russian Government, brought. and maintained by their bayonets; but his fifth-century predecessor came there by the power of the living extension of the Church, and he speedily developed into a metropolitan, with other bishops under him. Christianity could certainly be so proclaimed as to suit the oriental, when taught by easterns to their brethren; and when a religion, intrinsically eastern, was presented without the western externals which a western is apt to identify with its essence.

Yet if this oriental Christianity, oriental taught, could spread itself and flourish in these lands once, it has passed from them now; and with the exception of some scattered colonies of Armenians, may be said to have passed from them completely. How is it that it failed? How is it that another and a lower faith has expelled it? The question is a serious one for a writer who believes fully in the gospel of the Word made Flesh, and who holds that it, and it alone, can fully answer the cravings of the human heart. It is easy to say that this wonderful extension was "founded on Nestorius, and not on Christ," and therefore had no strength. But-putting aside the point that much of the growth took place before Nestorius was heard of-the explanation that a form of Christianity that has failed must have been heretical does not seem to cover the facts. Admitting for argument's sake (we must deal with the point more at length in a later chapter) that the Church of the Assyrians did teach what we mean by "Nestorianism," the fact remains that it is not the only great Church that has gone down before Islam, and that others have shared its fate to which the explanation given above will not apply. The Church of Africa was orthodox-and has perished; and the fall of the Nestorians has been only a little more complete than that of the unimpeachably correct Greeks of Asia Minor. It is a difficulty. If we could say what made the tree wither, we might also be able to say what would restore strength and vigour for fresh growth to its still living roots.

In the list of new sees there are three names of bishops which have some peculiar interest. First, "Adraq, bishop of the tents of the Kurds."[131] A nomad bishop, with a nomad flock, strikes us as unusual; and the fact shows that instinctive and natural adaptation to the habits of those to whom he ministered which was part of the strength of the oriental teacher. Perhaps with us a bishop of a new country, whose palace and cathedral are contained within the limits of one railway carriage, or one ox-wagon, is not a wholly unthinkable phenomenon.

Traces of this early spread of Christianity among the Kurds--those turbulent nomads and semi-nomads who are the bane of modern Assyrian Christians--exist to-day. It is probable that some at least of the Christians of Hakkiari are of Kurdish blood, though they themselves would strenuously deny it: and some tribes of Mussalman Kurds have clear recollection of the fact that their fathers were Christian; and retain a desire to return, if it be possible, to that unforgotten faith.[132]

The two other names that we may notice are, "Domit" (or Domitius), "Bishop of the Captivity of Gurgan," and "Hatit" (AEtius 7), "Bishop of the Captivity of Belashpar,"[133]--names that betray at once the Roman origin of their bearers. The existence of these "Roman captivities" is well known, and captives are frequently referred to in the *Acta Sanctorum*.[134] Thus, it was "Roman captives" who collected the bodies of Mar Shimun and his companions; and Pusai the martyr was "the son of a captive"; while another famous martyr, Bar-shbia, would seem by his name to have been so also.

When captivities were carried off *en masse* from the Christian empire, as sometimes happened, their bishops were taken with them. This we see from the history of the captives of B. Zabdai,[135] even if the story of Demetrius of B. Lapat be purely legendary.

Earlier kings like Sapor I made a special point of securing artisans and craftsmen, as the most valuable plunder in their colossal raids, and it was precisely among these classes that Christianity spread most rapidly. Indeed, this ancient habit of the Sassanids was one of the causes of the spread of the Church in "the East"; and in the times of their later kings, a cause of the extension of R1onophysitism within its bounds. We have no means of telling which of the numerous captivities are referred to here; but there is no impossibility in the supposition that they date back to Sapor I, one hundred and eighty years previously. A captivity-even when settled in its new home will retain its identity for centuries, particularly if its religion be also of a distinctive character. The Jews of Babylon are, of course, an instance of this, but other proofs can be given from much more modern times. The present Jewish colony in Mosul declare that they have been there since the days of Nebuchadnezzar, if not from the time of Sargon; and Julfa, a suburb of Ispahan, is populated still by the descendants of an Armenian captivity, brought from Erivan and Julfa on the river Aras in the time of our Queen Elizabeth. There is nothing impossible, then, in Roman captivities having a distinct existence in Persia.[136]

Early in this period of quiet Isaac the Catholicos passed away. The exact date of his death is not known; but it is clear that Yahb Alaha[137] was elected Catholicos in 415-416, and at least a year or two must be allowed for the tenure of the see by Akha, immediate successor of Isaac. We shall probably, therefore, not be far from the truth if we place the death of Isaac in the year 412.

Akha succeeded him. This man had been the pupil of the hermit Abda, whose life he wrote; and one of the helpers of Marutha, in his collection of the Acts of the Martyrs.[138] It was perhaps this circumstance that brought him to the notice of Yezdegerd, with whom he was a favourite, and from whom he received as Catholicos,[139] *amplissimam potestatem gregem regendi,* an endowment that no doubt saved trouble for the time, but was of evil omen for the future. A strict ascetic in his habits--for his food consisted of nothing but dry bread and olives--he was respected by that section of growing importance in the Church, the monastic party. His pontificate, however, was brief, and certainly did not include more than the three years that the mediaeval chronicler assigns to him.

Yahb-Alaha (whose not very euphonious name is the equivalent of Theodore) succeeded him. He had been the fellow pupil of Akha under Abda, and was, like him, a rigorous ascetic. Later tradition assigned to him the miraculous curing of a son of the Shah-in-Shah.[140] Yezdegerd, who still continued friendly with Rome, sent him on an embassy to Theodosius II shortly after his consecration, and from this he returned with splendid gifts for the adornment of his cathedral and private tent-chapel. On returning, however, he also found a somewhat disturbed Church awaiting him, and a situation that threatened that the religious peace established by Marutha would not continue for long. That Zoroastrians generally, and Magians more particularly, should be disturbed and angry at the rapid spread of Christianity-- "particularly among the nobles and freemen *(asatant.)*"[141]--was as natural, but ominous; however, the internal troubles of the Church were far more dangerous in reality. Unworthy men who had powerful Zoroastrian friends were making use of their influence, both to avoid discipline and to win promotion, even to the Episcopate; and dangerous quarrels and schisms were resulting.[142]

This use of pagan patronage to gain Church power was at once a scandal and a problem, and one very likely to arise under *melet* conditions of life. The interference of a non-Christian nobleman in the election of a bishop was, of course, the negation of all Church law; but it appeared perfectly natural, for instance, to the Zoroastrian *seigneur* to drop a hint to a village of his *rayats* that X. had done him good service more than once, and that, as they were choosing their religious headman, he thought that they might make a worse choice. The Shah-in-Shah nominated the Catholicos, why should not the Agha name the bishop? Supposing the man named to be not absolutely impossible, would the villagers neglect the seigneur's hint, and face the probability that double dues would be exacted next harvest? Similarly, discipline ought, of course, to be moved solely by the consideration of the law of the Church, and the guilt of the sinner. But supposing a bishop to have told a village of Christians that they ought not to tolerate a strange teacher in their midst, it would take some resolution to carry out the order in the face of a warning from the Agha over the hill, "if you dare to disturb my friend I will burn your village, as I did the seven others in your valley."[143] furthermore, though this use of pagan patronage was a very evil thing for the Church and a fatal thing for the spiritual life of those who availed themselves of it, it was, after all, only the correlative, in another sphere, of the reliance of Catholicos and bishops on the secular arm. If the Catholicos, who owed his throne to the fact that he was a *persona grata* at Court, used the power that the King gave him tyrannically, why should not the victims make use of their interest with lesser potentates to evade that tyranny?

The practice, evil enough, was a symptom only; and the real disease was ingrained quarrelsomeness, and the habit of mind that sticks at nothing if only the immediate end can be attained. Aden who used pagan patronage to get themselves made bishops, or to get censures removed, did not wish to injure the Church, or Christianity; they merely wanted to get their own way. Their present descendants act in precisely the same fashion, and when the inevitable results of their proposed action are pointed out, they are apt to reply, "Ah, but we will work a *pand*[144]and avoid that." Orientals are always inclined to think that they can call up the devil to do their work, and then cheat him and avoid paying him his fee!

Thus Yahb-Alaha came back, to find these tendencies running riot in the Church for which he was responsible. At a loss what to do, he fell back on the usual expedient of a council; and as the presence of another episcopal ambassador from Rome (Acacius of Amida, sent, it would seem, to return the visit of Yahb-Alaha) gave a convenient opportunity for obtaining leave, the assembly was able to meet in 420.[145]

The gathering was scantily attended, for only ten bishops, and among them only two representatives of metropolitan sees, were present with the Catholicos and Acacius; nor could they--or for that matter any assembly of bishops--really solve the problem that was before them. What was wanted was a change of disposition, and all that they could suggest was the acceptance of a number of rules. "We have not kept our old rules, therefore let us bind ourselves to keep them in future, and many more besides." It was decided (apparently at the suggestion of Acacius) that the Church of the "East" should not only re-enact its own canons, passed ten years ago, but should also accept as binding all the rules of several purely "western" councils, viz. those of Gangra, Antioch (the "dedication" council), Caesarea, Ancyra and Laodicea. All the canons of all these councils were therefore accepted *en bloc*, in spite of a hint from the Catholicos that it might be well to keep their own rules better before binding themselves to observe so many new ones. Perfect peace and concord reigned (so the argument ran) in the West (!), therefore the inspired rules that had produced that peace must be adopted in the "East." The expedient takes one's breath away. Putting aside the ignorance of things "western" shown in the placid assumption that peace existed there--and, also, the doubtful wisdom of attempting to control the schismatic spirit by the mere multiplication of canons--the adoption of an undigested mass of laws, made for other circumstances and other conditions, was necessarily useless. What, for instance, had the Church of the Persian Empire to do with canons like IV and XI of the "Dedication Council," composed specially to prevent St. Athanasius from ever getting a fair hearing? What had it to do with appeals to the Emperor at Constantinople? With the rules made at Laodicea for the reception of Novatians, Photinians, Quartodecimans and Montanists--none of whom ever seem to have gained a footing in Persia? With the purely local sect of Eustathians, whose practices were condemned at Ancyra? Or with the reconciliation of men who had lapsed under Roman conditions of persecution?

Of course adoption of such canons as were really fitted to their circumstances, coupled with a reasoned application of the excellent principles that underlay the others, would have been a very possible policy, particularly as the Assyrian Church seems never to have adopted any definite rules for dealing with "the lapsed" in her numerous persecutions; or to have attempted any control of irregular appeals to the secular power. But this was precisely what was not done. The councils were adopted bodily, and it was a question only whether the one hundred and eighty inconsistent canons thus added to the Corpus Juris of the Church would remain a mere *brutum fulmen,* or whether they would be the source of endless litigation and schism. Fortunately, and no thanks to the council therefor, it was the former alternative that resulted.

The council of Mar Yahb-Alaha presents an unpleasant contrast to that of Isaac. In the earlier, the canons of a much greater council were considered, and those adapted to Assyrian conditions adopted. In the later, Catholicos and bishops, having heard the advice of the ambassador who would seem to have been more saint than statesman, appear to have "opened their mouths and gulped down David whole."

The fact is that the Assyrian Church seems to have been in a frame of mind not unknown to their descendants. Suddenly realizing that things were unsatisfactory generally, they grasped at the first panacea that offered. In each case the feeling was, "All is wrong with us, and all is right with the West; let us therefore all be as western as we can." There was no consideration as to how far things were really wrong or right with either party; or whether things passably good for the "western" would for that reason be absolutely good for the "eastern." The panacea was adopted unanimously-till the reaction came.

As a general thing, when a change of habit or an abandonment of prejudice is in question, the oriental is found by the European to be "gifted with the noble firmness of the mule." But nature takes her revenge on him occasionally, for at times he will exhibit a positively sheep-like docility-a readiness to follow any leader along a new track, over a bridge or into a swamp as the case may be. Needless to say, no European can ever foretell with any certainty which disposition he will exhibit in a given case.

II. The Persecution of Bahram V

Troubles external as well as internal were soon to come upon the Assyrian Church. The increase of the number of converts from Zoroastrianism to Christianity was seriously alarming the Magian hierarchy; and it was obvious to those who had eyes to read the signs of the times that an effort would soon be made to check this flow of "apostasy" by drastic means. The best that could be hoped for was that a tolerant king would be able to keep the peace for his lifetime. Let another take his place, and the inevitable struggle between the two faiths could not be delayed.

Yahb-Alaha, the Catholicos, at least understood this, and prayed that his old age might be spared the sight of suffering. This prayer was granted; for the Catholicos died, perhaps before the, persecution had begun, certainly before it had become serious. His successor, M'ana, was hardly settled in his seat before the storm burst.

Its commencement was brought about by a deputation representing all the Magians of the kingdom, and headed by the "Mobed Mobedan," Adarbuzi, in person, which sought audience of the Shah-in-Shah, and practically called upon him to take action in view of the increase of apostasy from the State faith.[146] The great corporation was stronger than the King, who had to give way; and the prelate received power to turn back those who had fallen away, "not, however, by death, but by fear and a certain amount of beating." The 1lobeds had to be content with this for the moment, and perhaps felt some confidence that persecution could not long continue to be confined to converts only. In any case so it turned out; and we are enabled to trace the steps of the process in one of the most vivid pieces of hagiology in the Syriac or any other collection of that literature.[147]

One of the men whom Adarbuzi "turned back" from Christianity--by beating or otherwise--was a man of Seleucia, called Adur-parwa. This man had been converted to Christianity by a Qasha named Sapor, who had cured him in some illness, and for whom the grateful convert had built a church. Sapor, by the advice of a friend named Narses, had secured a regular deed of gift for both building and site, so that both were legally his property; but when the "trouble" began, and Adur-parwa was reconverted to Magianism, he (filled apparently with a renegade's zeal) demanded the restoration of what he had given. Sapor did not contest the point at law, but fled by the advice of Narses, carrying the title-deeds with him, and intending no doubt to return in better times and reclaim the church, which was legally his own. The 1lagians took possession of the building, and turned it into a fire-temple. Shortly after Narses, ignorant of what had happened, entered the church, and was surprised to find the sacred fire burning in it, and the whole place fitted up as a Magian sanctuary. He removed the furniture (no heavy task, if fire-temples in those days were furnished as simply as is the case now) and extinguished the fire, an act of sacrilege for which he was mobbed by the villagers. Being rescued from them by authority, he was sent to the Mobed Mobedan at Seleucia for trial. Here his Christianity was not urged against him, he being no doubt of the *melet* by birth; and Adarbuzi seems to have admitted extenuating circumstances in the matter of the extinction of the sacred fire, for the defendant was simply ordered to re-kindle it in the temple, and was promised his release on compliance. This he declared himself unable to do. All parties showed admirable restraint in the matter; the Mobed was anxious to release the prisoner, if he would give what was no doubt regarded as reasonable satisfaction; and Narses on his side indulged in none of the insults to another faith which mar some of the histories, but simply declined to purchase his own release by what he regarded as an act of apostasy, preferring to suffer the penalty instead.

On his refusal he was imprisoned at Seleucia during the winter-"among thieves and murderers," says his biographer, though, in all probability (an oriental prison not being provided with separate cells) this implied no special hardship beyond that of detention-and towards spring a bribe to the gaoler procured his release on bail and permission to reside in a monastery not far from the city.

In spring the Court made its usual move "to the hills"--*i.e.* to B. Lapat or to Susa--and it was decided to have a general clearance of the city prisons on the occasion. Narses honourably surrendered himself, and his case thus came before the King personally, and was decided summarily. "Let him collect fire from 365 places, and put it in the temple, or let him be put to death." Again he refused to comply, and was therefore ordered for execution-the first man, apparently, to die in this persecution.

Crowds of Christians accompanied him to see the end, exciting the fears of the official in charge, till both they and the martyr assured him that they had no thought of obstructing "the King's justice," but merely wished to see the last of a friend. So, without malice and without display, he met his death, the authorities doing no more than they judged their duty, and the sufferer making no complaint of the penalty that befell him for following his conscience. Both parties acted as became honourable men, the Christian as became his faith. Only the clumsiness of the impressed executioner (a Christian, who refused to act till the martyr bade him "strike," for it should not be imputed to him) marred the nobility of the ending. Its tragedy lay, not in the death of the man who preferred it to treachery to his religion, but in the circumstances which gave honourable men no choice but mutually to inflict and submit to death.

It was impossible, however, for persecution to continue in this gentlemanly style. Bloodshed infuriated both sides, calling out hot zeal in the one party and massacre-lust in the other. Narses could not have been dead many days when a great fire-temple of Seleucia,[148] which stood close to a Christian church, was burnt by Christians. A bishop of the name of Abda was arrested, both as being a prominent Christian, and as being suspected of this insult to the State religion; and these facts show that persecution was already drifting beyond the lines of Yezdegerd's original permission. As a matter of fact, it was not Abda who had been guilty of this act of incendiarism; it was an overzealous Qasha of the name of Hashu, who at once accused himself when he heard of the arrest of the bishop, and boldly justified his action; "it was no shrine of God that we destroyed." When told to hold his tongue, and let the accused speak for himself, he persisted in statements that were, under the circumstances, insults to the State faith, and provocative of persecution. "Fire is no god, it is but a creature given to us for our use." Admitting the burning of the temple, lie absolutely refused to admit that it was even a questionable act. Abda, however, seems to have been regarded as responsible; and it was he, not the zealot, who, according to Theodoret, was ordered to rebuild the temple,[149] and was executed on his refusal. With these two martyrdoms, and the feeling which the acts precedent to them would certainly call out (viz. that the Christians were making attacks on "the religion"), a definite persecution of Christians, as distinct from a "disciplining of converts," may be said to have begun.

About this time, too, any chance of the Shah-in-Shah using his influence on the side of moderation was removed by the sudden death of Yezdegerd from the kick of a horse. Both religions saw a divine judgment on a persecutor in the accident; the Magians holding it a punishment for his early acts, and the Christians (with somewhat less than justice to the memory of one who had been on the whole their benefactor) for the final episodes of his reign.

Bahram V, who succeeded his father Yezdegerd, was practically the Magian nominee. There was another candidate for. the throne, and the prince, to secure the support of the hierarchy,[150] was obliged to give pledges of some sort to the Mobeds-an act which of course implied that his full support should be given to the persecution of the Christians. Thus the religious war continued with peculiar ferocity, the hideous tortures which Theodoret details[151] being fully supported by the evidence of Syriac writers. It is not necessary to dwell on these horrors. Churches, of course, were destroyed, the tent-church of the Catholicos being made into a hunting-tent for the King; and all freemen (azatan) who were known to be Christians were deprived of their fiefs. Theodoret records the case of one of these last in particular: a Christian named Hormizdas, "who was of the ancient house of the Achaemenids, and the son of a. Marzban." He was degraded from his rank, and set to do the work of the lowest slaves (groom'-rig camels) without his staunchness being affected; and he died a martyr at the last. Probably this persecution, for the four years of its duration, was as savage as any that this much-tried Church was ever called upon to face.

As was the case previously, Christian persecution and war with Rome went hand in hand, though in this instance the former caused the latter, and not vice versa. Bahram made the amazing request that Theodosius should surrender all Christian refugees to his officers, and the inevitable refusal produced a renewal of war. The course of hostilities was dull and eventless. The Romans besieged Nisibis, only to find that the ramparts they had themselves constructed were too strong for them; while in the north the Persian army, under Bahram himself, failed in similar fashion before Theodosiopolis, or Erzerum. Persian siege engineering was always clumsy, and it was not till they had at last learnt to copy Roman methods that any attempt of theirs on a strong fort was formidable. The siege of Erzerum, however, furnished one picturesque incident at least. The bishop of the city, Eunomius-not content with the giving of moral strength to the garrison after the model of St. James of Nisibis-appeared in person on the ramparts, and himself pointed and discharged "the great ballista, blessed in the name of St. Thomas." He killed one of the sub-kings present in the Persian army, and earned for himself the doubtful honour of being the first of the company of fighting bishops. The whole episode, and particularly the giving of the name of an apostle to the catapult, has a very mediaeval ring, and prepares us for the exploits of Bar-soma, half a century later.

Another bishop, Acacius of Amida, already known in Persia, played a more episcopal part in the famous episode of the ransoming of the Persian captives with the Church treasures; an act which both facilitated the making of peace, and probably contributed to bring about the cessation of persecution that accompanied the conclusion of hostilities.

As an effect of the war the last relics of Armenian independence passed away. The notables of the nation, wearied of the misrule of their own native prince who was a Persian sub-king, disregarded the protests of the patriotic Catholicos of Armenia, and requested the Shah-in-Shah to put them under the rule of an ordinary Marzban. This petition the Persians naturally granted at once.

III. The Council of Dad-Ishu

Domestic confusions and troubles beset the Assyrian Church even during the course of the external trial. Armies have fought through an earthquake before now; and similarly it took more than a mere persecution to keep the members of the Church from quarrelling among themselves.[152]

Yahb-Alaha the Catholicos had died very shortly after the conclusion of the council at which he presided, and M'ana was elected or nominated in his stead. This prelate, however, was almost immediately deprived and banished to Fars-on account of the destruction of a fire-temple,[153] says one authority. It is quite possible that he somehow incurred the royal displeasure over the Abda-Hashu incident, and was exiled on that account. In any case, he held office for a very short time, and sometimes is not reckoned among the Catholici. It would seem that he died in exile.

Bar-Hebraeus, on the other hand,[154] states that M'ana or Magnes introduced the heresy of Nestorius into Persia, and was for that reason expelled by the orthodox zeal of his flock. This account we may reject without hesitation, as founded on the confusion of M'ana the Catholicos with a later namesake, the friend and helper of Bar-soma. The Catholicos, whatever his sins, did not introduce "Nestorianism" into Persia ten years previous to the Council of. Ephesus, while Nestorius was still an unknown monk at Antioch.

Al'ana being thus banished two claimants arose in his place. One was Marbokht or Farbokht, a man who procured an unauthorized consecration by purely Zoroastrian influence; while a second candidate, Dad-Ishu, was more regularly elected, by a council which apparently met during the actual course of the persecution. This must have taken place, use suppose, during the first stage, while Yezdegerd was still alive, and only converts from Zoroastrianism ran any serious risk. Even so, it was only rendered possible by the interest of one particular man, Samuel, Bishop of Khorassan, who had a claim on the royal gratitude for his services in checking an invasion of Turks.[155] Dad-Ishu was duly elected and consecrated, and the usurpation of Farbokht declared to be utterly void.

Farbokht's proceedings were apparently too irregular to be seriously defended; but that fact did not prevent him and his party from making the wildest accusations, *more orientali,* against a successful rival.[156] To the King they declared the Catholicos to be a Roman sympathizer; while to the Christians they asserted him to be debauched in morals, utterly unlearned, unable even to read the scriptures, a usurer, a pillager of churches, and an apostate who had stirred up the existing persecution! Bahram may have cared but little for the other accusations, but a Roman sympathizer was, of course, suspect, and the Catholicos was arrested, beaten and imprisoned.[157] This proceeding not improbably saved his life in fact; for being already in prison on a secular charge, he remained there forgotten till the peril of martyrdom had passed. His imprisonment continued until the war with Rome had come to an end and Christians had liberty to exist once more.

When the persecution and the war ended together, the Christian "melet" *ipso facto* resumed their own position towards the Government, as naturally as did Armenians, for instance, in a later age. Dad-Ishu was released; but his sufferings and the slanders combined had broken his spirit. He refused to take his place at the head of the Church, and crept off alone to the "Monastery of the Ark," in Cordyene,[158] intending there to spend his days in a hermit's cell, "weeping over the fall of the Church."

This, however, by no means suited the intentions of his brother bishops. They were now proposing to organize the Church again after the persecution, and, moreover, to emphasize its independent and autocephalous character; and for this, the presence of the Catholicos was a vital necessity. The pro-western wave of feeling, which had been in the ascendant four years previously, had now spent its force-the more so, that the panacea adopted under its influence had conspicuously failed to do what was expected of it-and the inevitable reaction was now beginning. Perhaps, with the *post hoc propter hoc* style of reasoning dear to the oriental, folk attributed both their suffering and disorders to the westernizing line they had taken recently; and in any case, they were now resolved to reverse it.

Accordingly,[159] a council of all six metropolitans and thirty-one other bishops met in the spring of 424 at the little town of "Markabta of the Arabs," a place chosen probably because, when persecution was barely ended, it was not prudent to attract attention by meeting at "the King's door." When they gathered there was one conspicuous absentee; the Catholicos indeed was there-brought by something very like force from his monastery, and put on to a throne to preside; but this time there was no ambassador from "the westerns" to be the moving spirit, as in 410 and 420. To make the gap more marked, Acacius, their visitor and guide four years before, was actually the guest of the King at the time: and this on an errand equally honourable to himself and to Bahram, viz. to receive the royal thanks for his most Christian treatment of Persian captives. He was not invited to the council that was to reverse his policy. Proceedings were opened by a pathetic appeal from the Catholicos (who recounted his past sufferings in detail) to be allowed to lay down a burden that was too heavy for him, and to retire to the cell whence he had most reluctantly been dragged; but though all the bishops present were moved to tears at the recital, they had absolutely no intention of acceding to the petition. Agapitus, Metropolitan of Bait Lapat,[160] then rose and made a speech of some length. This is a valuable historical document from which we have drawn freely in the previous chapters. He acknowledged in the fullest way Assyrian indebtedness to "westerns" in the past, showing how repeatedly their intervention had saved "easterns" from the consequences of their own acts, and how invaluable their influence with the Government had been. Then, in apparent contradiction with the lessons of this recent history, it was proposed by Hosea, Bishop of Nisibis, and carried by acclamation, that Dad-Ishu should be begged to resume his throne as Patriarch (the title is now used for the first time); that in future absolute obedience must be rendered to him, and, in particular, that no appeal should be made from his decrees to "Western patriarchs."[161] If there were cause for complaint against him, neither suffragans nor foreigners might presume to judge him; that office being the right of Christ alone, who placed him at the head of the Church. Dad-Ishu yielded to the prayer of the council, and resumed his throne, and this decision was solemnly placed on record.

The act of the council, as will be seen, wag twofold. It declared the "Church of the East" to be absolutely independent, and it did as much as a council could do to set up an oriental papacy over itself, in the person of him whom we may now call its patriarch.

Of these two, the first was probably the important point i7n the eyes of contemporaries, and the second necessary to guard it. Westernization spelt persecution and must be stopped, and the readiest way to stop it was to proclaim independence, and no longer to invite western bishops to concern themselves in eastern affairs.

The decision of the council (which was apparently not challenged by Antioch, though it may conceivably have been not quite welcome there) did not make very much practical difference. Political reasons-that is to say, the impossibility of Persian subjects existing under the rule of any Roman prelate-had' decreed the independence of the Persian Church. No oriental ruler who is strong enough to prevent it will have his *rayats* subject ecclesiastically to a foreign king, or a foreign king's subject; and just as Yezdegerd's firman had only formally declared the Catholicos and his *melet* to be that which they already were in fact, so this council declared formally an independence and supremacy which already really existed. Circumstances had previously made orientals welcome western interference: an interference which was not the assertion of a jurisdiction, but yet was something on which the assertion of a jurisdiction might be based if ever opportunity presented itself. It was a possibility that was repudiated rather than a fact. They now proclaimed the independence that was already theirs by right and custom, and declared their patriarch the supreme head of their branch of the Church.

The question now before us is: How did this independence, which was right and helpful, harden into the separation which we now see and deplore?

Chapter Seven - The Patriarchate of Dad-Ishu-- Persecution of Yezdegerd II

FOR more than twenty years after the important council of Dad-Ishu the history of the Assyrian Church is a void. The patriarch, whose tenure of office was longer than that of almost any other holder of his post, seems to have enjoyed a long period of peaceful rule, as compensation for his stormy experiences at its commencement; and we know nothing of any act of his until his death in 456, and practically nothing of the history of the Church from 424 to 447.

In secular matters Bahram V, after making peace with Rome, was busied for the rest of his life in the guarding of his north-eastern frontier against Turkish inroads; and on his death in 440 (he was drowned in a spring), his son and successor, Yezdegerd II, was similarly occupied for the first portion of his reign. It is true that his King did declare war on the Roman Empire at his accession, but no event of any importance followed,[162] and peace was made very shortly. Broadly, the State and the Christian Church in Persia seem to have had no history between 424 and 447; and the fact that such a gap should be possible in those twentythree years of the world's history shows how isolated was the Church's position, at any rate from the main stream of events.

In the further west, just that period saw the fall of the Roman Empire. Alaric had entered Rome in 410; and in the next generation, Goths, Vandals and other "barbarians" were establishing themselves in Gaul, Spain and Africa. Still, the *Hesperiae sonitum ruinae* which Horace had heard in imagination remained *inauditum Medis* when at last it actually came to pass.

Probably the activity of the Turks, which forced Persia to stand on guard on the Oxus, was but another manifestation of that mysterious outburst of energy in Central Asia which at the same time was sending Attila and his Huns to the West, and to the Catalaunian plains. Both empires were facing phases of a common danger, but each was ignorant of the other's fortunes.

In the nearer west, Asia Minor and Constantinople, events which were to have the most important influence on the history of the Assyrian Church were in actual course; but at that time its members seem to have been almost as ignorant of them as they had been of Nicaea and the Arian struggle. The Christological controversy, which had begun before the close of the fourth century, was rapidly becoming what it was to remain until the rise of Islam, viz., the dominant question in both Church and State in the Eastern Empire.

Hitherto we have been attempting to trace the story of the relations of the Church in the Persian Empire with the Government of that empire; and also, as far as our material will permit, the history of the internal life of the Church in question. Now a new element is introduced; and we have also to trace the effect of the impact of this great controversy, in its various phases, on the particular *melet* whose history forms our main subject.

It is, however, necessary to pause for a moment to discuss the problem, "How was it that questions so abstract and, as many men say, so unpractical roused passions so very concrete and mundane?"

Of course it is not really justifiable to call the point at issue "unpractical." The question (for though it is convenient to divide the great Christological controversy into minor heresies, yet it is essentially one question that is discussed throughout, and to which various solutions are propounded) is of supreme importance both theologically and practically. The answer given to it, however little the fact may be perceived, is bound to colour the whole of human life. Broadly, it may be stated thus: Admitting the full and proper Deity of "the Word," how is this Divine Being also man?

The question is most practical, for all its seeming remoteness. A man's conception of religion, and hence of worldly duty, is bound to be affected, in the long run, according as the object of his highest reverence is a Gnostic's Unknowable, or a God Incarnate; and this is not the less true because men who have turned their backs on the Star of Bethlehem may for a generation or two be able to walk by the light that streams from it, though they know not whence it comes. In the long run, the answer to the question whether a man is or is not bound to frame his daily life after the model left us by the Carpenter of Nazareth depends upon the answer to the question that He Himself set men asking, "Whom say ye that I am?" The connection between the highest problems of theology and the practice of daily life is as real and as strong as the force of gravitation which links the sun to every stone on earth's surface, and binds the universe in one. Neither is less real for being unperceived by the ordinary man.

Still, it was not because the supreme importance of the truth at stake was perceived and understood that men waxed so fierce in the controversy about them. To assert that it was so is probably no nearer to the truth than the gibe that the heat excited by theological controversy stands in inverse ratio to the importance of the questions discussed. No doubt men on each side felt, dimly or clearly, that it was Truth for which they struggled, and hence came their fierceness; but, speaking generally, nobody would dream of saying that the very ordinary men of the fifth and sixth centuries, who shouted themselves hoarse over these highest questions, understood their real, if unseen, practical bearing. Thus we are thrown back upon the question, How was it that ordinary men, of passions not wholly unlike our own, were moved to such fury by questions which to the ordinary man of to-day seem so unpractical?

Of course it might have been infinitely better, both for the Church and the world, if the problems of theology could have been confined to the study, and discussed calmly there till agreement was reached; if they could have been kept "out of the street," and so have avoided both the raising of the dust and the soiling of themselves in it. Had every theologian of the time possessed the temperament, if not the talent, of an Athanasius, that might have been possible. As, however, it was morally impossible that a party defeated in conclave should not appeal to popular support outside it, that "might have been" may be put aside; and it must be remembered that struggle, with all its unedifying incidents and consequences, is better for the souls of men than a peace based on indifference to all except things mundane.

To us it appears that the discussion, thus inevitably brought "into the street," raised heat simply because the *odium theologicum,* if a very ridiculous, is also a very human passion, and one that exists to-day in a slightly different form. We do not tear one another to pieces in the twentieth century over the matter of an iota in the creed; but we have seen quarrels over points of geology or archeology, or the question whether A, or B, was the first to reach a wholly conventional point of the world's surface; and these problems are surely at least as remote from practical importance as the question whether the central figure of a man's religion is or is not a proper object of worship. Man was then, and is still, a highly combative animal.

Further, under the Roman Empire religion was politics. Putting the military and civil services aside, the Church, and the politics of the Church, offered to the ordinary man the one real *carricre ouverte* in which lie could rise to importance locally or even imperially. All that his Church, and his office in it, means to the member of an oriental *melet* to-day, it meant then; with this addition that a man of power in the Church had the opportunity of using his talents, not merely in an institution that Government despised, but in the one institution that the Emperor could not despise. All that political life and its struggles mean to a constitutional country to-day was meant by ecclesiastical politics and struggles to a Roman subject of the fifth century; and interest was as real and keen in one as in the other.

Next, the theological strife of the period was the expression, not only of politics, but of nationality, and of a national feeling consciously opposed to the Government policy. In the empire religion and the Church tended rapidly, during the fifth and sixth centuries, to become instruments of government in a despotism that tended more and more toward what is suggested to us by the name Byzantine. Orthodoxy was loyalty to the Emperor, not to Christ; and heresy was not the display of a special variety of unchristian spirit, but an offence against State order. This was, of course, only the reappearance, under slightly different conditions, of a spirit that had dictated the persecution of Christianity under Decius and Diocletian, and that now dictated the persecution of pagans and "heretics."

And it must be remembered that while the empire was getting more and more into the habit of using the Church as its instrument, it was also itself becoming more and more Greek in its character; and so used the Church as the means to "Graecize," or rather to "Byzantine," all nations within it. This process was instinctively resented by nationalities that were not Greek; and Egyptian, "Latin" and Syrian fought against it. Under the circumstances it was perhaps inevitable that they should fight the battle of nationality on the religious field; and that when the Christological controversy came up they should tend to take an anti-Byzantine line.

The struggle continued till the nationalities concerned fairly split off from the Church of the capital and empire, and the bulk of them found under Moslem rule at least a semi-recognition of that independent life which the empire denied them. That part of the empire which was either really Greek, or which had been content to become so, remained subject to Constantinople; and was for centuries the most solid and permanent, and one of the most important facts of history.

Thus the battle was fought on the theological field, and around theological truths of the last importance; but it was not for these that the combatants fought, but for something that in their minds they represented.

As regards the merits of the controversy, the Greeks were the better theologians; that is to say, their expressions of infinite truths in finite words appear to us to be the least unsatisfactory and misleading. Of course every human expression intended to explain or describe the mystery of the Incarnation becomes false if its inadequacy is forgotten; and each party, as a rule, only half remembered this fact as regards their own terms, and quite forgot it as regards those of their opponents. Thus each usually insisted on stretching the language used by the other to its full logical conclusion; forgetting that logic does not apply to the case, and that this *reductio ad absurdum* line of argument, if used at all, was applicable equally to both. Each side vehemently asserted that the other was teaching a doctrine which the other as vehemently denied that he taught. A. stretched B.'s tenets (usually misunderstood, and sometimes misstated) to their full logical conclusion, and presented them to B. as B.'s doctrines. B. returned the compliment to A. Each denied holding the views that the other attributed to him, and anathematized what he insisted that the other must hold.[163]

Whether "heretics" of any variety really intended to deny the truths which the Greek theologians asserted, and which they intended their expressions to guard, is another and very difficult question. We shall have to examine it later as far as one variety is concerned. They very certainly did not intend to agree with the Greeks; in fact, they -,wanted to differ from them. On the other hand, the Greeks did not want to agree with them, but to subdue them. Rancour against Greek theologians, however, though it may be a wrong thing, is not necessarily rancour against truth; even though the Greek may think that it is, and though what he shouts as a battle-cry may be sound theology. Neither side in the battle made any attempt to "get behind words," and to see whether they could not, and did not, fully accept the principle embodied in the objectionable form of words that was the other's standard in the theological war. Again and again one is disposed to cry, as one studies the weary warfare, "Oh for one hour of St. Athanasius!"

Another question remains, and one which is of growing importance in our own day. Supposing, for argument's sake, that the "heretics" did hold at the beginning of each of the various schisms all that the "orthodox" imputed to them (a large supposition-a test of the size of which is the extraordinary character of the views which the "heretics" Imputed to the "orthodox"), do those views still exist to-day? It is of the nature of "heresy" to disappear, and of imperfect and inadequate conceptions to melt silently away when they are not maintained by opposition. The writer can affirm this much of his own personal knowledge: that where "heretics," of various complexions, state the beliefs they hold in non-technical language, so that they do not use the terms to which they cling as a sacred heritage (and which often have very different meanings as used by different Churches), they usually make a statement of faith indistinguishable from orthodoxy.

A formidable complication, which one does not see how to disentangle, still further increases the difficulty of the problem. It must. be remembered[164] that the great crux of specifically Christian theology, "How can Christ be at once God and Man?" was approached in the East from Antioch to Seleucia by minds steeped for generations in the dualistic conceptions that lie at the base of all oriental philosophy--conceptions which postulate the evil of matter, and the existence of an impassable gulf between Creator and creature.

Doctrines of this kind are called Manichaean, principally because disciples of Manes did much to popularize them in the West, but Manes did not create or give currency to the conceptions; he merely based his system upon them.

Minds bred in a "Manichaean" medium shrank inevitably from the conception of a real Incarnation of the Word, resulting in a true "God-Man"; and they explained away the difficulty in various ways. Some declared, with the Gnostics, that the nature assumed must have been a phantom merely; others adopted one of two explanations superficially. opposite but essentially the same, the concave and convex sides of the curve. They either declared the Incarnation to be a mere association of a man with the Divinity, which is Nestorianism; or that the manhood was annihilated by assumption into the Divinity, which is Monophysitism. In either case, belief in the absolute incompatibility of the human and the Divine lies at the root of the conception. Neither the "Nestorian" nor the "Monophysite" Christ (if the language they used be pressed) is a true Mediator, for a Mediator is impossible. The persistence of this inadequate conception may be judged from the fact that it also underlies Mahommedan theology.

So much for the general mental atmosphere, so to speak, in which the problems of the Christological controversy were approached by some of the combatants in the struggle, a statement necessary for our comprehension of it.

The Assyrian Church, however, had not to face it until it was pretty far advanced. Isolated as ever, it might have escaped this controversy as thoroughly as it did that of Arianism, had it been no more prolonged and equally decisive in its issue. The patriarchate of Dad-Ishu saw in the West the assembling of the first council of Ephesus, and the deposition of Nestorius; the scandal of the second council of that name, and the assembly of the fourth "general council" at Chalcedon. It saw, in a word, the rejection of Nestorianism and the rise of Monophysitism in the Roman Empire. But only the faintest echoes of this strife appear to have reached the Church of Assyria, which was in the peaceful state of having nothing to record during most of that period. Mshikha-Zca, writing about a hundred years later,[165] has absolutely nothing "local" to say of the two bishops, Daniel and Rkhima, who during this period were the metropolitans of Arbela. Concerning the controversy he tells us that the first of them, Daniel, heard of the persecution of "the martyr Nestorius" by "the second Pharaoh, Cyril of Egypt"; and, being a prophet, foretold the "extinction of the true light in the West, and its shining forth in the East." If (as we are given to understand) this worthy prelate died before his time, owing to his grief at the persecution referred to, we need certainly not question his status as a prophet--seeing that he died on Low Sunday, 431, and the council of Ephesus did not meet till June of that year.

Rkhima, his successor, was a hard-working bishop within his own diocese. He certainly, and other bishops probably, warned their flocks against "the perversion of the faith" current in the West; and men's minds were thus prepared for the separation that was to follow fifty years later. For the time being, however, the Church took no corporate action. How little they knew of the rights and wrongs of the matter appears from the fact that they believed Cyril to have proclaimed, in his "sacrilegious council of Ephesus," the doctrine of "one nature and one qnuma," with the express object of severing communion between East and West.[166]

A man of some fame in later ages appears to have arisen during this period, though he probably reached maturity a few years after this date. This was Isaac of Nineveh; who as ascetic and mystic was honoured by all sects in after time, and who, therefore, probably dates from a period antecedent to their division. Though his writings on the contemplative life and the various grades thereof were to exercise a great influence on Eastern monasticism, he did not exert, and, indeed, carefully refrained from exerting, any sway over his contemporaries. If his biographer tells the truth, he may share with another bishop mentioned in this chapter the distinction of having the shortest episcopate on record. He was (much against his inclination, no doubt) dragged from his cell on the mountain of Mar Mattai (where his monastery still exists), and consecrated Bishop of Nineveh. The new bishop made the six hours' journey from the monastery to the city, and was installed; but either that evening or next morning two litigants brought a case of debt for the episcopal decision. "What says the Gospel?" began the bishop. "Oh, never mind the Gospel just now, Holiness," said the creditor. "But if you don't mind the Gospel, what am I doing here?" said the prelate, who apparently did not admit that he was there to get them to mind it, or that if they did mind it they would hardly need a pastor at all! So, "seeing that his solitary life would be disturbed by the episcopal office"--which was, indeed, inevitable, but might perhaps have been foreseen-the bishop resigned at once, and betook himself to the desert of Scete; where he remained until death, undisturbed either by office or by the troubles that arose in the Church before the time of his final departure.[167]

At the time, however, things were peaceful; and the time of peace was also one of growth. In the life-story of Pethiun,[168] evangelist of the country about the sources of the lesser Zab, we have a picture that must have been repeated in many another province at the time. There we read the story of the lad Yazdin, son of a wealthy Magian, who, being unhappy at home, found happiness, and was led to Christianity in the house of one Jacob, a Christian dependent of the family, and apparently foster-father of the youth. Jacob refused his charge baptism when he applied for it, "from fear of what your father will say"; and Yazdin ran way from home and found an asylum with the Bishop of Karka d'Bait Sluk, who received him into a monastery. After some years he returned home, to find his father dead and his brother Gushnasp (now owner of the family property) a Christian also, baptized by the name of Dad-Ishu, and more than willing that his rabban brother should build the cell he needed on the estate, and receive his son Pethiun under his care. Neither Government nor clan openly resented, at the moment, this conversion of a family that was obviously of some local importance.

Still, this exemption of an active Church from Government interference and from doctrinal quarrels could not last; and about the year 448 we find Yezdegerd II declaring war against Christianity in his dominions. At about the same time he started a vehement persecution of both Armenians and Assyrians; in the former case avowedly because Christians could not possibly be loyal subjects of Persia, and, in all probability, for the same reason in the latter case also.

The persecution seems to have been intended to be general all over Persia,[169] but we have only details of it as far as it affected the province of B. Garmai. It is probable that it was far more severe there than elsewhere, and perhaps was unknown in some districts altogether.

According to the rather late account that remains to us, a massacre of appalling magnitude took place; ten bishops and 153,000 (!) clergy and laity being martyred in several consecutive days of slaughter on a mound outside the city of Karka d'Bait Sluk. Local tradition still asserts that the red gravel of the hillock was stained that colour by the martyrs' blood, and the martyrium built over the bodies remains to this day?[170]

The fact of a great massacre of Christians in this persecution at this spot need not be doubted, even if the number given by the historian be impossibly large, and if there be some other errors to the narrative.[171] Nor need we question the perfectly historical character of the episodes recorded; such as the act of the woman Shirin, who with her two sons came of her own accord to seek the martyrdom that she received;[172] or the conversion of the chief agent of the persecution, Tamasgerd, who was led by the sight of the endurance of those whom he was butchering to own that the faith that gave them strength must be from God, and joined himself with them in their confession and their fate. The place of martyrdom and the memorial church that stands there still bear the name, not of any of the bishops that perished then, but of this convert who was there "baptized in his own blood."

As John, the metropolitan of Karka, was led to death,[173] a youth among those who stood by called to him to be of good cheer and play the man; and the bishop, turning to him, declared that he was worthy to take his place. So, in their prison, or perhaps on the very place of execution, the other bishops laid hands upon the youth Dindui; and for a day or so he remained as metropolitan of Karka, until he too, marked by the persecutors, received his crown.

Like other persecutions, this trial passed at last; and when peace came again, the bishops of two provinces gathered at the spot,[174] and decreed a solemn annual memorial of those who had perished there. More than fourteen centuries have passed, and the Christians of Kirkuk own now a jurisdiction that was strange to their ancestors; yet still they gather year by year at the little church upon the red hillock, and still the 25th day of Ilul is the holy *dukrana* of those who died for Christ in the year 448.

Other martyrdoms, of course, took place elsewhere, and in particular we know of the death of the Pethiun mentioned above. This teacher was put to death near the modern Sulimanieh (the ancient Kholwan), and with him perished his disciple and companion in "rabbanship," Anahid,. the beautiful daughter of the Mobed Adur-Hormizd. The nun, however (who, as usual, was offered life "if she would marry as women ought"[175]), was for some reason taken to Nisibis for execution.

However extensive the massacres in the Assyrian Church, the sufferings here can hardly have been greater than those inflicted in Armenia to the course of what Armenians describe as the first great persecution of their national Church. We perhaps should describe it rather as a rebellion or civil war, prompted by the attempt of the Government to destroy the national faith.

In this case,[176] Yezdegerd, by rather treacherous means, was able to procure a more or less forced apostasy from most of the Armenian nobles, as a preliminary measure; and then attempted, through them, to force Zoroastrianism on the mass of the people. A national rising followed, the rebels making a fruitless appeal to Rome for help; and a fierce "guerilla" warfare waged for several years--the Armenians finding, as usual, patriots who were able leaders on a small scale, but somehow producing no great general.[177] As usual, too, their worst foes were those of their own households, and none did so much to subdue Armenia as Armenian renegades.

Finally, a sullen submission was secured; and Zoroastrianism drove Christianity out of sight for the moment, so that the Shah-in-Shah could plume himself on a new country won to Magianism--a conversion which lasted, of course, for just so long as it could be enforced. It is worth mentioning that the history of their country, between the years 448 and 456, affords an ample explanation of the non-appearance of the Armenian bishops of Chalcedon, and of their consequent non-acceptance of that council. The Assyrian Church was not represented at it either, any more than at the preceding councils; nevertheless, they seem to have accepted, at some subsequent date, what they understood to be the decision of this synod.[178]

Chapter Eight - Bar-Soma and Acacius

Y<small>EZDEGERD</small> was succeeded on the throne by Piroz. Not altogether peaceably, for there was a rival claimant in the person of Prince Hormizdas, and he was only overthrown by Turkish help-help that had to be paid for by the cession of a frontier fortress. Piroz, however, succeeded, and ruled for twenty-eight years. Christian writers give him a high character, in that lie was (then declare[179]) ruled in all things by the advice of a Christian of whom we shall hear much-Bar-soma of Nisibis. Bar soma was a favourite of Piroz, no doubt, and his adviser in some things, and no very good adviser either. Still, it may be doubted whether the power of the Christian counsellor was as great as other Christians thought, particularly as they always tend to believe that a man in any post of authority is practically omnipotent. If the power of Barsoma was anything like as great as Christians believed, Magians must have judged the precedent a very bad one, for no king of the Sassanid house was so consistently unlucky as was Piroz. He was unfortunate in war abroad, for in fighting with the Turks (a war brought on solely by his own perfidy[180]) lie was manoeuvred into a hopeless position and forced to capitulate; as the price of life the "King of kings" had to do homage, and to swear never again to lead an army past the boundary stone of his empire.

At home he was even more unfortunate; for a terrible drought of seven years brought, of course, famine and pestilence in its train. Even the snow-fed Tigris had no water in its bed, and all other streams failed completely. Nevertheless, either the King or his advisers managed the great relief works that were instituted so well that not a single man, or, according to another account, one only, died of starvation.

At the beginning of this reign Babowai became patriarch of the Assyrian Church-a man who was a learned philosopher, according to one historian, and *mediocriter doctus* according to the other. Adore important, however, than his learning, or lack of it, was the fact that he was a convert from Magianism-an "apostate" Zoroastrians would say-and therefore always liable to death, though many reasons might make it impossible to carry out the sentence. Still, as convert, he had much to suffer. He was imprisoned for seven years and tortured repeatedly, though- it is not clear whether this was before or after his consecration made him conspicuous to his enemies.[181] As it was in his days that the Church of the East was disturbed by the impact of those disputes that for the last half century or more had been agitating the West, we must here say a word on the stage that the Christological controversy had reached when it did at last arrive in Assyrian Church territory.

There is a general impression, even in the minds of historical students, that when once a council which after ages were to style "oecumenical" had given its decision on a point, that question was settled finally; and that any one who did not subscribe to it, wrote himself down heretic at once by his refusal. As a matter of fact no settlement was authoritative till it was generally accepted. In the eyes of contemporaries, Ephesus was simply an assembly, whose dictum needed re-enacting and "stiffening" (according to one party) at the second council held at that place, which we usually call by the name of the "Latrocinium"[182]; while according to the other party (the majority) its decision needed restating, and co-ordinating with other truths at Chalcedon.

This latter council, too, no more settled the question at issue than did that of Nicaea. Each was the beginning of a period of strife, not its conclusion. But whereas the dispute argued at Nicxa did come to an end (for the time) within three centuries after the dispersal of the council[183] tile problems "settled" at Chalcedon are causes of schism still, and will remain so, while Armenian, Copt and Jacobite remain unreconciled.

The council was rejected, either at once or after a very short interval, by whole provinces of the empire-not altogether, it is true, for theological reasons-but that does not alter the fact. Broadly, it was rejected absolutely by Egypt and Palestine, the former of which will have none of it to this day. A large majority of the Christians of the Antiochene patriarchate and a considerable minority of those in Asia Minor opposed it also; and one of the two national Churches outside the empire (the Armenian) repudiated it as noon as it had opportunity to speak. Only Rome and what we call "the West" were heartily for it, and that mainly because it was the only oecumenical council where the Pope played a prominent and worthy part.

At first the Emperor, of course, felt bound to maintain its decision; for the gibing name of "melkite,"[184] given to its adherents in Syria, had this much of truth in it to give it a sting-that the Council of Chalcedon was at least as much under royal influence as it is good for a "general council" to be. As time passed, however, certain facts came out, and were impressed on that imperial consciousness that never seems to die with its possessor.

Any emperor who held Constantinople, held Asia Minor up to the Taurus range: held, that is, the Pontic and Asian themes, and could keep them tolerably quiet and obedient. On the other hand, no "Chalcedonian" could make loyal subjects of the inhabitants of Egypt, Palestine and "Syria,"[185] and no "anti-Chalcedonian" could do so with Rome and the West. The empire, in fact, was parting asunder like a ship on rocks. Nothing could keep its eastern and western extremities, the bow and stern of the figure, from tearing themselves off by their own weight; but when once they had gone, the strongly knit midship section, left on the rocks on which the ship had splintered, had passive strength enough to resist any waves for many a long year. Had it not been for a gang of wreckers who called themselves crusaders, it might be there still.

The rending process also took time, for the rivets of Roman organization did not "give" readily; and it was not completed till the Khalifs sat in Damascus at one end, and Charlemagne had been crowned at Rome at the other. Successive emperors might give special attention, now to one of the sections that tended to part, and now to the other. At first their attention was drawn to the East. Zeno and Anastasius regarded the West, subdued by Goths and Vandals, as lost already and irrecoverably; they might indeed, as opportunity offered, let loose a second horde of "barbarians" against those in possession, but no more. Thus Anastasius watched Theodoric go against Odoacer with much the feelings, one imagines, of a man who sees the pack of wolves who have been hunting him turn against the second pack that are already ravaging his flocks. The country was lost, and they "cut their losses." They would not run any risk of estranging the subjects who remained-the Monophysites of Syria and Egypt--to conciliate the "Dyophysites"[186] of Italy who were lost to them already.

Hence these two emperors are monophysite in sympathy; and, under them that confession is dominant in the empire, till at last all the great patriarchates save Rome only are held by its followers. Roman Christians, abandoned by the empire, are loyal to an Arian ruler, and Rome anathematizes all the "Eastern Empire."

With the rise of a new dynasty there is a change. Justin and Justinian were Chalcedonian-orthodox -by conviction, and resolute to recover Italy and Africa politically. Hence the portion of the empire that really depends on Constantinople becomes orthodox once more, and continues so to be. As it becomes clear that it has definitely adopted this bias, the lapse of two or three generations sees the Monophysite portions surrender themselves to the Mussulman, rather than be conquered by him; while in another century or so, for different reasons, Rome and the West are lost to the empire also. Fate decreed-or shall we say that the Devil contrived-that it was in the time of Monophysite supremacy in the empire that the Christological problem should first be presented to the Assyrian Church; and further, that when the Church of the empire had abandoned that inadequate conception, and settled to orthodoxy, knowledge of what "orthodoxy" is, and of what the "Greeks" held, should be hidden from the Assyrians by the *bulk* of interposed Monophysitism.

It ought to be clearly realized-for it is a fact of the last importance for the formation of a right judgment on the attitude taken by the Assyrian Church--that when the Christological controversy came before its members, the Church of the empire, so far as known to them, was Monophysite. The doctrine of "the one Nature" was not a heresy professed by a handful of Egyptian and Syrian nobodies, who were clearly and avowedly out of Catholic communion; but it was the doctrine that was dominant over all the empire of Constantinople held by every patriarch except only the Roman and he was in any case beyond Assyrian ken.

We can now approach, with some possibility of just comprehension, the story of the great controversy as it affected the Assyrian Church.

Babowai, as patriarch, had no easy time of rule. It was not only the hourly danger that he, a conspicuous "apostate," must run from the Magi; but he had under him a suffragan of the most awkward character to control, viz., Barsoma, metropolitan of Nisibis. This was the man who was to be protagonist in the first part of the drama that was to be played; one of the most striking and picturesque, but not one of the most saintly, figures in the history of his Church.

By birth he was of Cordyene, and was possibly slave-born,[187] though he must have attained freedom, in that case, early in life, for when Ibas was Bishop of Edessa this youth, with several other Assyrians destined to high office in their Church, was a student in the college there. This college, though of no great antiquity (for it owed its foundation to St. Ephraim, and was therefore of later date than the migration of that saint from Nisibis to Edessa, after the cession of the former city to Persia in 363), had become the centre of theological and Western culture to the Christians of the East. There were in Persia, as far as we know, no Christian schools, though Magian colleges abounded, and the teacher was a recognized and honoured grade in their hierarchy. The Christian who desired learning (and the Assyrian thirst for it is keener than even his thirst for money) must cross the frontier to where Christianity ruled.

To Edessa, then, went many an Assyrian, during the long period of peace that marked the patriarchate of Dad-Ishu; and Bar-soma had for companions (amongst others) Acacius, afterwards patriarch of Seleucia, Narses, called "the harp of the Spirit," and first head of the college that was to spring from Edessa, Wana, afterwards Bishop of Ardashir, and Papa, afterwards metropolitan of B. Lapat. It adds a touch of nature to the history to find that the oriental student of theology was human enough to give nicknames to his fellows, and these lads were known one to another as "Bean-maker," "Dagon," and "Piggy"! Bar-soma's own sobriquet was "Swimmer among the nests."

During the episcopate of Ibas (435-457) one Marun of Dilaita, an Assyrian from the district of Mosul, was head of the college, and the whole atmosphere was pronouncedly "dyophysite"--something, that is to say, which its enemies (and its enemies were rapidly becoming the dominant theological party) would call "Nestorian." The question whether the bishop himself was or was not a "Nestorian," as we understand the term, is one that we may be thankful to leave undisturbed. The fact that one and the same letter of his was accepted as orthodox by one oecumenical council (the fourth) and condemned as heretical by the fifth, may suffice to show how impossible it is to apply the clear-cut distinctions that a later age thinks it can draw, to the men who were actually engaged in the conflict. In looking at a landscape from a distance it is easy to say "that rock lies on the hillside, and that other in the valley." On the spot, one sees that it is a misuse of terms to say "here valley ends and hillside begins."

At Edessa Bar-soma shared the stormy fortunes of his chief, and was expelled with him from school and city when the notorious "Latrocinium" sent Ibas into exile.[188] The. fact that one who must have been still comparatively young was marked out for condemnation by what was meant to be an oecumenical synod, is evidence that he already attained a reputation-of a kind. When Ibas was acquitted at Chalcedon and returned to his see, his pupil seemingly returned with him and remained for about six years. In 457 Ibas died, and the wave of monophysite feeling that he had kept in check swept over the place; Nonnus, whom the Latrocinium had put in as bishop in his room, now regaining the see, of which the Council of Chalcedon had deprived him. Bar-soma and most of his companions were either expelled, or voluntarily quitted a sphere that had ceased to be congenial; and the party returned to Persia, where, as stated, most of them rose to high office in the Assyrian Church.[189]

Bar-soma in particular became Archbishop of Nisibis, third see in the Church, and was a particular favourite with King Piroz. Further, he was very active in secular business, and (according to one account) actually united with his office as archbishop the post of "Lord of the Marches" of the Roman and Persian Empires--a combination that makes us think we are already in the middle ages. It appears from his own writings, however, that he was not personally "Marquis of Nisibis," though he certainly acted as the assistant and right hand of that official in the border province of Persia.[190]

For the time being at any rate there was no confinement of promotion to men who had been markedly "dyophysite" at Edessa. The high promotion of Papa,[191] who certainly had belonged to the other party, and who is noted as "orthodox" by the monophysite Shimun of B. Arsham,[192] is a proof that there was no controversy in the Church as yet. Still, things were uneasy. In particular there was trouble, if not with the Government, yet with the Magians, in spite of the royal favour to particular Christians. It is possible that we ought to date the imprisonment of Babowai the patriarch somewhere in the period 470-480,[193] and it is certain that those years saw what we may call a minor persecution. Churches were burnt and Christians imprisoned, though we have no evidence that there were any martyrdoms.

A more dangerous thing was, that the relations between the patriarch and Bar-soma became exceedingly hostile. We have no information as to what the *casus belli* may have been; but both were Assyrians, and therefore not prone to peace; and of Bar-soma we know that he had separate quarrels with almost every authority, colleague or subordinate, with whom he came in contact. Babowai used discipline,[194] righteously or otherwise, on some bishops, who fled to Bar-soma and found the pre. late of Nisibis ready to take their part. Bar-Hebraeus hints, and quite possibly with truth, that the attempt to enforce episcopal celibacy was at the root of this trouble between the two. Apparently this was a point on which party feeling ran high; and though there was no canon on the matter, a strict section wished to enforce it, while a majority were strongly opposed to its enforcement. Whatever the cause, the two quarrelled fiercely. even while persecution was threatening, and while things were so the patriarch made a fatal blunder. He wrote a letter to some "Roman bishops," asking them to use their influence with the emperor, and procure his intercession with the Shah-in-Shah to avert persecution; and in the letter, he used one very unfortunate expression "God has given us over to an accursed kingdom. This was dispatched by a special messenger, who was directed to smuggle it over the border in the hollow of a cane; but things went awry somehow and the document fell into the hands of Bar-soma.

It is too much to ask of an oriental controversialist, that when the imprudence of an opponent has put the means of ruining him in his hands, the combatant should refrain from using it, merely because the consequences to the writer may be very unpleasant! Further, it was easy for Bar-soma to persuade himself that his mere duty to the Shah-in-Shah demanded that he should forward the letter to him; and it was the fact that he would himself be ruined if the King should ever hear that he had seen--and suppressed--such a document.

Given the choice between using the chance of ruining an opponent and running the risk of ruin himself, it was not likely that Bar-soma should hesitate. He sent the letter to Piroz. It was not generous, but few orientals would have acted otherwise. He may or may not have sent accusations with it, nor does it greatly matter; a man does not reach high office under an oriental despotism without knowing what the writing of such a letter means to its writer if it be discovered.

Piroz was furious when the letter was read to him: the patriarch was summoned at once to "the King's door," and when he entered was shown simply the foot of the folded paper, with the query, "Is this your seal?" He admitted the fact, and the letter was read in full diwan. It was vain for the terror-struck Christians to explain that "accursed" was simply a figure of speech for non-Christian; or, as some gallantly attempted, to say that it was no more than a slip of the pen, and that "sublime"[195] was what was really meant. The unhappy prelate was sentenced to a horrible death, being hung up by his ring-finger till he expired. The Church in after days reckoned him a martyr, as having been put to death, if not for Christianity, at least by Magian malice.

The post of patriarch was seemingly left vacant for a while, as might easily happen under the circumstances; and for about three years Bar-soma was the most real authority in the Church. Authority in such vigorous hands was not likely to lie idle, but we have unfortunately no very reliable account of the use he made of it. Bar-Hebraeus indeed is explicit enough, giving an account borrowed (as Monsignor Chagot points out) from a Monophysite writer of the seventh century, Michael the Syrian.[196]

According to him, when Babowai was dead, Bar-soma advised Piroz to establish or promote "heresy" in the Church of his empire, for political reasons. It would be very much better for him, if his Christian subjects were entirely separated from those of the Roman Empire. Piroz agreeing and giving his favourite a "free hand," Bar-soma took Persian troops and with them marched through the length and breadth of the land, forcing all Christians into heresy. At Tagrit on the Tigris he was repulsed-the men of that place declaring, "If you dare to interfere with us, we will expose you and your crimes to the King,"[197] and he dared not enter Armenia; but he drove the "orthodox" monks from Mar Matai, and destroyed with fire and sword all who would not follow him into heresy. Ninety priests in particular were massacred in Nineveh, says the historian, and 7,700 of the faithful in all. Collecting some bishops at B. Adrai in Nuhadra, he forced on them a canon allowing Episcopal marriage-an act repeated at later councils at B. Sluk[198] and Seleucia. As a result of these acts, "Nestorianism" was spread all over Persia; and with it came such an appalling increase of immorality among the clergy, that all the dust-heaps and roads were full of exposed and abandoned children, and special orphanages had to be made for their reception, to save them from being devoured by dogs!

Finally, some bishops who had fled from Bar-soma consecrated Acacius as patriarch; but the terrible "Bar-sola"[199] was able to force him into Nestorianism also, and the schism was complete between the Assyrian Church and the rest of the Church Catholic.

This statement is of course the work of a partisan, not of an historian-and of an oriental partisan. To such an one the throwing of mud is "common form," and truth is not so much an object as adhesiveness. Ages of controversy have made him an adept in judging what mud will stick, and he has a full appreciation of the power of a half-truth! Still, even in oriental controversy, regard should be paid to the probabilities, if not to the decencies; and (putting aside a few small blunders) it is simply impossible to believe that the licensing of clerical marriage should have led to the spread of open immorality, and the exposure of thousands of unacknowledged children, and the like. The only result of the wild slander of Bar-Hebraeus, is to throw doubt on every statement that he makes to the discredit of his opponent.

It must also be remembered that Bar-Hebraeus is a Monophysite, and writes as one. Hence, where he says Catholic or orthodox, we have to substitute the name of that heresy.

Certain broad facts, however, stand out as true. Thus it appears that after the death of Babowai, Bar-soma organized the Church on a footing of separation from, not merely independence of, the Westerns. Piroz of course approved. It was obviously to his interest that his Christian subjects should be separated from those of Rome, and no doubt he threw the weight of royal influence on Bar-soma's side. As the "Henoticon" of Zeno had recently been published (these events took place 482-484), and the Church of the Roman Empire was officially Monophysite, to make an official confession of the "two Natures in Christ"--which to Bar-Hebraeus was "Nestorianism"--was to separate from them--and this was done.

There can be little doubt that the great mass of Christians in Persia were on Bar-soma's side in what he did. Bar-Hebraeus of course declares that they were "dragooned" into it; but, putting aside the fact that Assyrian Christians were not wont to be very pliant under persecution, does the work of a "dragonade" last as that of Bar-soma has done? It cannot be doubted that the mass of Assyrian Christians were "Dyophysite" to the core, and were perfectly willing to separate from those who held the doctrine of "one Nature." Their reasons for wishing to separate, however, were not purely doctrinal. That, as we have stated, we hold to have been the case nowhere; even though the oriental has an appetite for abstract theology and philosophical disputation that the Western cannot appreciate. The spirit of nationality, too, had probably less to do with it in their case than in that of others, for their full ecclesiastical independence was won already. The cause was something more mundane, but very natural all the same. For about one hundred and fifty years now they had been always under the shadow, and frequently under the edge of the sword of persecution; and this persecution had been never separate from the feeling," Rome is Christian, therefore no Christian can be loyal." A Persian war with Rome and a persecution of the Assyrian Church had usually gone together, and the answer to the question "which caused which?" had made little difference to the persecuted.

Their faith was a thing they could not and would not give up; but when already estranged from the Westerns by the theological quarrel, was it wonderful that, weary of suffering, they should say, "Let us at all events do something to show that we are a different brand of Christians to the Roman, and so need not be persecuted every time the Emperor and the Shah-in-Shah have a quarrel."

Bar-Hebraeus also informs us that a motive force in the matter was the desire for legalized marriage among the clergy and bishops (though marriage is not the word that the historian employs). That this was so, particularly in the light of the fact that the passing of a canon to that effect accompanied the separation, is very probable. There is not much evidence available on the point; but it does seem that the oriental mind was revolting against the false doctrine about celibacy current in "the West"; and while asceticism had a place, and a prominent one, in their religion, there was yet a perfectly true instinct in their minds that marriage was a holy thing to all not specially called to another life, and that sacred office was no bar to what was a duty rather than an indulgence. It has been suggested,[200] that desire to assimilate themselves to their Zoroastrian neighbours also moved them. The writer does not think it likely that there was conscious desire for assimilation. At the same time, the ideas and conceptions of the religion of the land have a way of soaking into the mind even of the alien, when resident, as we see in our best Indian officials; and how much more must this be the case with the native? It is probable that the Zoroastrian atmosphere they breathed kept their ascetic conceptions (which as orientals they were bound to have in one form or another) within the very reasonable bounds which at present prevail among them.[201]

As an incident of his work Bar-soma held a council at B. Lapat, and issued a confession of faith, the first of several of the Assyrian Church's declaring, that concerned itself with Christology. It does not survive; but there can be no doubt that it was emphatically "Dyophysite," and opposed to the then dominant creed of "the West." Bar-Hebraeus declares it to have been "Nestorian," and so it very possibly was, even in our sense of the word. The point is of no great importance as the confession was formally repudiated soon after; but as the council ofChalcedon was "Nestorian" to all good Monophysites, the evidence of this writer (*valeat quantum*) would rather point to its being orthodox. Next, the council of B. Lapat proceeded to practically canonize Theodore of Mopsuestia, whom they described (truly enough) as having been "honoured in life, and honoured in death," and whom they further added, "all should follow."[202] Another canon, the only one to be regularly re-enacted later, declared the lawfulness of marriage for all Christians, including every grade of the hierarchy, and Bar-soma himself took advantage of the permission thus given. Seventeen other canons followed, which concerned themselves, so far *as* the few fragments remaining will allow us to judge,[203] with Simony, nepotism, and like matters, which were, in fact, rules highly profitable for the Assyrian or for any Church--if they could be executed.

The council of Bait Lapat was the "high-water mark" of Bar-soma's power. He had become head of his Church, and he had bent it to his will. It had declared itself opposed theologically to "the West"--to the Church of the Emperor and his Henoticon; it was independent and separate, and friendly to the King of Persia, and Bar-soma was its ruler. No doubt he had won this position not only as bishop, but also as warden of the marches. The people and clergy were willing to go with him, but if not he had military as well as theological arguments to urge! The story of extensive massacres of "the faithful," given by Bar-Hebraeus, one may put on one side without hesitation, as on a par with that historian's orphanages; but the fact that Bar-soma's admirer, Amr,[204] hints at some bloodshed, makes it probable that force was sometimes used. Still, as Shimun of B. Arsham, that very hostile contemporary writer (who must have been a young man, at or near Seleucia, at the time), who knows the career of Bar-soma well enough to be able to give us his school nickname yet knows nothing of any slaughter, we may conclude confidently that if there was any, it was insignificant in amount. It must be remembered that nobody would be shocked at the fact of Barsoma's making an episcopal tour with an escort drawn from the frontier corps that lie seems to have commanded, or much shocked if blood should be shed. Orientals like to have proof that the "Hukumet" is behind the man they are willing to obey. They revere power; and its concrete embodiment in a few soldiers does not strike them as at all unepiscopal. Of course his opponents would exclaim at the sacrilege--and would imitate it, if they got the chance!

Though there is no doubt that the great majority of the Christians of Persia were willing enough to follow the lead given by Bar-soma, there was a minority opposed to him. Papa, Bishop of B. Lapat, was one of them, and there were other bishops with him. The men of Tagrit, too, and the monks of at least one important monastery (Mar Matai by Mosul) clung to the confession of one "Nature"-or adopted it, in opposition to a man they hated-and some monks about Seleucia-Ctesiphon were of the same way of thinking.[205]

It is impossible to say how far this minority at the time was Monophysite in doctrine and by conviction, and how far it was merely opposed to Bar-soma, though there is good evidence that its principal bishop, Papa of B. Lapat, acted from the latter of these two motives. Still, here was the root of a Monophysite party in the Church, opposed to the Dyophysite majority. In later days it was to gather strength and to make a bold effort at the capture of the Church itself. Failing in this, it was able to win recognition as a separate *melet.*

No doubt Bar-soma hoped and expected to be patriarch in place of Babowai, and the prize must have seemed in his grasp when he held the council of B. Lapat in 484. At that very moment, however, it was snatched from him, and the support of much of his power cut from under his feet, by the death of his patron, King Piroz. That sovereign's defeat by the Turks, and his disgraceful homage to their sultan, had of course rankled in his mind; and, oath or no oath, lie was resolved to avenge it. Thu$ he made war against them, and to keep the letter of his bond, made elephants drag in the van of his army the boundary stone that he had sworn that he would never pass. The Turks gathered for battle, and their sultan, like another of his race in another continent, reared the broken treaty on a lance, and bade his troops fight under that banner. As at Kossovo, the God of Battles accepted the appeal, and in the utter rout of the Persians that followed, Piroz himself was killed. The Turks, mere nomad tribesmen still, could not follow up their great success; but Persian power was paralyzed for the moment, and Armenia recognized the opportunity and sprang to arms. The new King, Balas, was glad enough to retain his sovereignty over them at the price of the recognition of their national Christianity.

Balas also filled up the vacant patriarchate of the Assyrian Church, but it was not Bar-soma that he selected. The late King's favourite seldom stands too well with the new ruler, and Balas ordered the consecration of the old school-fellow of Bar-soma, Acacius. This destroyed the very base of the power that the Bishop of Nisibis had wielded. He was, of course, metropolitan still; but he was not head of the *melet,* and another was. To use a homely metaphor, there had been a new deal, and a change of trumps. All the old figures remained unaltered, but their relations to one another and their relative values had changed.

For a little Bar-soma refused to admit the situation, and would not acknowledge Acacius. We do not know what ostensible reason he gave, but it does not matter, for it was his own power that he fought for, and the dispute was not long. The metropolitan of Nisibis had to admit that he was powerless against the patriarch backed by the King, and finally to submit, making the best terms for himself that he could:

Thus, in August 485, Acacius came north; and a gathering of bishops (for it was hardly a formal council) took place at B. Adrai,[206] in the province of Nuhadra. Bar-soma had still a strong party behind him, for the metropolitans of Bait Garmai and Fars, with the bishop of the important see of Kashkar, were his supporters; and Papa of B. Lapat was the only bishop of importance who accompanied the patriarch. The metropolitans of Arbela and Prat D'Maishan were not present. Still he had to submit; to acknowledge Acacius as his patriarch and superior; to consent to the full annulment of his own council at B. Lapat, and to agree that another council should be held to review its canons and to re-enact as many of them as should be desirable. On these terms a reconciliation of a kind was effected, and Bar-soma was recognized as' metropolitan of Nisibis, whither he now proceeded to hide his diminished head.

Bar-soma had had to submit to his rival, more or less *in camera;* but it was not likely that he would make a public "journey to Canossa" if that could be avoided and circumstances came to his aid. Opportune frontier disturbances made it impossible for the soldier-bishop to leave his post. One may suspect that the prelate who knew the frontier so well that it was impossible to spare him in time of trouble, knew also enough to make (if necessary) the trouble that made it so impossible that he should be spared! There is, however, absolutely no evidence behind that supposition. All that we know is that an Arab raid put Bar. soma's attendance at the council out of the question; and we cannot deny ourselves the pleasure of giving a free translation of the letter in which he announced the fact to his superior.[207]

"People who don't know think that the Bishop of Nisibis has a fine time of it; but for two years we have been having plague and famine, and now the Tu'an Arabs have been on the raid, plundering round Nisibis and across the Roman border; and the Romans, with their Arabs, the Tai'ans,[208] are threatening reprisals. The marquis is trying to make terms on condition of mutual return of plunder; but that necessitates a meeting between him and the Roman general, with a big official from Seleucia, and all the chiefs of both Arab tribes, and goodness knows how long that will take to arrange!

"Last August (when I did come to a council, to oblige you) we got the general to come to Nisibis for a talk; and those Tu'ans must needs choose that time to go a-raiding, and of course the Romans thought it was our treachery, and there was no end of a fuss. I cannot possibly come to any council now, in spite of your request and the King's order. The marquis will not hear of it, and will not even summon my suffragans and let them go. Besides, you are just starting on this embassy of yours to Constantinople, and you really had better put off the council till your return. By the way, among the Romans there is the devil of a row ecclesiastically, and you will be delighted at the contrast with our splendid union (!). If you will have the council, I will agree beforehand to all of its decisions that are in accordance with the faith. We have already dropped the Bait Lapat canons. Your humble disciple and subject. Take care of yourself, and pray for us."

Neither the dispositions of men nor the conditions of life have changed in all these centuries in the country where that letter was written; and in course of time even episcopal functions have come to be once more pretty much what Bar-soma made them!

In spite of (or was it because of?) the absence of his formidable suffragan Acacius determined on holding the council, which met accordingly. Either before or during it he received another letter from Bar-soma,[209] to inform him that the marquis had written to the King (who had clearly authorized the holding of the council) to say that he could not spare his active helper. He reiterates his guarded assurance that he will accept "all that the council does for the preservation of the Faith and in accordance with the canons"--an assertion which, of course, meant that he would accept just as much as he approved-but declares that he is not to be expected at it.

The council met without him in February 486, and was scantily attended. As its first Canon it passed a Confession of Faith, which was declared to be the more necessary as some "false ascetics" were busy spreading false teaching among the Faithful, particularly round Seleucia. The Confession (which speaks of a Trinity in Three perfect "Qnumi"--a point to be noted, as being the first official use of that term in the sense in which it is afterwards habitually employed) is orthodox: but it emphatically asserts the Two Natures, and is (perhaps with intention) so worded that a Nestorian could accept it. Thus it speaks of the ܢܩܝܦܘܬܐ ܓܡܝܪܬܐ, *naqiputha gamirta*, or the "perfect conjoining" of the two natures, and also of the Unity of the Person[210] of Christ.

After a second Canon ordering the false ascetics spoken of (who were Monophysite monks) to be confined to their monasteries, and in particular to refrain from schismatic celebrations of the Eucharist-an indication that the Monophysite party were already beginning to try to secure for themselves a separate existence; the council goes on to affirm emphatically the right of all, including bishops and clergy, to marry and to take a second wife if the first should die. Celibacy was to be a matter of choice, scandals having taught the Church that any attempt to make it compulsory led to disaster. A professed celebate, who broke his vow of chastity in secret, naturally received special censure; but it is not clear whether a "Rabban" who found his chosen life too high for him, might (as he may at present) openly declare that fact, and live as an ordinary layman with the wife of his choice having departed from a holy purpose, but broken no irrevocable vow.

The disciplinary rules seem to an Anglican to be excellent, and the doctrinal canon acceptable,[211] its indefiniteness being to our thinking no fault. Apparently it either was or could be interpreted as being similar to that of B. Lapat; and indeed that council seems to have been fudged irregular rather because of the conduct of Bar-soma, and the absence of the Catholicos, than for any other reason. Bar-soma accepted the council, and Acacius and his turbulent suffragan had peace awhile; the patriarch being soon invoked positively to protect the metropolitan, who was by no means at ease in his own diocese, and who wrote to the patriarch, begging him to excommunicate the malcontents, lest serious trouble should arise and rebellion and persecution follow.[212] One cannot say that the accusation of tyranny, which was the charge against Bar-soma, is improbable in the light of his career; and it is noteworthy how very humble the sometime ruler of the whole Church had for the time being become. He professes himself "the humblest of the servants" of Acacius, deplores the "human passion" which led to his "unchristian synod" at B. Lapat, and his "unchristian rebellion" against the lawful authority of Babowai. However (standing and immemorial excuse of the Assyrian when his sin has found him out), all this was dust because human nature is fallible: and the Devil is the person really responsible--a doctrine which all orientals find very consoling.

Acacius made peace somehow without launching the excommunications which Bar-soma (true Assyrian in this as in all) was sure the judge must pronounce, after hearing the plaintiff's side only; and a little later lie had to ask the Bishop of Nisibis to try and bring the Bishop and people of Susa to a sense of their duties to one another and to the patriarch-thus affording Bar-soma the chance of appearing in the one -role which that versatile hero had never played yet, that of peacemaker. The veteran fighter, magnificently declaring as a preface that he had always been a lover of peace (!), did his best no doubt, but failed. Indeed, one has some sympathy with disputants_ who failed to recognize the dove of peace in a messenger whose previous career so much more nearly resembled that of a game-cock.

Before long, however, Bar-soma found worthier (his worthiest) work to do. His. old school, Edessa, had been suspect by the authorities for thirty years, since Ibas had died and the doctrine of the "one Nature" had been predominant. In 489 Zeno the Emperor ordered its dispersal; telling the bishop, Cyrus, to purge his city of Nestorian venom. According! the great school, the centre of culture for the Last, came abruptly to an end; the college by the "spring of Abraham" was destroyed and a church built on the site; and the main channel summarily blocked, through which the Persian Church could receive Western philosophy and theology. By its means they might have been taught that the Greeks were not so far removed from them, after all, and through it they. might have made their contribution to the fulness of Catholic life. The Church of the Empire now turned her back on the Church without the border; and the act is another and important stage in the gradual separation of the Assyrian Church from the rest of Christendom.

This circumstance brought to Bar-soma the great opportunity of his life, and it must be owned that he took advantage of it as an enlightened statesman and prelate should. He did a work for which his Church was to be his debtor during a thousand ears of existence, and which may weigh in the balance against much that is evil in his chequered and stormy career.

The university that had been destroyed in Edessa he set up in Nisibis. Selecting an able head, Narses, he gathered tutors and pupils once more; found quarters for them somewhere; and established the great school that was to be the nursery of patriarchs and bishops for future generations, and which was to supply to the Church of the East that which Edessa had given her, and of which she was now deprived. It was a great deed, and one that was to have influence that the doer could not dream of. When we remember how much of the culture of mediaeval Europe was to come to her through the Saracens, and that the "Nestorians" were the teachers of the Saracens, one is set asking whether Oxford, Cambridge and Paris do not owe an unsuspected debt to Bar-soma, though the road from Nisibis to those centres may run through Baghdad and Salamanca.

While Bar-soma was superintending the growth of his school, and the Church was assimilating the reforms that he had forced upon her, the Armenian Church to the north was also taking one of the important steps in her history. The bishops gathered in council at Dvin,[213] and there formally repudiated the council of Chalcedon, an act which they have never since really withdrawn. They were led to this step by a rather curious coincidence, through the influence of another Barsoma; that Barsumas (to give him the name by which we know him) who won an unhappy notoriety at the "Latrocinium," and who was afterwards a vigorous preacher of Monophysitism in Asia. His disciple, Samuel,[214] had been sent by him to Armenia.

Of course, this act did not for the moment separate them from the Church of Constantinople, which then professed the Henoticon. That effect came to pass thirty years later, when Chalcedon was acknowledged once more, and Armenia clung obstinately to her national confession. Formal reconciliation has been affected more than once, but it has always been unreal, and this Church has always continued in separation on that point, and has professed some sort of Monophysitism.[215] Thus (a fact which must have been very gratifying to all Persian statesmen) the two Christian *melets* to their dominions were separated, not only from the Christians of the Roman Empire, but also from one another.

In the Assyrian Church quarrels soon broke out once more. It would seem really not to have been in Bar-soma's power to be long at peace with anybody, and by the year 491 he was again at open war with Acacius.[216] We do not know the cause of quarrel; but as open anathemas were exchanged, it was obviously pushed further than any previous disagreement of theirs. On this occasion there was no reconciliation, though (when both were dead) some attempt was made to "whitewash" both parties by the next patriarch. Bar-soma had yet another quarrel on his hands at the time with Narses, head of the Nisibis college. Bar-Hebraeus declares it to have been over a woman; but Barsoma must at the time have been over seventy, and Narses cannot have been much less.

It was probably during this final quarrel (though the date is uncertain) that Acacius was sent by the Shah-in-Shah on an embassy to Constantinople.[217] Here he was catechized, of course, by the bishops of the empire concerning his faith. Having heard his statement they demanded that, as further proof of orthodoxy, he should anathematize Bar-soma. Acacius made no difficulty in doing that; and in fact the man was, in all probability, already as much under anathema as his patriarch could make him, though for acts which neither the bishops of the time, nor we moderns, would regard as his greatest sins l On the doctrinal point Acacius gave, presumably, the only official statement of faith the Church knew other than the Nicene creed, viz., the Confession that the council of 486 had endorsed; and declared that the "Easterns" knew nothing of Nestorius and his heresy, and had simply kept the faith as they always had received it. This was probably perfectly true, as far as Christology was concerned; for up to that time the Assyrian Church had only retained the loose phraseology of an earlier age, either not knowing that the terms they used were changing their meaning in the "West," or thinking that the fact did not concern them. There is much strength in the position "they may change their terms if they like, but why should they think we ought to?" and had the Assyrian Church always acted thus, their position would be much less equivocal. Acacius was admitted to communion, and this may be taken as in some sort a healing of the separation that Bar-soma had brought about; but the memory of the rift remained, and was of evil omen for the future. As a matter of fact, the Church of the capital was herself too torn by dissensions to act very decisively, and the point is important. When we speak of the Assyrian Church "separating herself from the union of Christendom" we ought not to forget that the phrase presupposes the existence of an united body to separate from; and that such a body did not exist after the council of Chalcedon. What really happened was this. When all was in confusion and schism rife everywhere, one portion of the Church, isolated and independent before, took an independent line which led her into further isolation. Whether her teaching was really different from that portion of the Church which we now call "orthodox," and whether, granting that, it is now so different from that of another and younger portion of the Church that these two cannot enter into fraternal relations; these are two distinct and difficult questions, neither of which admit of an offhand answer.

Acacius returned to Persia. He had anathematized Bar-soma, and engaged to depose him-perhaps with a mental reservation, "if he could"; but their quarrel was ended before he arrived, for the Bishop of Nisibis was dead. He was killed, says Bar-Hebraeus, by the monks of Mt. Abdin;[218] but he was dead in any case, and that most strangely mingled character had passed to its account.

A man who did much good, and much evil. Who. would win the power he desired by any means; and would use it at once for his own advancement and for what he judged to be the good of his *melet*. In his status lie reminds us of the medixval prince-prelate, rather than the oriental ecclesiastic. May we judge him by the same rule that we apply to them? Yet he is, withal, the epitome of his people. We see in him their qualities; but those qualities are exaggerated, and he is cast altogether to a larger mould than is the wont. In his quarrelsomeness, in his unscrupulousness, in his love for his Church and love for learning, joined with personal ambition, he is a true son of his annoying and attractive nation. One who has studied the history of the Church must feel some gratitude towards the man who wrote some of its most picturesque pages; and one who has learnt to care for the people must own to a kindness for so representative an Assyrian.

Chapter Nine - Disorder and Reform - Patriarchates of Babai, Silas, Mar Aba

THE quarrel between Acacius and Bar-soma had been a personal feud-devoid, so far as we are aware, of any great influence on the Church. But while it was raging, a controversy of another kind had arisen in Persia, culminating in one of the strangest episodes in the history, not of the Sassanid house only, but of kingship itself.

Kobad (or Qawad) had followed Balas on the throne; and in his days one Mazdak, a Magian of high rank, had started the preaching of doctrines which purported to be only a reform in the religion of Zoroaster, but which were in effect productive of a revolution both in Church and State.

All men were equal, according to this very modern-spirited zealot;[219] and all life, including animal life, was sacred and inviolable. 'All property was common, and "property" included women. The gospel proclaimed by this new prophet was a Socialism of the most communistic variety, coupled with Vegetarianism, Humanitarianism, and perhaps a few other polysyllabic "isms" which some believe to be the offspring of modern thought alone.

We know too little, unfortunately, of the inner life of the Assyrian Church to say what effect, if any, was produced on it by this new gospel. Thus the opportunity of studying an early version of Christian Socialism is denied us, interesting and profitable though it might be.[220]

In the nation at large, as might perhaps have been expected, Mazdak's teaching was most warmly received and widely propagated. It is true that it was ultimately trampled out; but obviously there was much resentment current at the "caste-system" of Magianism: and the welcome given to this reformer may help us to understand the rapid downfall of Zoroastrianism before the political and religious teaching of Islam, when that wonderful system made its appearance in Persia 150 years later. Nor was the discontent confined to the commonalty. Some of the nobles and princes became converts to a system which robbed them of their rank and wealth, and this fact makes one suspect the existence of some such wave of republican enthusiasm as that which swept over the French *noblesse* in the early days of the revolution. Most marvellous of all, the King of kings himself became a convert, and an adherent of the new teaching! The spectacle of an autocrat suddenly turning Communist is suggestive of the realms of Gilbert and Sullivan, rather than of sober history; but the explanation would seem to be that Kobad was moved, not solely by religious zeal, but partly by the hope that he would be able to break down by this means the dominion of the great clans, the Zoroastrian *noblesse*, and specially that of the Magian body. One historian has it that a sham miracle (the familiar voice from the sacred fire) converted the doubting monarch. One would have thought that this particular fraud was too familiar to deceive; but after all it is the old tricks that succeed, so there may be truth in the story.

Kobad, says the same writer, followed the teaching of his new creed with a peculiar thoroughness; surrendering (by a sort of reversal of the policy of King Cophetua) even his harem to his brothers in the faith, and descending from the throne himself when warned that he had had his turn at kingship, and ought to let another try his hand!

As a matter of fact, though one abandons so Utopian an episode with distinct regret, it appears to have been the nobles who deposed the King. They procured what modern Ottomans would call a "fetva" from the Mobed Mobedan,[221] to the effect that it was lawful to depose a prince who had departed from "the religion" (recent events have familiarized us with this strange outcrop of constitutionalism in the midst of autocracy); and the Shah-in-Shah was consigned to the Castle of Oblivion.

Zamasp, his brother, became King in his room, and, with a generosity unusual in an oriental, refused to kill the dethroned monarch. After a while Kobad escaped from prison-smuggled out by his sister (or wife) in a roll of carpets which ignorant servants carried off, while the, lady occupied the attention of the guard. Kobad found a refuge among the Turks, and (after a year or so) help from them also, by means of which he regained his throne. Zamasp disappears, but apparently was not murdered, and was allowed to live in retirement. Exile had effectually cooled the King's reforming zeal. Henceforward, whatever his private opinions, he would be a Zoroastrian ruler, prepared, as facts were to show, to deal most drastically with his former brethren.

The Assyrian Church as such was apparently not affected by either the revolution or the counterrevolution, any mote than the same Church in modern times was affected by changes in the Ottoman Empire, though, of course, the daily life of every member of the body was profoundly influenced. Acacius the Patriarch died during the changes, and was succeeded by Babai, a married man, who was allowed by Zamasp to assemble the bishops of the Church in council to 497. A firman was necessary for this, as for anything out of the ordinary routine of life; for the oriental official is always afraid (or the *rayat* is afraid that the official will be afraid) of anything not absolutely familiar. The doctrine that the assembly of any council, general or otherwise, needs the commandment and will of the prince seems perfectly natural to an Eastern.

The firman gave a significant hint that it would be well to re-affirm the canon permitting the marriage of all clergy-for. a conspicuous dissimilarity of custom does more to provoke race hatred than any abstract doctrine-and the rule was passed accordingly. It is worth noting that this canon-so far as the writer has been able to ascertain-has never been repealed; and therefore presumably remains the law (though not the practice) of the Assyrian Church to this day. At present it held usually that all clergy up to the grade of bishop may marry; and they do so freely. But bishops, in all the various communions that we unscientifically "lump together" under the name of "the Eastern Church," must be strictly celibates.

When Abd-Ishu of Nisibis, during the thirteenth century, collated the various councils that were of authority in the Assyrian Church, and compiled from them "the Book of the Sunhadus" which is the present manual of canon law, he passed over the point of episcopal marriage in discreet silence. It had long ceased to be the custom (a fact brought about largely by the force of the example of Mar Aba), but there was no canon to forbid it. Still it had become so unheard of that he did not venture to transcribe the canon that expressly authorized it. However, there still survives some recollection of the fact that a few at least of their patriarchs were married men; and with it a certain amount of feeling that it might possibly be well to revive the custom.

After passing a second canon annulling all the anathemas discharged at one another by Bar-soma and Acacius--and doing all that was possible to "whitewash" both deceased prelates-the Council had to discuss the case of a man who had been concerned in their quarrels, Papa of B. Lapat. This old representative of the Monophysite party in the Church had refused to attend the Council, and was now threatened with anathema if he did not subscribe to its decisions within one year. He had, it will be remembered, been always believed to be a Monophysite; and though he had attended, and subscribed to the confession passed by the Council of Acacius in 486,[222] he was still believed to be so at heart. If Papa were an Assyrian of the twentieth century, one would suspect that he had swallowed some theological prejudices in order to be able to strike efficiently at his enemy, Bar-soma; and had reproduced the prejudice as soon as the overpowering necessity had passed with Bar-soma's death!

Papa's own death probably followed soon (for he must have been a very aged man in 498), and prevented the uneasiness from becoming an open breach. The bulk of his flock were Dyophysite in sympathy, and his successor was of that way of thinking.

Papa's career, however, serves to remind us of the existence of an undercurrent of Monophysite feeling; though the fact that they were unable to take advantage of the opportunity which the quarrels of the Dyophysites soon gave them is enough to prove their relative insignificance. Shimun of B. Arsham became, on Papa's death, their most prominent man-the word "leader" implies more coherence as a party than they seem to have possessed. This bishop had leave to "itinerate" among his people;[223] and his disputes with the Dyophysites once attracted the notice of the Government, with the result that both parties were contemptuously snubbed. Babai, or perhaps his successor, entered on some sort of persecution of the party; and Shimun himself was imprisoned, till the intercession of the Emperor Anastasius procured his release. This "persecution" (which the authors of it would consider to be only the disciplining of disorderly members of the *melet* its recognized head) failed of its object-the Monophysites remained a party, and Tagrit in particular was their stronghold. It was centuries before a single church of the Dyophysites was built there.

Yet another of the many wars between Rome and Persia was started in 502. It was a case of frontier manoeuvres only, noticeable chiefly for the ridiculous smallness of the force employed on the Roman side. An army of 15,000 men was all that Anastasius could put into the field; and those were put under divided command, to avert all danger of their achieving anything decisive.

Theodosiopolis and Amida were taken by the Persians, though the black ramparts of "Kara Amid"[224] all but foiled King Kobad. Both were returned at the peace, when (in flat defiance of the terms of it) Anastasius built the great fortress that was to balance lost Nisibis; Daras, where the ruined walls and vast indestructible grain-pits remain till this day.

The war with Rome did not disturb Christians in Persia. They were practically separated from the Church of Constantinople; though it would be very difficult to say exactly what the formal relations between the two bodies were at the time, or what was the theological status of either. Acacius had been admitted to communion; but the Church in the Roman Empire, so long as the Henoticon was its confession of faith, was officially Monophysite notwithstanding. No cut-and-dried theory will fit the anomalous facts. What most concerned the Assyrian Christians was that they had achieved the result they desired-freedom from persecution during Romo-Persian quarrels. Questions of inter-communion might stand over until the Byzantine Church should know its own mind.

During the war Babai the Patriarch died; and his successor, Silas, was duly chosen and consecrated, a fact that shows how free from all risk of persecution the Church was at the moment. He too was married--to a wife who had a tongue and who ruled him, says Bar-Hebraeus--and, according to all authorities, he was both lax and covetous, selling even the church in his greed. The eighteen years of his patriarchate (505-523) seem to have passed without incidents, though the patriarch was more concerned with his family than with his duties. The metropolitan of B. Lapat (Buzaq, the successor of Papa) had influence with "the Porte," and secured peace for the Christians.[225] The decadence which had no doubt under Silas, continued and worsened at his death in 523; when there ensued what is known as "the duality," a period of sixteen years during which rival claimants to the patriarchate hurled anathemas at one another's heads, consecrated opposing bishops to the sees as they fell vacant, and generally brought confusion and schism into the Church.

Silas, when he felt himself failing, had endeavoured to secure the succession to his office-to one Elisha, his own son-in-law and archdeacon, and head of a school recently founded in Seleucia.[226] The act was, of course, both improper and uncanonical, being directly forbidden by the first canon of the Council of Isaac, but was not for that reason opposed to oriental ways of thought. Ideas which in another Eastern land have produced caste were consonant to the Persian mind; and those who had the existence of a priestly clan constantly before them is the Magians were not shocked at the thought of a sacred office belonging naturally to one house or family. We can see the custom beginning in the election of the nephew and archdeacon of Mar Shimun to the vacant throne when the latter Was martyred; and the strange semi-hereditary system of to-day shows how persistent, and how far superior to all canons, the habit can be.[227]

The election of Elisha was contested, and a somewhat lengthy dispute resulted. Finally the candidate, seeing that it was impossible to secure any unanimous choice, procured an irregular consecration from his own supporters (of whom the Bishop of Merv was chief), probably in the hope that his opponents would be obliged to accept a *fait accompli*.[228] This, however, they would not do; and after a fruitless appeal to Kobad, chose and consecrated one Narses. This claimant was a man of Huzistan, with some reputation for learning. He had, however, few supporters; and his own diocesan appears to have been none too willing to accept him. Ultimately, however, the latter withdrew leis opposition, apparently on the ground that Elisha was too impossible, and the consecration was performed. Elisha, however, would not give way, and each claimant began consecrating bishops in the sees of those who refused to recognize him. A destructive schism followed-almost every diocese and province being divided against itself, and spiritual life and power naturally suffering.

Narses ultimately died; and Elisha hoped for the moment that his claim would now be acknowledged. But though all longed for peace, all were disgusted with him and his conduct, and not a man would accept him.

A synod of some kind was gathered, and the pseudo-patriarch formally deposed. It was declared that neither he nor Narses were to be counted legitimate holders of the office; and Paul of Khuzistan, Archdeacon and Bishop-elect of Bait Lapat,[229] was elected. This man stood high in the favour of Chosroes I, who was now Shah-in-Shah, because of a service he had rendered to him as crown-prince in giving an opportune supply of water to his army.[230] It was hoped that his high character would enable him to really heal the open wounds of the Church.

While all had, been in confusion among the Dyophysites, their opponents were hardly in better case. Shortly before the duality in the Assyrian Church gave the Monophysites their opportunity in Persia, that whole sect had been deprived of a main source of its strength by the accession of Justin at Constantinople, and the return of Dyophysitism to power in the empire. This act was proclaimed by an ostentatious reconciliation with the see of Rome.

Neither Justin nor Justinian persecuted the Monophysites; but they depressed them, and, so far as possible, secured that they should not consecrate any bishops. It was probably owing to this that when Shimun of B. Arsham died, about 534, only one bishop of his way of thinking, Qaris of

Singar,[231] was to be found in all the East; and the monks of Mar Matai had to apply to the Armenian Church for the consecration of the domestic prelate whom they kept (and **still** keep) resident in that monastery.

Magianism, too, was having its troubles. Mazdak and his teaching were by no means disposed of when Kobad was officially reconverted; for at least one member of the royal house, beside several nobles, remained in the new faith- a fact that makes one suspect that a doctrine that could thus win men against their own obvious interest must have had more to commend it than its adversaries would allow! A little oriental experience gives a great distrust in that account of a man's religion that his enemy gives. The opponent may not be consciously caricaturing, but he invariably represents his own deductions from A.'s principles as A.'s actual tenets.

Mazdakites were numerous enough to be formidable, and when, in 523, Kobad proclaimed his favourite and youngest son Chosroes as heir-apparent, they made a determined attempt to substitute the Alazdakean prince in his room. Kobad and Chosroes together determined to read the rebels a lesson, and a grim and treacherous one it was. The Mazdakite chiefs were invited to a royal banquet, the Shah-in-Shah himself receiving Mazdak alone. The banquet over, the King asked his guest and old teacher to come out into the garden "to see some trees of the King's planting." He came, and was shown them-the feet of his own adherents projecting from the row of pits in which they had been buried alive. He himself was seized, and impaled publicly; and a massacre of 100,000 of his followers put the crown' on the horrible work. The party of reform among Zoroastrians, if not destroyed, was driven out of sight.

Another war with Rome began in 528, which was of no great importance, except for the fact that it showed Justinian that he had at last found a general in Belisarius. It brought to the Romans the satisfaction of winning the first victory in the open field that they had won for more than a generation-the battle of Daras. Virtue had altogether one out of the Roman armies for the time; and tough the victor of Daras was to restore it, the tactics which he, most dashing of cavalry generals, adopted on that day show how little confidence he had in his own troops.[232]

In the Church it seemed as though fate was determined to give no peace to the Assyrians; for Paul, the patriarch elected after the long "duality," lived only for two months. All were bitterly disappointed at his death; but for once the blow proved to be a blessing in disguise, for the man elected in his place was one of the greatest gifts of God to the Assyrian Church.

All men were weary of strife; and for once the election was unanimous, without a prompting from the King. The electors chose a man whose reputation for wisdom, learning and holiness already stood high; and which was so well founded that trials could but increase it--Aba, a professor in the college at Nisibis.

An oriental always reverences character and sanctity, however unequal a battle that reverence may sometimes fight with his self-interest; and for once those who chose the patriarch allowed this feeling free scope, and called a man to be their leader who for saintliness, for statesmanship, for loyalty both to his God and his king has no equal in the long series of "holders of the throne of Mar Adai." Oriental conditions do not favour the selection of great men for episcopal rank. As a rule, those who control the choice prefer a nonentity, and it is well if the nonentity is respectable. Sometimes, however, the power that lies in the character of a saint overcomes all obstacles; and as in our own time such an one as Megerdich Khrimian can rise to the throne of the "Catholicos of all the Armenians," so it was in the sixth century, when the whole Church of. Persia turned to the lecturer of Nisibis as the man who could save them from their enemies and from themselves.

Aba, Mar Aba the Great, was by birth and education a Zoroastrian, and a member of the great Magian clan. Learned in the theology and philosophy of his faith, he had risen to the rank of "Andarzbed," or "instructor of Magi", and was also secretary to the governor of the province of B. Aramai--when the call to another service came to him. That is to say he was of mature age, and he knowingly abandoned a promising career.

It was the courtesy and humility of a Christian of Jewish descent that first drew the Magian official to Christianity. Exactly in the fashion of a modern Ottoman official, he had ordered this man, whose name was Joseph, to clear out of the ferry-boat that was going over the Tigris, and let his betters go first.[233] Twice they attempted to cross, and twice the clumsy craft was driven back by squalls of wind, and it was not till they asked the Christian to enter the boat that the passage was accomplished.

Aba frankly asked Joseph's pardon for his discourtesy, and made his acquaintance; thus discovering that he was a Christian, and not, as he had thought, a Marcionite.[234] The influence of his new friend drew him towards Christianity; and he was accused of being an apostate by his fellow secretary, who discovered that he frequented the Christian services. On this he gave up his official career and sought baptism, intending to embrace the solitary life; but before doing so he went to the college at Nisibis, to spend some time in preliminary study. Here he distinguished himself, "learning 'David' in a few days"; but was not permitted to hide his talents as he had intended.

M'ana, Bishop of Arzun, realized the ability of the new proselyte, and insisted that it was his duty to teach others, thus persuading him to take for a while the post of teacher in the school which he had established in his own diocese. Thence Aba went on pilgrimage to Jerusalem, visiting Egypt, Greece and Constantinople, where he stayed for a year with a companion whom he had picked up at Edessa. Both employed themselves in teaching. and were apparently received to communion as a matter of course by the authorities of the Church at the capital, where Justinian had brought back Dyophysitism. and the acceptance of the Council of Chalcedon. After his residence there he returned to the East, which he reached somewhere about the year 536, or perhaps rather before that date.[235] Here the state of the Church after the years of duality shocked and horrified him, and he thought once more of fleeing from the world into a rabban's cell; but again he responded to the call of duty and service of the Church, and remained as a teacher at Nisibis, where his learning and sanctity soon won him wide fame in the *melet*. Time passed; the Narses-Elisha schism came to an end; Paul the Patriarch was elected, and died; and now all turned to the converted Magian, the man of wisdom, experience and holiness, to come forth from his retirement and heal the wounds of the Church.

Aba accepted the call; a deed which was, for him, an act of the highest self-sacrifice, for he cannot have been ignorant of the fate to which he was exposing himself by so doing. To one born in "the *melet*" the patriarchate might present itself as a prize; for it was the highest position open to him-it carried with it wealth, consideration, power. To the convert the case was absolutely changed; to him-an apostate in the eyes of every Magian-to be patriarch was to be a conspicuous apostate, whose daily duty it would be to stand between Christians and Magian oppression, and to invoke the protection of the *hukumet* for the former against the latter. His very existence was an outrage and a provocation to all good Zoroastrians; and his occupation the balking of their desires. The fate of the last patriarch who had been a convert, Babowai, was an example of what, his own would probably be. Aba, who had given up a career for his faith's sake, can hardly be accused of the ambition that takes no count of danger. When he accepted consecration, it can only have been in obedience to what he felt to be the solemn call of duty to God and man; and with the full knowledge that the duty would have to be fulfilled at the constant risk and, in all probability, at the ultimate cost of his life.

The state of the Church when Mar Aba assumed the government might have been the despair of a weak man, but yet it offered a great opportunity to a strong one. The patriarchate had been restored and unified; but all else was in the most admired disorder, and it was the patriarch's part to put all straight, if indeed it could be done. But if all was in disorder, all men were sick of disorder, and were ready to follow almost any lead that gave a hope of better things-and in Mar Aba they had found a leader who, believing in and trusting his God, believed in and trusted himself and the power given him. 'Men will follow such an one; and orientals will follow him more readily than most men.

In things external the barometer seemed to be tending more and more towards "stormy." Magians were uneasy and suspicious, and the clouds were once more banking up for persecution--a trial that the Church had been spared since the official adoption of a Monophysite confession by the Church in the empire, and the repudiation of it by the "easterns" under Bar-soma. The reason was that the Church of the empire had now ceased to be Monophysite, and a Chalcedonian (Justin or Justinian) had been on the throne now for twenty-two years.

Their policy, viz. that of depressing and suppressing the Monophysites, had been carried out as consistently as an active-minded empress would allow, and it was now bearing fruit. Almost all the bishops of the empire were Dyophysite; and the opposite party, alarmed by the prospect of extinction, were taking exceptional measures to preserve themselves.

The secret consecration of Jacobus Baradaeus was practically. contemporary with that of Aba; but there had been no time for the work of that name-father of his communion to show; and the Monophysites, except in their Egyptian stronghold, had been driven out of sight for the time being. This meant a distinct *rapprochement* of the Persian and "Byzantine" Churches, with its automatic consequence, a danger of persecution to the former. The commencement of Justinian's great war with Persia was nearly simultaneous with the accession of the two prelates named (540), and this of course increased the danger that Chosroes would follow the example of Sapor II. So, in a measure, he actually did; commencing a definite, though not very general, persecution, as we shall see a little later. It may be remembered that when peace was made between the two empires in 562, Justinian inserted a special article, quite in the style of his predecessors, to the effect that Persian Christians were not to be persecuted.

There was this danger, then, to face; but when we turn to the question of the relations between the Assyrian Church and that in the Roman Empire, we find it still very difficult to say what they were, and can only repeat our warning that the facts will not square with any cut-and-dried theory of what ought to be. Things would be simpler if we could accept the general idea that, by rejecting the inspired and infallible Council of Ephesus, the Church of Assyria had cut herself off from Catholic communion, and was thenceforward openly and avowedly heretical; but that idea has no relation to the facts. The Assyrian Church had certainly not accepted Ephesus-nor had they formally rejected it--nor had they ever been asked to do either. But they had accepted, or at least were under the impression that they had accepted, Chalcedon as an orthodox council,[236] and Leo's tome as an authoritative explanation of Christological doctrine. There was no formal act on either side; and the question whether communion was or was not restored under Justinian depends on the question whether it was or was not in a broken state previous to his accession. When last there had been any dealings between the two bodies the "westerns' had accepted Acacius as orthodox. Since then the Assyrians had not changed, but had kept to, and still used, terms that were anterior in date to the controversy; and the most rigid anti-Nestorian can only say of *e.g.* the confession of Aba,[237] that it is not very definite. On the other hand, the Assyrians were quite entitled to say that the Church of Constantinople, so long as they had accepted the Henoticon of Zeno, lay at the least under grave suspicion of heresy. Now, however, they had cleared themselves; and therefore there was no reason why the Patriarch of Seleucia could not follow the laudable example of his brother of Rome, and admit--his brother of Constantinople to communion!

If one may use a figure, these two parts of the Christian body, the Greek and Persian Churches, were like those masses of foam that one sees so often on a swollen river. They had a common origin, and in essence they were one; but an eddy had drifted them apart, and they pursued separate ways on the surface of the one stream, each having its own history and adventures. Then another swirl of the current brought them together once more, and they touched, and it would seem as if they were on the point of coalescing finally; but there came another swirl and they separated again, and were carried by a force outside themselves further and further from one another.

All that Aba could do for the Church had to be done under Chosroes I, or to give him the name that he would have used himself, Kosru, or Cyrus, II. Claiming as they did to be the heirs of the Achaemenids, the Sassanid kings used their names; and they may fairly have a grudge against the Greek historians whose perversity has so thoroughly disguised the fact. Greeks never seemed able to get an oriental name right, and were not even consistent in their crooked versions of them.

On the whole, Chosroes was no unworthy representative of his namesake, for there was much that was fine in his character. Of course he was very warlike, as may be judged from the fact that twenty-five of the forty-seven years of his reign were spent in war against the Roman Empire, and most of the remaining twenty-two in fighting with other foes. One must own, too, that he could be (like all orientals) not so much cruel for cruelty's sake, as absolutely merciless in taking what he most likely called "precautions." Thus he shared in his father's massacre of the Mazdakites, and perpetrated another on his own account a little later. Further, he seems to have been the first Sassanid king to signalize his accession by a massacre of all his brothers, a precedent followed often in later days.

On the whole, however, he deserved his title of "just"; and in reorganizing Persian society, much shaken by the recent attempt to establish Socialism, he showed much ability. We cannot deny him the merit of supreme insight into the needs of his people when we remember that the system of taxation that he devised exists in those lands to this day,[238] and does not seem likely to be abolished except in one particular.

He could be generous in the grand oriental style; and as a general was no mean strategist, being able to see where to strike. Thus in his Roman wars he was not content, like his predecessors, to raid and plunder Syria; but struck for Lazica, and a footing on the Black Sea. It is true that he failed to hold it, for it is not easy for one who rules from Seleucia or Baghdad to stretch his hand over the Taurus mountains; but had Chosroes I succeeded in his aim and made Persia a maritime power, Chosroes If might not have been stopped by the Bosphorus, and the Persian might have anticipated Mahomet the Victorious.

Mar Aba's first work was to repair the ravages of the duality, and the total breach of all discipline that the schism had produced. With this end the council that followed his consecration passed forty canons,[239] most of which are simply re-enactments of rules nominally in force; they are taken in fact from the six councils adopted *en bloc* by Mar Yahb Alaha in 420, to which (an important addition) that of Chalcedon is now added. Wiser than his predecessor, Aba only adopted such rules as experience had shown to be needful and suitable for those for whom they were destined. The one doctrinal canon (XL) is important. This declares that the Church of Assyria accepts the faith of Nicaea, as expounded by Theodore. The question of doctrine, and the point whether the Church did in fact preach the peculiar tenets of the great theorizer of Mopsuestia, or (a distinct question) whether it or anybody ever taught those condemned as his in 553, requires special treatment. For the moment it suffices to note the fact of this re-enactment of Bar-soma's canonization of the great Antiochene, who, it will be remembered, was still uncondemned in the West. It was destined to prove important, in the light of the attitude adopted by the Assyrian Church in future controversies.

The canons of past councils had often been left unenforced, but this was not to be the case with Aba. Further, the patriarch knew his countrymen, to whom authority that is not visible is too often authority forgotten; and he determined that the patriarchate should show itself alive and vigorous to those who needed its rule. Of course those who most required discipline were the least likely to come and ask for it (with one exception, certainly, for the most disreputable of several claimants to the see of B. Lapat came to curry favour with the new patriarch, and got more discipline than he either expected or desired); therefore discipline should be taken to them. Matters were soon put straight at Seleucia, where Paul had probably been able to do some work; and in October 540 the patriarch set out on a prolonged "cold weather tour" in the provinces of Maishan, Fars and Khuzistan, where the schisms of the duality had been worst. The northern provinces (Adiabene, B. Garmai, Assyria) had either been less affected by the evil, or (which is more probable) the troubles had been already diminished by Aba's personal influence during his residence at Nisibis.

Setting out accordingly the patriarch went first to Kashkar, where he met several brother bishops who accompanied him for the journey. In fact, it was not a mere patriarchal tour of visitation round the provinces that now took place; it was a perambulatory synod that went to all centres of disturbance, and did summary justice with full synodical authority, though its *personnel* varied from time to time. Halting at all the principal towns, Kashkar, Bassora, Ri-Ardashir, and others, the council heard cases and established Church order and discipline, and no doubt summary sessions could be held under any convenient tree at any midday halt![240]

Usually the procedure was much the same in all cases. When a town was reached all claimants to the bishopric, whatever their number, appeared. Where there was but one (a thing that did not happen often), he was confirmed in his see, no matter which of the two rivals had appointed him. Where there were two or more, the patriarch in synod heard and decided with plenary authority; paying due regard to such features of the case as priority of consecration or personal character, and sometimes allowing the unsuccessful claimant the *jus successionis* and the privilege of receiving the Eucharist in the sanctuary.[241] One specially bad case, that of Abraham, *soi-disant* Bishop of B. Lapat, may be described, as giving both an instance of procedure and a rather lurid light on the state of the Church during the schism.

This man had, as a layman, been censured by the bishop, Buzaq, for immorality; and an appeal to the patriarch, Silas, had only resulted in his being declared incapable of receiving ordination. Notwithstanding, he had contrived to get ordained by one party or the other during the schism, and aspired to the bishopric by the help of some powerful Magian friends. He offered a heavy bribe to Taimai, Metropolitan of Bassora, if he would come and consecrate him; and when that apparently equally disreputable prelate was prevented from doing so by some more respectable bishops, Abraham came secretly to Bassora, and by another bribe induced Taimai and two suffragans to break a solemn oath and consecrate him.

Paul, then patriarch, excommunicated all four; and the synod which elected Mar Aba confirmed the sentence. Undaunted, Abraham presented himself at Seleucia, hoping for the countenance of the new Catholicos; but Aba refused even to see him, and Abraham, finding himself shunned by all Christians, presented himself afresh as a penitent, in which capacity he was received. He confessed his ordination as priest to have been irregular, his consecration as bishop simoniacal, disclaimed the episcopate, and begged for leave to exercise qashaship only. On these terms he was absolved; but returning to B. Lapat, refused to submit to the sentence, and appealed to his Zoroastrian supporters, hoping to be bishop still. Even the Magians refused to help him, however, and he fled. Things stood thus when the perambulatory synod reached B. Lapat, and by its sentence the criminal was degraded from all clerical rank and excommunicated. Only on penitence could he be restored even to lay communion. All the clergy present, and the more prominent Christian laymen of the town, signed the sentence.

The work of the synod and the effect of it were alike admirable. Its picturesqueness, its summariness and its efficiency all appealed strongly to the oriental imagination; and one wonders that so good a precedent has not been followed. Of course circumstances favoured it. Had not Government looked kindly on the patriarch, so suspicious an outburst of activity would have been stopped at its first stage. And the time fitted also; for had not men been weary of strife, they might not have been so docile. Even with all' deductions, however, the work of the council remains a marvellous instance of the cheerful obedience which the oriental will yield, not to law (that does not appeal to him in the least), but to the man in whose disinterestedness he believes. This faith is hard to win; but when it is won, much may be done by its means. That his fellows had such faith in him is not the least testimony to Aba's lofty character.

It was during this memorable journey that the patriarch wrote-for the information of certain villagers-that confession of faith which still remains as his, and which was probably spread broadcast wherever it was required.[242] Immediately on his return he put forth another document-his pastoral "De Moribus."[243] The first of these we treat of elsewhere; and the second deals mainly with the law of marriage and with "the prohibited degrees"-a matter on which clear regulation was specially necessary for Assyrians., seeing that with them the temptation to assimilate themselves to their Zoroastrian neighbours was always present, and the Christian law meant always odium and sometimes danger. The patriarch drew up the table under which his Church is ruled to-day, and it is one of several legacies for which she stands indebted to him. As we shall see, his work in this direction was to cost him personally much affliction.

On his return to Seleucia, probably in the spring of 541, Mar Aba settled to a busy life. The night, says his biographer (who, being an oriental,[244] thought of the day as beginning at sunset), was given to correspondence; and from dawn till 10 a.m. he expounded the Scriptures in the school of Seleucia, the school which, if he did not found, he at least remodelled after the fashion of his own Nisibis. From 10 a.m. till evening he was busy with "affairs," settling disputes between Christians, or between Christians and heathen. The various works of scholarship attributed to him (Commentaries, and a translation of the New Testament into Syriac) can hardly be of this period, and most likely date from his residence at Nisibis.

The perambulatory synod had done wonders; but it could not, of course, prevent the subsequent arising of troubles in the provinces. B. Lapat and Nisibis, those special homes of unrest, gave cause for anxiety once more; and this time the patriarch was unable to visit the places personally, for Government was uneasy about the loyalty of Christians during the war with Rome, and therefore (it is always the first act of an oriental official when anxious) all itinerating was forbidden.[245] At B. Lapat the trouble was a disputed election; but at Nisibis the prelate (probably Kusai) was suffering from what in anything less than a metropolitan archbishop one would have called a fit of sulks! Having quarrelled with his flock, he had shut himself up in his house, and "would not be their bishop any more." The phenomenon is not unfamiliar to those who have to deal with Mar Kusai's present descendants; and one can only say that there is in the oriental a vein of childishness that is extremely puzzling and annoying to the Western. To call him "half devil and half child" is not to give an exhaustive description of him; but strains of both of these types appear in him most disconcertingly, and one is, often tempted, when the latter is to the fore, to apply the appropriate childish remedies. Unluckily one cannot use these on the person of an archbishop !

Mar Aba tried to meet the difficulty by the proclamation of the supremacy, not to say the autocracy, of the patriarch; declaring that every suffragan must come to council at his call, and regard all as void which had not his approval. Let all men take example from the obedience and discipline that prevailed across the border, where, even if there were disagreements about the faith, all obeyed their patriarchs and bishops without hesitation or question. The example was not too happily chosen at a time when the "Nika" was still a recent memory at Constantinople, and Justinian was trying in vain to find some means of keeping Monophysite and Chalcedonian from one another's throats; and one must own that Mar Aba, like many another great ruler, forgot in his own disinterestedness that others might be self-seeking. If the patriarch is to be an autocrat, some means must be found of securing always a virtuous autocrat!

In a measure he recognized this difficulty, and by the scheme he drew up for the future election of patriarchs[246] he endeavoured to secure that there should not be another case of "duality," and that only men of tried worth should be chosen to his high office. The method of the election of the Catholicos, it will be remembered, had been left open by the council of Isaac; and now Afar Aba made an effort to fill this gap by the formation of an electoral college, which should do something like justice to the three elements that had a right to a voice in the matter--viz. the clergy and laity of Seleucia-Ctesiphon, of whom the patriarch was diocesan; the bishops of B. Aramai, of which province he was metropolitan; and the other metropolitans and their suffragans. According to the scheme, the clergy and laity of the capital were to assemble, with the bishops of the province, and the metropolitans of Prat d'Maishan (Bassora), Arbela and Karka d'Bait Sluk, each of whom was to bring three suffragans. This body elected the patriarch. On paper, the plan was probably as fair as any that could be devised, though the omission of Nisibis from the electing metropolitans strikes one as peculiar. Practically, however, it must be owned that no account is taken of the most important element of all, the Shah-in-Shah. Whether the intervention of a non-Christian in the choice 6f a patriarch be correct or incorrect, the King would always have the last voice, and frequently the first also, in the choice of the "meletbashi"; nor did the *melet* think it possible that it should be otherwise. Aba's scheme might give the machinery by which the patriarch was to be elected, and by which, in fact, he was elected for many a year; but that election was usually performed under the shadow of what we should call a *conge d'elire*.

Afar Aba, it would seem, had something of the idealist in him; and would not have been the great prelate and spiritual father that he was had he not had it. His vigour and devotion breathed a new spirit into the Church; his wise regulations repaired the body where repair was needed;-and the ready response to his calls showed that there was zeal enough ready to be roused, and that (as so often happens) it was leaders who could lead that the Church needed; of men who could follow she had plenty. From the inspiration that he had given, and the renewal of spiritual life which followed it, came, moreover, the great revival and reform of monastic life which (under Abraham of Kashkar) also marks Aba's patriarchate. Of this we shall have a word to say in another chapter; and here need only note that it was natural among orientals--and doubly natural in the sixth century--that a great "movement" or "revival" (to use the Western terms) should choose instinctively that special form of self-expression. We must now turn from the story of the patriarch's reforms to the tale of the sufferings and oppressions, in which he showed a moral greatness and strength equal at least to the disinterested statesmanship which had reformed the disordered Church-though one must own that to a Western who lives among orientals it is the latter virtues that strike us most in Aba; and all the more because of their rarity in his *melet*. The Church of the East has many martyrs, but not a statesman who can be named in comparison with him.

The work of organization and reform had not been accomplished too soon; for not many weeks can have elapsed after the patriarch's return from his tour when his persecution at the hands of the Magi began-a trial that was to continue until his death. Some at least of the synodical documents that the Church has preserved must have been composed when this trouble was actually upon him. Nor was the patriarch the only sufferer; for a certain amount of persecution fell upon the whole Church, though it would appear that converts were the only actual martyrs. We have the acta of two of these, Gregory and Yazidpanah,[247] both of whom were men of position; and the same source informs us that some at least among the bishops, besides the patriarch, were imprisoned. This revival of persecution after an interval of sixty years (for there had been none since the death of Babowai) naturally produced a panic among Christians; and the "good lead" given by Grigor, the first martyr, was therefore doubly valuable for those who had not been bred up in the knowledge of what their faith might mean to them. The fact that the Church of Persia was no longer clearly separated from that of the empire would expose it, of course, to the old dangers and suspicions.

Naturally it was not long before an "apostate" so conspicuous as the patriarch was attacked; he being accused to the Kind by the Mobed Mobedan in person, and charged with despising the national "din," and with proselytizing.[248] Chosroes, who always both liked and respected the patriarch, and who was no fanatic personally, was not anxious to have the question raised at all; but he was also desirous not to offend the established hierarchy, a body whose resentment not even the Shah-in-Shah could despise. Thus, for the moment, he found some excuse for putting off the case (the circumlocution office itself might learn much from the oriental in that respect), and departed to the war in Lazica. When he was gone, however, Dad-Hormizd, the Mobed

Mobedan, proceeded with the affair on his own authority, as head of the Magian inquisition (or of what more or less corresponded to the Holy Office)- being able to do so on account of the fact that Aba was a "renegade" from Magianism.

The patriarch was arrested, and tumultuously accused as an apostate and a proselytizer, both of which charges he fully admitted, and was threatened with death. Had he been a mere rayat he would probably have been executed at once; but the head of the Christian *melet* was too conspicuous a man to be disposed of summarily, so as they could not frighten him, and were afraid to kill him, some more formal accusation had to be made. Of course there was little difficulty about this. The Rad of Fars (the title is that of the chief Mobed of a province) was produced, and bore testimony to Aba's proselytizing in his diocese; and further, to his warning Christians not to eat "the flesh of Murmurings,"[249] or food over which Magian incantations had been pronounced. Aba was given no opportunity of defending himself, but was declared guilty and worthy of death. On this he appealed to the King, who had by this time (for the proceedings took time) returned from the war to Seleucia.

Chosroes heard the case, the Mobeds demanding the death of the enemy of "the religion," and called on the patriarch for his answer. "I am a Christian," he said; "I preach my own faith, and I want every man to join it; but of his own free will, and not of compulsion. I use force on no man; but I warn those who are Christians to keep the laws of their religion." "And if you would but hear him, sire, you would join us, and we would welcome you," cried a voice from the crowd. It was one Abrudaq, a Christian in the King's service, and the words, of course, infuriated the Mobeds, who demanded the death of the blasphemer. The King, however, not wishing to lose a good servant, sent the man away on some business of his own, and adjourned the case once more. He was obviously in a difficulty. He wished not to condemn Aba, both because of his respect for his character, and because the Christian *melet* was powerful enough to make the King hesitate about offending them; on the other hand, he could not afford to enrage the Mobeds, and there was no denying the fact (which the prisoner admitted) that the law was on their side! There was no doubt that Aba was an "apostate," and the law of the religion said that apostates must die. The Magians probably understood the situation, and cast about for means of overcoming the King's reluctance. Accusations of oppression of his own people was their first idea, and this was their next move against the Catholicos; though Magian zeal in such a matter must have worn a rather ridiculous air--the wolf solemnly accusing the sheep-dog of bullying the sheep! Still a false accuser was found and produced in court-where he broke down utterly and ignominiously, confessing himself that all his accusations were false. Such an end to such a charge against a man who had done Aba's reforming work is as high a testimony to the character of that work as could well be given.

Foiled on this tack, the persevering Magi tried another. During the "duality" discipline had gone to the winds, and many Christians had contracted marriages of a type lawful by Zoroastrian

law, but incestuous to all Christian thinking. Aba had disciplined these cases, and the fact had brought into prominence the ever-present dislike which Zoroastrians felt for a practice which (by implication) accused their habits.

"Who are these dogs who say that our holy law is sinful?" was the feeling that all Zoroastrians, even the King, shared more or less. Hence the Magians approached the patriarch on the matter, hoping to trap him into some sort of defiance of the King. "Let those marriages stand at least which were entered into before your time." "I cannot," was the answer. "God's law is not mine to alter." "But if the King orders you to do so?" "Let his Majesty issue the order first." "But if he does order it?" "I will see what the order is but at the last I must obey God rather than man." Shortly afterwards Chosroes met Aba in the street (the patriarch was apparently allowed a measure of personal liberty), and to the horror and rage of the Magi returned his salute with marked friendliness, and summoned him to an audience. Here he told him frankly that, as a renegade, he was legally liable to death. "But you shall go free and continue to act as Catholicos if you will stop receiving converts, admit those married by Magian law to communion, and allow your people to eat Magian sacrifices." Obviously the Mobeds had been influencing the King; but the royal offer sheds an instructive light on the rapid growth of the Church, and on the position of the patriarch as recognized head of his *melet*. To the terms, however, Aba could only return his steadfast *non possumus*, and the King, annoyed at the attitude, ordered him to prison under the care of the Magi. This was equivalent to a sentence of death, though it was probably not so intended; for when he was in prison it would be easy to dispatch him by the hand of some underling, and represent that an act of possibly mistimed zeal towards a notorious apostate ought not to be judged severely. This was understood, and the attitude of the Christians of the capital became so threatening that the order was recalled. Chosroes, feeling, it would appear, that the matter had got to be settled somehow, sent the Catholicos into exile, to Azerbaijan. Amid the passionate grief of all Christians he departed, and reached the appointed province; but the local Rad, Dardin (a man selected for his notoriously hard character), soon showed such respect and regard for the patriarch that he was removed thence, and sent to "Sirsh," the very centre and stronghold of Magianism. This place was in all probability "Takht-i-Sulieman," about sixty miles south-east of Lake Urmi; where the ruins of the great Magian temple still stand on their mound, close by the mysterious crater of Zindan. Here his confinement was purposely made very severe at first, in the undisguised hope that his death would be caused by it; and the hard winters of the high Persian plateau must have been a further trial to one bred in the land of Radan, which is practically the Babylonian plain. Later, however (perhaps in response to a hint from court), he was allowed to live in a house of his own, where he furnished a room as a church, and his friends were allowed to visit him. Here for seven years he continued in a captivity which may without irreverence be compared to that of St. Paul; and acted as patriarch from his prison in the Magian stronghold. He consecrated bishops, reconciled penitents, governed by interviews and correspondence. Men came in numbers to see him, and "the mountains of Azerbaijan were worn by the feet of saints"[250] who came either on Church business, or on what tended to become a pilgrimage to a living saint. Cures were worked by him-such cures as are wrought to-day among a people among whom the "ages of faith" have never passed away, and the reality of which we therefore need not doubt, any more than we doubt the similar incidents in Bede or Adamnan. The power of the patriarch when going from place to place with his synod, strong in the favour of the Government, was not greater than when he sat in prison among his enemies, and ruled the flock committed to him from a cell.

Finally his persecutors, disappointed no doubt at the failure of their double plan, to deprive him of his power or to compass his death, determined to be done with him for ever. An assassin was hired, one Peter of Gurgan, an apostate Christian priest; and a plot formed for the murder of Aba, who, it was to be explained, had been cut down in attempting to make his escape. The plot failed, and was discovered, and the wretched instrument fled. Aba, however, recognized that the attempt would be repeated, perhaps with better fortune, and took a bold resolution. He left his place of exile with one or two companions; but went, not to any place of concealment, but straight to Seleucia and the King, before whose astonished gaze he presented himself. The Magians were, of course, delighted, thinking that their enemy was at last delivered into their hands. The patriarch was, of course, arrested; and the amazed Chosroes asked what he expected, after thus flying in the face of the royal command. Fearlessly Mar Aba replied that he was the King's servant, ready to die if that was his will; but though willing to be executed at the King's order, he was not willing to be murdered contrary to his order. Let the King of kings do justice! No appeal so goes home to an oriental as a cry to "the justice of the King." Slackness in government, self-seeking in officials, fear of disloyalty, all produce infinite suffering and oppression; but things have gone very far to the bad when Majesty will make no effort "to deliver the poor when he crieth," as the ideal King should do. Chosroes was not unworthy of his name of "Just"; for though he could be frightfully cruel at times, he did as a rule endeavour to live up to the higher side of the saying, "the King is the shadow of God"--the representative, that is, of a power beyond him self. Now he heard the stream of accusations that the Magians poured out, and then addressed the patriarch. "You stand charged with apostasy, with proselytizing, with forcing your *melet* to abstain from marriages that the State accepts, with acting as patriarch in exile against the King's order, and with breaking prison--and you admit the offences. All the offences against the State I pardon freely; as a renegade from Magianism, however, you must answer that charge before the Mobeds. Now, as you have come of your own accord to the King's justice, go freely to your house, and come to answer the accusation when called upon." The decision shows at once the strength and weakness of the King: he could pardon offences against himself, and he could respect a noble character; but he dared not defy the Magian hierarchy.

As usual, the half-measure proved so irritating that the King might just as well have defied the Mobeds once for all; for though the Christians were, of course, delighted, and escorted the patriarch to his house with frantic joy, the Magians were furious, and rebuked the King to his face as a "fautor of apostates." Nor were Aba's perils over; next day he had to attend the royal divan at a hunting-lodge, and a plot was formed to kill him at the gates as he came up. A body of Christians, however, escorted him, and the attempt was postponed from fear of a tumult; while a Zoroastrian noble, who had become aware of the plot, informed the King of it. and warned him of the political danger of allowing the head of a powerful *melet* to be assassinated. Still fear of the Mobeds prevailed with the King, and he allowed them to arrest the patriarch and convey him to prison, secretly, for fear of riot; though it must be owned that he gave strict orders that he was on no account to be killed. For months Aba remained in prison, and in chains; though, as is usual in oriental prisons, his friends were allowed to visit him (probably by grace of the great power Bakhshish), and he was allowed even to consecrate bishops while in confinement.[251] Still a captive, he was obliged to accompany the King on the whole of his "summer progress"; though at every halting-place Christians crowded to see him and receive his blessing, and to petition the King for his release. Even Mobeds respected him, and promised to intercede for his pardon if he would but promise to make no more converts.

Finally, soon after the royal return to Seleucia, his patient constancy was victorious. Chosroes sent for him, and released him, absolutely and unconditionally. It is true that when the King left the city soon after the Mobeds pounced on their prey, and the patriarch found himself in prison once more; but though Chosroes might hesitate long, he was not the tool that the Mobeds imagined him to be, and this open contempt of the royal decree roused him. A sharply-worded order for the instant release of the prisoner came back; and Mar Aba, worn in body and broken in health, but victorious, came out once more, and finally, from his prison. Nine years of persecution and danger had been his portion, but he had endured to the end, and he was saved.

One last test remained to be faced. One of the sons of Chosroes, Nushishad, was a Christian. The King had shown no resentment of the fact, beyond confining the prince to the palace; but he had escaped thence and risen in rebellion against his father, calling on all Christians, and specially those of Khuzistan, to join him. Mar Aba was suspected of complicity, on account of a recent consecration of bishops for that province, and the Mobeds, of course, supported the accusation. He was arrested and brought before Chosroes, who broke out in one of his rages, denouncing him as guilty and sentencing him to one of the horrible Sassanid punishments-viz. to be blinded, thrown into a sand-pit, and left to die. "If that be the King's will," said the fearless patriarch, "I am ready. I am not guilty; but I welcome the end of a long trial." As so often, the power of his high character recalled the King to his better self; he examined the case, and it soon appeared that Magian malice was the only evidence against the prisoner. Chosroes released him at once, only calling on him to write to the Christians of Khuzistan, and to warn them not to join the rebellion. This he at once agreed to do, and soon after was actually sent to the disturbed district by the King to remove all danger of a Christian rising.[252]

This, however, was his last journey, and his last earthly service to his melet. Worn out by his trials he fell ill on his return to Seleucia; and though Chosroes sent his own physician to tend him, it soon appeared that hardship and imprisonment had done their work, and the long-desired release was given to this faithful servant. The hatred of some Magians might pursue him after death, and an attempt was made to procure a royal order that his body should be cast to the dogs; but Chosroes absolutely refused to allow this insult to the memory of one whom he had always respected, and whom at last he had learnt to trust. Other important Mobeds, sent to certify his death, could not refuse the tribute of their reverence to the great opponent of their faith.

Thus Mar Aba the Great passed to his reward. His career as patriarch had been a martyrdom, though he was not actually called upon to undergo, for his Master's sake, the death that he had faced so often and so fearlessly in His cause. Greatest and noblest of the patriarchs of the East; worthy companion of Hugh, of Anselm, and of other Western saints who have withstood kings to the face for the glory of God; we may apply to him the words a great English writer has written of another Father, abler perhaps, and more famous, but hardly more "royal-hearted"-in all that is recorded of him (and we know him better than we do any other figure of the period) "we find nothing but what it well became a wise man to do and a righteous to suffer."

Chapter Ten - The Patriarchates of Joseph, Ezekiel, Ishu-Yahb I, Sabr-Ishu (552-604)

CHOSROES' admiration of Mar Aba had been sincere; but it did not find expression in any very careful choice of his successor. The man whom he nominated to the electoral college was his doctor--probably the same man whom he sent to attend Aba in his last illness--a layman of the name of Joseph. This man was a scholar of Nisibis;[253] trained as a doctor in the Roman

Empire, and obviously a favourite with the King. He may have been a good doctor, but he made a very bad patriarch; for he had all of his predecessor's belief that the holder of that office ought to be an autocrat, very little of his high sense of duty, and none of his disinterestedness. For two years after his consecration he ruled alone; making excuses when the metropolitans demanded that he should call them to the customary synod. And though his personal conduct gave no cause for complaint in this first portion of his reign, yet he was obviously a bad ruler; for when, in 554, he was forced to gather a council, the bishops declared that the state of the Church "was as if no canons had ever existed."[254]

The council administered a rebuke to the patriarch which was severe, but probably not undeserved; for they passed a canon (Canon VII of Joseph's synod) to the effect that the Catholicos was not, in future, to make important decisions on his own authority only; but was first to take the advice of at least three of his colleagues. These were easy to collect, in spite of the governmental nervousness about councils for which there was no firman. Several of the centres of the great urban district of Seleucia-Ctesiphon had now bishops of their own--as at B. Ardashir and Dastagerd; while the constant presence of bishops at the capital, on Church or personal business, formed a sort of "Sojourning synod" comparable to the well-known one at Constantinople.

In spite of the rebuke, or possibly in his anger at it, the conduct of the high-handed Joseph grew Steadily worse as time went on. He took bribes; he tyrannized over priests; in at least one case he imprisoned a bishop--Shimun of Anbar or Piroz-Sapor--in his own patriarchal palace. Here, he would not even allow him to attend the Eucharist; and when the prisoner consecrated a miniature altar in his cell, the patriarch himself desecrated and destroyed it.[255] Nor was it the clergy only that he bullied; the laity came in for ill-treatment too: and if, as Bar-Hebraeus tells us, fie had a habit of putting a donkey's head-stall on inconvenient petitioners, and tying them up at his gate, we cannot wonder that he acquired a good deal of unpopularity l Finally, a council was held, to consider his acts and the situation at large; and it declared him deposed,[256] an act of very doubtful legality, in view of the express declarations of the synods of Dad-Ishu and Aba. But neither legality nor consistency are held in great regard by the oriental, when they happen to stand in the way of the immediate need.

To decree the patriarch's dep6sition, however, was one thing, and to get rid of him another. Joseph had the support of Chosroes; and while that was secured to him, he could point triumphantly to the canons declaring his supremacy, and snap his fingers at a council. The Shah-in-Shah, when appealed to, only said, "He is Catholicos, and what would you?"

Finally Moses of Nisibis--Joseph's successor as royal physician--contrived to secure his removal. Coming to the King to make a petition as for himself, he told a story of a poor man to whom the King of his bounty had given an elephant, which ate its owner out of house and home till he begged to be relieved of it. Chosroes laughed. "Well, what is it you want?" he said. "Oh, King, if you would only take away your elephant!"

Joseph was removed from office accordingly in 570: and spent some of his retirement in the composition of certain letters, which still remain, purporting to be written in the fourth century by Ephraim Syrus and James of Nisibis to Papa, explaining the impossibility of dethroning a Catholicos. Possibly the same ingenious pen did something to improve the acts of the Council of Dad-Ishu. All were delighted to be rid of him; the name of the degraded patriarch was not put upon the diptychs, and even those ordained by him were held to be in some sense "irregular" and to need some sort of reconciliation.[257]

Ezekiel, the man whom Moses of Nisibis suggested as Joseph's successor, is little more than a name to us. He is said to have been married.[258] But in that case was perhaps a widower at the time of his consecration; for the example of Mar Aba, and possibly the mockery of the Monophysites, made Assyrians unwilling to have more married patriarchs, though married bishops were by no means unknown as yet. His council, with its thirty-nine canons,[259] is an important document for the history of oriental canon law, and gives us a picture of Church life at the time to which we shall refer later. But his twelve years of rule (570-582) were not marked by political or ecclesiastical events of importance; excepting the death of Chosroes 1, and the accession of Hormizd IV, or Hormisdas, in 578.

The reason for this emptiness of history is not far to seek. The latter part of the patriarchate of Joseph, and the first of that of Ezekiel, saw a terrible outbreak of plague in all the East-a return of the same scourge as that which had devastated both the Roman and Persian Empires in 541, and of which Procopius has left us a description. Syriac writers call the sickness the "Shar'uth,"[260] ܫܪܥܘܬܐ; but it was probably what we know as oriental plague, and its destructiveness was as awful as usual. Whole households died; and none dare enter the empty houses to gather the gold that lay there ownerless. The King, by payment of a huge reward, got together a company of grave-diggers, who collected the corpses in the capital, interred them, and claimed their fee. It was paid them; but all were found dead a few hours later, the pile of gold lying undivided by their side.

Finally, two of the metropolitans-those of Karka and Arbela-instituted solemn services of intercession, litanies and Rogation processions; calling on all men to show penitence under the shadow of God's judgments, as the men of Nineveh had done of old, in order that they too might be spared. The patriarch scoffed;[261] and called the leaders of the processions "blind leaders of the blind"--a faithlessness punished by the failure of his own sight. The plague abated, and ever since the Church of Assyria has perpetuated the observance. The third week before "the Great Fast" still sees the celebration of the "Bautha of the Ninevites," the "Rogation days" of this Church.[262]

Ezekiel was followed on the throne by Ishu-yahb of Arzun, the first of several patriarchs to bear that name. Two names, as in the modern Armenian fashion, were presented to the King by the electoral college;[263] and Hormizd chose Ishu-yahb on account of a political service he had rendered in giving information of some Roman military movements on the frontier. Hormizd was a pro-Christian ruler, if we may, credit a story given us by the Arabic chronicler.[264] It is said that the Magi tried to rouse him to persecute the Christians, on the ground that they were a danger to his throne. Ay throne stands on four feet, not on two," said the King. "On Jews and Christians as well as on Zoroastrians"; and so the matter dropped.

The whole of this reign was occupied with the weary war which Justin II, Tiberius, and Maurice waged from 572 till 591; a war conducted apparently with the object of securing the maximum of suffering to the provincials, with the minimum of strategic result. Campaigns that were mere raids followed one upon another; the Persians once pushing to the gates of Antioch, and securing an enormous number of captives, who were, after the plague, probably as valuable a form of loot as any available. Two hundred and ninety thousand prisoners were carried off to Persia, and settled in new Antioch and similar cities. One flash of pure comedy, not to say farce, enlivens the dreary story. Justin sent to Mondir, the Arab king, bidding him come on important business to meet the Roman general Marcian; and wrote also to Marcian, bidding him execute the Arab on his arrival; put the letters into the wrong envelopes and so dispatched them!

The war was only ended by a palace revolution, which brought about the death of Hormizd; and immediately there followed a foretaste of that outburst of anarchy which was practically to destroy the Sassanid monarchy a generation later, after another and greater struggle with Rome. Bahram the Persian general, who was already in revolt, owing to a personal insult offered him by Hormizd, made an attempt to secure the throne for himself, when that king was dethroned by the adherents of his son, Chosroes.[265] For a time lie succeeded; defeating Chosroes, and forcing him to take refuge in Roman territory: But, outside his own army, Bahram had no supporters; and when his one force was defeated by Roman troops supplied by Maurice, the general's cause was lost. Chosroes II, surnamed Parviz, was thereupon recognized as king.

Many embassies were, of course, exchanged in the course of the long war; and of one of them at least--possibly that which brought about the final peace--the patriarch Ishu-yahb was a member, and he thus came to have an interview with the Emperor Maurice.[266] Diplomatic business done, the theological question came up; and the Emperor asked, "What is your faith in the Persian Church? Since the time of the Council of Chalcedon, we have heard nothing whatever about you." The patriarch in answer wrote a confession, which was submitted to the patriarchs of Constantinople and Antioch, and received by them as absolutely orthodox. This confession may have been that given in the *Liber Turris,* or may have been one of the two theological canons included in the Synodicon as the work of this patriarch.[267] In either case it is hard to see what other decision the two prelates consulted could have given, seeing that the confessions are elaborately orthodox, and one of them cannot even be called indefinite.

The incident shows that, a full century and a half after the, time of Nestorius, Constantinople did not know how to class the Assyrian Church in the controversies of the time. It was regarded as something outside current ecclesiastical politics; while at the same time it was certainly not classed as Nestorian. Nevertheless, it as in the days of this patriarch, just when there seemed a fair prospect of a clear understanding, that a more definite step was taken towards separation than any since the time of Bar-soma; for it was at this time that "the easterns" first heard of, or first realized, the condemnation in the West of the man whom they regarded as the greatest of all commentators and theologians--Theodore of Mopsuestia.

We cannot enter here into the details of the weary "Three Chapters" controversy, but must recapitulate a few of the main facts. Justinian had come to the conclusion that something must be done to reconcile the Monophysites of Egypt and Syria to the Council of Chalcedon; and thereby to abate the chronic disloyalty of those provinces, which indeed had become a public danger. For the conqueror of Italy to estrange the West by repudiating Chalcedon was impossible, even if the imperial theologian could have brought himself to it. There was hope, however, that if the men most objectionable to them were anathematized, the Monophysite party would consent to swallow their objections to the council; and this was the line that the Emperor on the advice of Theodora and Theodore Ascidas the courtier. bishop-determined to follow. Theodore of Mopsuestia, Theodoret, Ibas, and a little later Origen, were selected as the victims, and were condemned.

It was a political move, not a religious act characteristic of the time when religion had become politics; and it deservedly failed of its political object. The Monophysites were not reconciled; and were only furnished with another argument for controversial use. "You have condemned Chalcedon, in condemning the men whom Chalcedon acquitted. Now be consistent, and condemn the council."

Many, too, felt, and quite rightly, that the condemnation of men dead "in the peace of the Church" (whatever defence might be found in the doubtful precedent of King Josiah and the idolaters' bones) was a scandal and a wrong. Of course, more than one of Theodore's theories had a strange sound; even as had others of Origen's, his fellow in condemnation. But nevertheless, to condemn the man who had passed from the earthly tribunal to one where absolute justice would be done him to condemn him when he could neither defend nor abandon his tenets-was contrary to all justice. The two great irregular thinkers were far enough from one another in time, in way of life, in cast of mind. Love of meditating on the deep things of God, and love of their

Master's service, were about the only things they had in common. Nevertheless, there was a sardonic fitness in the fact that these two great minds should be linked in a common condemnation, by one so immeasurably below them as that imperial pedant, the Caesar-Pope Justinian.

Theology that could not be expressed in a code, conceptions that "broke through language," could not enter into that legal mind; and the condemnation appeared to him to stand on all fours with the confiscation of the property of a rebel, who could not be executed because he was dead.

Thus it was that, even in the West, the condemnation of the "Three Chapters" was felt to be a very questionable transaction, and one that stood much in need of explanation. Vigilius the Pope had to give it, as he travelled towards the home he never reached; and he, poor man, was in the singularly unfortunate position of having to give an explanation, not only of his condemnation of the Chapters, but of his refusal to condemn them also! With some ingenuity he had got himself gored by both horns of the dilemma. Africa and Gaul refused at first to accept the council. Aquileia and the north of Italy held out against it for one hundred and fifty years. Only the original Roman patriarchate seems to have accepted it at once. Of course, ultimately, all the West came into line, as they realized that there was no objection to their continuing to honour the Council of Chalcedon; and that the second Council of Constantinople could be neglected, as it has been in fact; for, after all, it was not their men that had been condemned.

But if the West felt so much uneasiness on a point which did not concern them directly, what was the East likely to feel upon the point? Theodore had been their teacher, and was "their man." For more than a century his name, uncondemned in the 'Nest, had been held in special honour by them. And now, without consultation with them, and frankly as a move in a political game for the reconciling of heretics, he was to be declared anathema.

Whether they, as a Church, actually held the doctrines of the man they honoured, is another matter. Some of their writers did so. But if it be fair to describe Theodore's conception of the Hypostatic Union as "a connexion, gradually growing more complete as the spiritual growth of the Christ proceeded," then they, as a Church, certainly did not hold it. And as certainly they did not hold the opinions condemned as Theodore's by the Council of Constantinople.[268] However, the Assyrian Church did not pause to consider these refinements. Their man had been attacked, and they defended him. With characteristic oriental wrong-headedness, they assumed that because Theodore had been unjustly condemned, therefore he was a writer of infallible correctness in all points; and they passed a decree accordingly.[269] A domestic disagreement, of which we treat in the next chapter, made them still more eager to affirm the orthodoxy of the Mopsuestian.

There is a positively Mephistophelean irony in the situation. For some time past the Assyrians had been obliged to define their own thoughts on the Christoiogical problem more accurately; owing, probably, to the exigencies of argument with the Monophysites. In consequence the Assyrian theologians, though working on their own line, had reached a conclusion practically identical with that reached at Constantinople. Granting, for argument's sake, the absolute Nestorianism (in the worst sense) of men like Bar-soma and Narses, yet Ishu-yahb's confession is orthodox; and this occupies a position of authority in the formal documents of the Church which is not given to the writings of either of the other two. But just at the moment when it was put forward they realized the condemnation of their hero; and, to use a figure they will employ of themselves, they "shied like a horse." To fall back on the metaphor we employ above, the swirl of the current had caught the foam patches just as they seemed uniting--and they swung apart once more. Justinian could hardly have intended or foreseen this result of his political move; but perhaps it would not have affected him had he known it. He had the Church in the empire to manage; what was the Church outside it to him?

Henceforward, the Assyrians do seem to have regarded themselves as separate from the Church of Constantinople; but separated far more by the "names of the doctors" than by any abstract point of Christology. Soon, too, suspicion grew between the two bodies, each thinking that the other's words and intent must be wrong; and a temper most antagonistic to true union came to prevail in the minds of both.

Ishu-yahb continued to be patriarch until his death in 596; but lost the favour of the King in his latter years. Chosroes II, as stated above, was forced to flee to Rome almost immediately after his accession; and had expected the head of the Christian *melet* to accompany him--no doubt in the belief that such a circumstance would make it easier for him to obtain the help he desired from the Emperor Maurice. Ishu-yahb avoided coming with him perhaps because he was worshipping the rising sun (though there is no evidence on this point)--and did not go out to meet him on his return. This last is a great breach of oriental etiquette towards a superior; and is generally taken as implying either hostility to the person you do not meet, or a guilty conscience towards him.

The patriarch died in 596 while on a visit to the Court of Khirta, the residence of the Arab sub-King Naaman, who was a Christian. There had been a bishop among these Arabs for many years; but the conversion of the prince was an event of Ishu-yahb's patriarchate, and was due mainly to the hermit-bishop of Lashom, Sabr-Ishu, the successor of Ishu-yahb at Seleucia. Monophysite missionaries also attempted to obtain a footing in this sphere; and an unseemly wrangle between the two Christian bodies resulted. The existence of this independent Arab Church is yet another instance of the ground once held by Christianity, and (alas!) lost again.

The man whom Chosroes selected in Ishu-yahb's place was Sabr-Ishu of Lashom, a man whose asceticism and sanctity had won him wide fame. Shirin, the King's Christian wife, had the greatest reverence for him;-- Chosroes himself was accustomed to ask for his prayers; and the Emperor

Maurice once sent him a relic, a piece of the true Cross, asking him to send his cowl in exchange.[270]

Chosroes revered him because, during his campaign against Bahram,[271] he had in a dream seen his horse led forward by an aged man, whom Shirin, when he told her the vision, declared must be Sabr-Ishu. Indeed, Chosroes is said to have recognized the figure of his dream, when he met the bishop.

Sabr-Ishu was bred a shepherd, and had been an ascetic from his youth; a fact which at one time led him toward Marcionism. He had been a hermit in "the mountains of Radan"[272] (the rugged parallel ridges of limestone between Kirkuk and Sulisanieh), and in other places, till he had become a power in the land as saint and healer. The reality of the cures he worked, many of which are recorded in his life, seems to be attested by the fact[273] that the Alagians regarded him as an enchanter. On this charge they summoned him to Karka d-B. Sluk; and the metropolitan and people immediately insisted on consecrating him to a bishopric that was then vacant, at Lashom, a small town distant about twelve miles from the city of Kirkuk, or Karka.

On the death of Ishu-yahb, the electoral body presented five names to the King for his selection; but that of the Bishop of Lashom was not among them. When Chosroes asked why he had been left out, the answer was made that indeed there was no holier man in the land, but that his great age was against him. Chosroes insisted; and Sabr-Ishu was elected, with an episcopal *vekil* to make the more fatiguing journeys.

Though a saint in his cell, Sabr-Ishu (like some others) was not quite a success as bishop. Physically, indeed, he proved tougher than had been anticipated, thanks no doubt to his shepherd training; but his episcopal decisions were apt to be harsh and unjust. A conspicuous instance of this was the case of Gregory of Nisibis. This prelate had some trouble with his flock, who always appear in the history as very unruly sheep (and indeed the combination of a frontier district, a large military garrison, and a big university, is not one that makes for orderliness); and sheaves of complaints were sent against him, both to patriarch and King.[274] He had offended the school, which constituted an extra-diocesan *imperium in imperio*, by his share in the condemnation and removal of their great teacher, Khenana (see next chapter). He had offended the clergy by a too vigorous discipline, particularly in the case of a man known only by his nickname, "the Fox's son," whom he had caught sacrificing a white cock in the woods outside the town.[275] And he had offended the monks, more particularly those of Singar, by his policy of weeding out from among them the sectaries known as Msaliani.[276]

Sabr-Ishu, apparently without due examination, accepted all these charges as true; and, with the consent of the King, deposed Gregory, and sent him to a monastery. In wrath, the metropolitan shook the dust of Nisibis from his feet, and withdrew-foretelling that judgment would shortly fall on both accusers and over-hasty judge.

In fact, shortly after, a local rebellion at Nisibis brought sharp discipline on the city from the King; and by his injustice, Sabr-Ishu is said to have lost thenceforward his power of working miracles.[277]

It must have been shortly after this episode that the Romano-Persian war broke out again; and the rivalry of four hundred years entered on its last and most magnificent phase.

Chosroes had at least a good reason to allege for his recommencement of it: to avenge the death of his friend and benefactor Maurice, and to win back the crown of his young ward, Theodosius, from the usurping Phocas. But though that was his excuse for beginning the war, and indeed may have been at first his real intention in fighting, for he made Sabr-Ishu solemnly crown the young refugee as Roman Emperor,[278] the intent and the youth soon vanish from sight together in the prospect of winning back, at last, the whole Achaemenid heritage: and Chosroes fights and conquers for his own hand.

In one of the first campaigns, the Shah-in-Shah insisted on the aged Sabr-Ishu accompanying the force, to bring good luck to his banners;[279] but though the amazing success that befell the Persians might seem to justify their belief in their episcopal mascot, the fatigues soon proved too much for the old man, who was well over eighty. He was carried back from Dara to Nisibis to die; and the city, of course, claimed his body, as that of a saint. However, after a wrangle, it was interred, according to his own wish, in his own monastery at Lashom.[280]

Chapter Eleven - The State of the Church in the Sixth Century

THE death of Sabr-Ishu saw the close of that period of relative quiet which had been accorded to the Assyrian Church since the accession of Aba. In the nest generation it was caught in the confusion of the mighty struggle between Heraclius and Chosroes, while at the same time it had to repulse the great attempt made by the Monophysites to capture its organization. This period saw also the definite crystallization of its hitherto fluid *formulae* in the shape which they still preserve; so that by the middle of the seventh century-when the Shah-in-Shah has given place to the Khalif, and Zoroaster to Mahommed--the Church settled down into the uneventful life of a subject *melet* in the Mussulman State, definitely separate from all others.

The close of this period of quiet, then, gives a good opportunity for attempting to sketch the condition of the Church, so far as our authorities reveal it to us.

The Church was an organized *melet* in the kingdom, as described in a previous chapter. Its patriarch was one of the great dignitaries of State, ranking apparently nest to the Mobed Mobedan,[281] and therefore very high indeed;

while many Christians held important posts-in the domestic service of the King for instance, and in the civil service. All this, however, does not necessarily mean, in the East, any real power of independence; and is quite compatible with a position of acknowledged inferiority, as a *melet.*

In Turkey under the old regime, the patriarchs of the various Christian bodies were great men in dignity. They had right of audience of the Sultan, and could (if so disposed) be tyrants, each over his own *melet;* but yet had less power in politics than a third-class Kaimakam. Similarly, to the provinces, the bishop might be one of the council of the governor-general (Vali); but his power there was usually nil. The vice-governor was always a Christian and next in dignity to the Vali; but supposing that official to be ill, it was never by any chance the vice-governor that took his place, but some other official. In theory, every position was open to the rayat, excepting only army rank. In practice, no power in the State was ever put into his hands, and no Turk would ever dream of obeying him. Power over his Christian fellows might be his, and individual Christians might have influence in the highest quarters, but no equality was possible.

The impression left by a study of Syriac authorities on the mind of a writer to whom the present position of Christian *melets* in the Ottoman Empire is more familiar than to most Europeans, is this that their position has changed very little since Sassanid days; and that the present Government has simply taken over the system that existed before them. There is, of course, a danger of "reading back" odd, but familiar, modern conditions into ancient authorities; but yet one rises from a study of, e.g., the very varied sources that deal with the career of Afar Aba, with the feeling that (given the change of Islam for Magianism) much of that history might belong to the present day, or at least, to a period immediately previous to the revolution of 1908-to. the nineteenth century instead of the sixth. Even the surface of things changes little in the East; and the substance hardly at all.

The Church was a *melet;* tolerated, but with no real political power; though members of it might have some, or much, influence. Even in the East, however, a *melet* has one lever of power, that of passive resistance, or absolute submission. It can say to authority, "Kill us if you will, but we will not do this thing"; and as authority, when not frightened, is usually unwilling to massacre (partly from good-nature, partly because nobody kills his own cattle wantonly) the *Melet* can sometimes get its object in this way.

On the other hand, outside the circle of Magian influence, in Herat and Khorassan, what little we know of the Church (and it is very little) shows us. Christianity as a growing force, able to win Turks and other Mongols.

The seventh century was the period of missions to China; and the strangely Christian like ceremonial of modern Lamas was quite possibly borrowed from Assyrian sources. Perhaps the greatest "might have been" in Church history, is what might have been had the magnificent Turkish stock adopted Christianity, and not Islam, as their national faith. A race that has all the military virtues in amplest measure, might have shown a Christian knighthood which the finest Norman chivalry could not surpass.

The dangers of the Church were those which always beset a subject *melet*. First (for the Assyrian is ever his own worst enemy) came their quarrelsomeness, and the habit of grasping at any weapon to gratify the immediate personal spite. Usually the handiest tool was the use of Magian patronage or Magian suspicion. Thus, we hear of a certain man,[282] who being refused ordination as priest because his villagers would have none of him, promptly stirred up the Magians against that village, by the accusation that they were "new Christians"--converts; and produced a local persecution. "They won't have me for priest, there shall be no priest and no people," was his feeling, no doubt.

Similarly, the same council tells us of a village, where there were two churches. The congregation of the original building, jealous of the other, got hold of a letter from the bishop "to the Clergy of the New Church of X," and took it to the local governor. "Excellency, here is a new church, built without leave; here is the proof thereof"; and the church was destroyed. The second of those incidents (the fact is worth recalling, as showing how exactly modern conditions reproduce the ancient ones) has an absolute parallel in the writer's own experience. The Romanist minority in a particular village complained of the act of the mass of the people, in rebuilding their own half ruinous church. "Excellency, they are building a new church without a firman." If they had no church of their own, they must of necessity come to that of the complainants, was the feeling. Proselytizing zeal, and not mere jealousy, was the motive.

The Assyrian Church has enemies in plenty; but none would be now, or ever would have been, really dangerous to her spiritual life, if she could be saved from the quarrels of her own children.

Of course, as we have seen above, this recourse to pagan patronage often made discipline an impossibility. A man censured, or. put to penance, might be able to get double *corvee*[283] a inflicted on the priest; or an utterly unworthy man might "pull the strings" with some Zoroastrian friend, till the bishop, from fear of the consequences to Christians, might feel that he could not refuse him the unmerited ordination he demanded-demanded, because Holy Orders carried (and carry) with them, always consideration, and sometimes power. Bishops might not be above using the influence of a Zoroastrian noble to get a portion of another's diocese into their hands; for a large diocese meant a large income, and this fact was a standing temptation to some metropolitans to keep dioceses in their provinces vacant.

The use of pagan patronage might appear in a hundred ways. This was bad for Church discipline, so specially necessary in a people who lack the instinct of self-government. It was worse for spiritual life. But it generally achieved its immediate object; and given quarrelsome people, it was almost sure to be resorted to.

We have said above, that in the position of a *melet* circumstances are against the election, as a rule, of really able bishops. Usually the ruler does nothing worse than dread genius and devotion, because it is so disturbing. But often he may want a tool, or a bishopric maybe, as in the case of the Patriarch Joseph, a way of rewarding a friend; or worse, a convenient way of paying a supple rascal for dirty work done.[284] Further, the fact that the bishop, as- chief of the *melet*, has much of the government in his hands, makes both bishop and people think of that most conspicuous side of the office, to the exclusion of any higher one. People want a bishop to be-and come to think he ought to be-a good ruler and manager, rather than a right reverend father in God.

It is probable that the growing habit of episcopal celibacy (for after Mar Aba's day, married bishops became few and far between[285]) was a useful means of checking this secularization of the bishop's office. So much worldly work came to him of necessity, that if he was not too immersed in it, he must be one of those who had markedly drawn themselves apart from the world.

Socially, the state of Christians was then, apparently, pretty much what it is still. The mercantile and artisan classes were largely of the faith; the villagers, the agricultural class, were so to a very considerable extent; the 'squire class, the feudal seigneur and his family, very seldom; and soldiers, hardly ever. Men of the civil service were Christians pretty frequently; while law was an ecclesiastical matter for all faiths, and its votaries were divided accordingly. Christians had almost a monopoly of the medical profession.

Thus, at B. Lapat, in 540, the chief of the artisans, the president of the merchants, and the head of the guild of silversmiths, all sign the condemnation of Abraham bar Audmihr.[286] While on another occasion, we see that the "Keeper of all the Oueen's camels"[287] was a Christian; and in the time of Chosroes, the chief financial officer of the empire was so too.[288]

That Christians had to wear some distinctive dress, appears not only from the story of Mar Aba, quoted above, but also from the life of Mar Giwergis, where the hero appears before his sister "in the humble dress of a Christian."[289] The same authority shows us, that in these later days, the risk that a Zoroastrian ran in becoming a Christian had much diminished. King Hormizd IV, for instance, on hearing of the conversion of this man, a Magian noble, only observed, "Well, let him go to hell, if he prefers it;" and his sister wrote to him that he would run no risk if he appeared at Court, and might even save his property by so doing. It must be owned that this man was martyred later, but under rather exceptional circumstances.

The Church was becoming wealthy; for in the long freedom from persecution, endowments accumulated. There was, however, a constant leakage, owing to the fact that the clergy or bishops, in whose name the real property was necessarily registered, were so very apt to regard it as their own, and to leave it by will accordingly![290] This habit also exists to-day;' the oriental being apparently quite unable to distinguish between funds entrusted to him for certain purposes, and his own absolute property. It was hardly to be expected that Magian law would guarantee the security of Christian Church property; and the modern expedient of securing honest and immortal trustees by registering lands in the name of the patron saint of the Church had apparently not then been thought of.[291]

Monks and Monasteries.--A sketch of the conditions of Assyrian Church life in the sixth century must include some reference to the monasticism that was one of its most marked features; though the institution was not a thing apart, but a branch only of the great system which spread from the cave of Benedict at Subiaco, to the lands eastward of Teheran.

Traditionally, the man who brought the monastic system from Egypt to "the East" was one Augin, or Eugenius, who was led from the Red Sea to Assyria at the very beginning of the fourth century, and established himself upon Mt. Izla near Nisibis, which was then Roman territory. The foundation of many monasteries besides that named is attributed to him; among which is included Deir Zaaferan by Mardin, the present residence of the patriarch of the Jacobites; and one of his many pupils is said to have been St. James of Nisibis.

Neither Theodoret nor Thomas of Marga, however, have any knowledge of Mar Augin; but his existence need not therefore be questioned, though it may be doubted whether the monastic system existed in any organized form at so early a date. That ascetics of both sexes, *Rabbans* and *Rabbanyati,* existed in considerable numbers, e.g., during the persecution of Sapor, is abundantly clear, and they often gathered in groups round some one leader. Organization and rule, however, hardly existed; and "nuns" were often simply women self-dedicated to a life of celibacy and good works in their own homes, wearing plain garments, but no recognized uniform. Among modern Assyrians, it is interesting to note, the institution has now reverted to this, its primitive form.

To speak of the organization or introduction of monasticism into the East, is really to use more formal language than the facts seem to justify. Augin or another wandering ascetic brought the seed, but in a soil so congenial as that of Mesopotamia it took root and grew naturally.[292]

A period of slackness, however, followed its first introduction, and its first growth. A Catholicos like Tamuza (see p. 26) discourages celibacy, though doubtless for good reasons; and in the time of Bar-soma celibates of both sexes are made to understand that their profession is purely voluntary as regards both the adoption. of, and continuance in, the life. It is not until the general revival of Church life under Mar Aba that monasticism really regains vigour; and then it formulates for itself a rule which, starting from Mount Izla, becomes the recognized way of life for all "oriental" monasteries.

Abraham of Kashkar, the contemporary of Mar Aba, a pupil like him of the college at Nisibis, and at one time also a pilgrim in Palestine and Egypt, was the great organizer, and in a sense the founder, of Assyrian monasticism.

His rules[293] are eleven in number; but four only are important, and these inculcate "tranquility," fasting, prayer and study, and silence, as the four great principles of the life. Chastity, of course, is assumed, and poverty also, for an intending monk, as a matter of course, gave all his goods to the poor; but there are no rules about dress or food, though there was a tradition on both those points; and the gap between the monasticism of East and West is marked by the absence of any vow of obedience. Eastern monasteries had their abbots; but the abbot's rule was one of personal influence rather than of law: and it may be broadly said that an eastern monastery had more of asceticism, and far less of discipline, than its western counterpart. An incident recorded by Thomas of Marga[294] will illustrate this. Some of the monks living in the "outer cells" at Mount Izla, brought women to stay with them there; and the abuse must have gone on for months, or even years, before it was brought to the notice of the abbot by a monk who happened to leave his cell at an unusual hour. Then, the guilty were expelled. Now, a Western monastery might be as corrupt as even Messrs. Legh and monastery might would have us believe; but the existence of such a state of things as this, without the connivance of the abbot, would be a physical impossibility.

In the West the life of the monastery was, of course, coenobitic. Monks lived in the common cloister, slept in the common dormitory, met in the common chapter-house. Prayer and fasting there might be in plenty, and study too; but "tranquillity" and silence hardly at all. A monastery was the barrack of a regiment organized for active service in the army of the Church.

In the East there was a certain amount of coenobitic life; but this was far less of a "common life" than in the West, for each monk had a cell of his own, where he spent the greater part of each day in solitude; and the life of a monastery was simply a preparation for the life of absolute solitude in a cell (or frequently a cave) in the neighbourhood The contrast between the buildings of monasteries of specially strict rule, like Fountains or Rievaulx, with great Eastern houses like Rabban Hormizd, or the monastery of the ark on Judi Dagh, shows the two ideals of monastic life. We all know the great English foundations, with chapter-house, refectory, school, guest-house and hospital, placed indeed far from the haunts of men, but becoming each a centre of life and culture in itself. Rabban Hormizd lies in a gorge of naked uncultivable rock-the church almost the only building; while cells by the hundred, hewn in the mountain-side, but placed without plan and often almost inaccessible, were the lodgings of the monks.

The one is a great organization; the other a gathering of ascetics only.

Kipling's "Purun Bhagat" is the ideal Eastern monk. He retires from the world, that he "may sit down, and get knowledge:" Fast and vigil are his instruments; constant repetition of some holy formula (a "Name" in one case, the Psalms and offices in the other), the "Key to unlock the secrets of Paradise"; and, says Isaac of Nineveh, in the highest stage of the life of contemplation a stage that can only be begun in this life, the mind, free from its captivity in the body, "flits through immaterial realms."[295]

But, if this degree is to be attained, absolute solitude is a sine qua non. Human companionship is like frost, to the buds and fruit of the contemplative life, says Isaac of Nineveh; and of Sabr-Ishu it is recorded that he left the spot where people came to him to be cured, because his contemplation was disturbed thereby. As with the Indian hermit of the story, it never occurred to him to doubt the reality of his miraculous powers, or to be surprised at his own possession of them.

If, however, this contemplative ideal could produce, at times, saints of exceptional elevation of character; there is no denying that it was frightfully liable to abuse, and might readily produce either a mere idler, or something worse. This we see in the curious sect of Christian Fakirs, the *Msaliani* or praying-men, who at this period troubled all Church authorities from Ephesus to Seleucia. These men (of whom we hear first in the year 350, and who were not extinct in the twelfth century) professed to occupy themselves only in prayer; but had no cells or monasteries, and wandered about, living by begging. They must have much resembled the dervishes of to-day.

According to their theory, a demon was innate in every man (this is a sort of caricature of the doctrine of original sin) and was to be expelled only by a life of continuous prayers. After its expulsion, the Holy Spirit entered, giving the beatific vision, and subduing all bodily passions. To one who had reached this stage, Church ordinances were indifferent. He could do what he would without sin, and he had supernatural powers.

It will be seen that men of this type might be harmless mystics; or might be simply useless idlers (many of them gave themselves over to sleep under pretence of seeing visions[296]); or might be sunk in the lowest profligacy. As many of them used to wander with female companions, the last was probably often the case. In the West they were soon condemned. Flavian of Antioch came to Edessa to detect them, and by a treacherous show of friendship,' got their local leader, Akha, to reveal the secret tenets. These were repudiated both by a local synod and afterwards by the general council of Ephesus.

In the East they were not conspicuous till much later; or possibly the way of monastic life current there, enabled them to pass undetected much longer. Ezekiel is the first patriarch to refer to them. He speaks (Canon I) of the existence of "false ascetics, who lead captive silly women and seduce them from their duties"; who also "Broke all laws and despised sacraments." Ishuyahb takes much the same line. His declaration (Canon VIII of his council) that all religions must have a monastery or some other proper abode (whence one may infer that the existence of a Rabban who lived in his own house was still not uncommon); and that those who desired to wander, whether for study or any other purpose, must have a commendatory letter from the bishop of their diocese; was reasonable enough. An Eastern monastery certainly did not err to the direction of not giving facilities for the contemplative life; and as a rule, the Msaliani were either a nuisance or a scandal.

Incidentally, one notices with interest that the "roving strain" so conspicuous in some modern Assyrians, goes back to this early period of their history.

Monasteries were, in theory, diocesan, and subject to the bishop. But just as in the `Vest, at a later period, it was the ambition of all monks to get their houses declared subordinate to the Pope alone, so in the East (as the council of Sabr-Ishu shows us) many sought to escape the rule of their bishop, and to be put "under the hand" of the patriarch only.[297]

In that case, any bishop available was secured for the performance of pontifical acts.

In a later age, any church where a patriarch had been buried claimed the privilege of independence.[298]

Schools of the Assyrian Church.--Education is one of the things that never fails to stimulate the Assyrian, and their schools have always been a feature of their Church life. As we have seen, no centre of education of any great importance existed among them at first; though the fact that special search was made for "teachers" in Adiabene during the persecution of Sapor is evidence that there were such schools during the fourth century.[299] These, however, could hardly have been very advanced affairs; and for all higher education, the college of Edessa served until its suppression in 489. Then the school of Nisibis was founded; and the next century, when the Church had relative peace, saw the rise of a large number of really important "education centres" in Persia. Babowai the patriarch started a school at Seleucia,[300] of which his successor Acacius was the first head. Aba refounded or remodelled it, and gave it a library; and in later days, when the patriarchate was transferred to Baghdad, the school followed it. Other schools of note existed at Dor Koni and Makhozi d'Ariun; while Amr speaks of colleges for Tartars at Merv, and for Arabs at Khirta and Prat d'Maishan.[301]

Every bishop probably maintained a school of greater or less importance (a thing that was necessary in a land where the Government colleges were pronouncedly Magian), and the Chorepiscopus of every diocese appears to have had. education as his special charge.[302] Scribes and doctors were highly honoured. One school, that of Seleucia, seems to have had a half recognized right of interference in the election of the patriarch (much, perhaps, as the school of Westminster has in the coronation of the King of England), and once, by schoolboy arguments, compelled a reluctant man to accept consecration![303]

Of the curriculum of these schools we have information in one instance only, Nisibis, the rules of which have been preserved. This, however, was the most important of all, and was probably representative.[304]

This school formed a self-governing corporation, which could own property, and was extra-diocesan, its head being apparently subordinate only to the patriarch. It was quartered in a monastery, the tutors being brethren of the same; and its students were so far under monastic rule, that they were expected to live a celibate life during the three years' course. The head of the school was known as Rabban; and the tutors, who shared that name with the head also, as teachers and expounders, ܪܒܢܐ ܡܦܫܩܢܐ, while a college steward, acting with a council, managed the finances. Education was free: but students were expected to maintain themselves, apparently by their own work, during the long summer vacation that the climate of Nisibis imposes; and they therefore presumably paid the cost of their maintenance in one form or another to some authority, probably to the steward. Begging was forbidden; but students might lend money to one another at one per cent., and the steward had a certain number of bursaries in his gift.

The course was purely theological, the sole textbooks being the Scriptures, and more particularly the Psalms (to this day many Assyrians know the whole psalter by heart; and in theory, none should be ordained deacon till he has that knowledge.) The Church services also formed a part of the regular course; and no doubt all the approved theological works of the Church were to be found in the library.

The students lived in groups of five or six in a cell, where they ate in common. Hence it was that Sabr-Ishu, during his residence, was enabled to observe his rule of eating only once in the week, a fact which he persuaded the "sons of his cell" to conceal. All lodged within the monastery precincts; but orientals pack close, and where bedsteads, chairs and tables are not in use, a very small cell will accommodate six. A space of ten feet by seven gives ample room for all to lie at length, and what more is needed? Thus, though the college in Sabr-Ishu's day contained eight hundred pupils, one need not assume the existence of courts like those of a Western college, and the architecture was probably always what we should consider very humble. No institution under Mussulman rule likes to give the impression that it has more money than it knows what to do with! Leave to quit the precincts had always to be obtained; and of course a special permit was necessary for the crossing of the frontier line that ran so attractively near to the West.

Monophysitism in Persia.--The latter half of the sixth century saw a considerable increase in the number of the small discontented minority that had developed into the "Monophysite Church of the East." In the empire this faction had gradually resigned their hope of winning the Church of the capital; and as Justinian succeeded Justin, and the acquiescence (to use no stronger term) of the Church of Asia Minor in the confession of the council of Chalcedon became a plain undeniable fact, they began to organize themselves in Syria on a separate footing. In Egypt Monophysitism had become a national faith, and even emperors did not wish to stir tip a hornets' nest by interfering with it. A "Melkite" patriarch was maintained there, but he ruled over an insignificant minority of officials, and the vast majority of Egyptian Christians would have none of his services.[305]

In Syria, from Antioch to the Persian border and beyond it--Jacobus Baradmus was wandering to and fro as a monk or beggar, consecrating bishops literally by the score, and starting the Monophysite Church once more under the name which that communion bears to this day, the "Jacobites." Efforts were, of course, made to find and stop him; but to quote the apposite remark of an Ottoman official, "To find one special beggar is like trying to find one special flea"; and Monophysites, under his influence, speedily became the dominant party in Syria, and, in company with the Armenians, have remained so to this day. Naturally this revival of their brethren in the Roman Empire had its effect on the Monophysites in Persia, who again received a "metropolitan" (though he probably had no suffragans) in the person of Akha d'Imeh. This prelate was consecrated by Jacobus Baradaus himself,[306] but was martyred in 575 for some untimely proselytizing from Magians which brought the wrath of Chosroes I upon him; and no successor was found to him, until after the death of that monarch, in 578. Qam-Ishu was then consecrated; but though the monastery of Mar Mattai and the town of Tagrit remained as their strongholds, the Monophysites, by the admission of their own historian, were a small body.[307]

Still, they were soon to receive recruits, and in a somewhat unexpected fashion. Already, in 540, Chosroes I had brought a huge train of captives from Antioch to Seleucia, where he had built "New Antioch" for their reception; and most of these were probably Christians, and most of the Christians were Monophysite in creed. The experiment had probably succeeded; for in 573 the same King repeated it, raiding the unhappy provinces once more, and bringing back a captivity that might have roused the envy of Sargon and Nebuchadnezzar. Two hundred and ninety thousand new subjects were brought from Roman to Persian territory, and settled in various towns, where they formed a welcome reinforcement for the hitherto not very important Monophysite body.[308] It was shortly after this event that we get the first formal admission, in Assyrian councils, of the existence of organized bodies of "heretics" outside the only recognized Church.[309] They were soon to force themselves on the notice of its authorities in an unpleasant way; and meantime their position was anomalous, even for the East. They were Christians; and therefore, in the view of the Government, members of the Christian *melet* and subject to its head. But they regarded themselves as out side that body; they had their own bishop's, and used, if not their own services, at least an expurgated version of those in common use. After a little their recognition as a separate and independent *melet* was to regularize matters; but in the interval there was an excellent opportunity for anybody who deemed himself censured unjustly by his bishop (or even not given the promotion he thought he had earned) to evade discipline by "going over to the opposition" and joining this Monophysite section. The act did not imply apostasy, for the Jacobites were Christians. It did not imply abandonment of an old confession, for the confession was still unformulated. Of course, the position was destructive of discipline and *morale* in the Church, and is exactly paralleled to-day in the relations of the "Evangelical" and "Romanized" Assyrians towards the parent body.

Kenana and his doctrines.--During this period some theological troubles arose in the Assyrian Church; and the influence of a great teacher, who might have saved them from the separation to which they were fast drifting, was contemptuously rejected. This man was Khenana of Adiabene; a man who in 570 had become head of the school of Nisibis, and who therefore held what was probably the most influential position in the Church for the formation of its theology.[310] Of course, he was a writer on doctrine, and he had composed works "On the Sacraments" and "On the Observance of Palm Sunday"-which festival he, with the then Bishop of Nisibis, seems to have really introduced into the Assyrian calendar. He was also partly responsible for the Bautha services.

It was his doctrinal and exegetical works, however, that roused odium against him. These were a book "on the Orthodox Faith," and a commentary on Job, both of which were vehemently attacked. The leader of the assault on the former was one Giwergis, a converted Magian and a monk of Mount Izla, who had great weight in the Church; and somewhere between the years 577-580, there was a bitter controversy between the two men.[311]

Giwergis, who declared that the influence of Khenana was ruining the school, accused him of teaching (a) Fatalism, in that he asserted that all things were fated and decreed by the stars; (b) A unity of Nature between God and Man; and (c) That there were in Christ two natures, but only one "qnuma."

The first two charges probably meant no more than that the Professor taught "predestination" in some form; and that he emphasized such texts as "we shall be like Him," "partakers of the divine Nature," and the like. All the gravamen of the accusation lay in the third heading. Giwergis insisted that the phrase was a simple impossibility. "One qnuma means necessarily one nature, and if, as Justinian asserts, half a nature and half a nature make one qnuma, then you have something that is neither God nor Man, a thing apart."[312] Here, as again on a later occasion, the Assyrian controversialist showed great ignorance as to what "Western" teachers actually did assert; for of course no theologian ever produced the monstrous doctrine here attributed to Justinian.

Each side was convinced that they were right, and the other wrong; and neither wanted to hear that the other's doctrine did not deserve all the abuse they poured on it. A peacemaker who strove to show (as Khenana apparently, and a later writer certainly did) that each could accept and use the other's terms, found himself hounded out. Khenana had not contradicted authorized phraseology; for the point was still open in his time, and remained so for a generation after.

The theological question does not seem to have been threshed out on this occasion. Khenana was condemned by his bishop, Gregory, certainly, and by the patriarch probably. But he was condemned on a minor point, viz., because in his commentary on Job he had ventured to contradict the "Interpreter," and ascribe that work to Moses.[313] Neither Ishu-yahb not Sabr-Ishu ventured to condemn the doctor by name; and one is inclined to suggest (for it would be characteristic of oriental ways) that as it was difficult to reach any clear decision on the Christological problem (for in all probability the views of the Patriarch Ishu-yahb were pretty much those of Khenana on that point), it was found convenient to get rid of the doctor by condemning his views on the minor point, and to let the larger question rest. Of course, this shirking of the difficulty was useless in the long run.

Khenana left Nisibis, accompanied by fully three hundred of his pupils, but no schism followed, though the danger of one must have been considerable. Most of this school, we may conjecture, were probably absorbed by the Monophysites, seeing that their indeterminate position would make such a process easy. The condemnation of the man who was trying to teach that "Western" expressions were of a kind that could be accepted in the "East," was a very grave misfortune; and it shows how misunderstanding, resentment and suspicion were now causing the two bodies to drift apart from one another.

Chapter Twelve - The Vacancy in the Patriarchate--Struggle with Monophysitism--608-628

THERE was no difficulty in obtaining leave for the election of a successor to Sabr-Ishu. Chosroes readily gave permission for the gathering of a council, and the electoral college met early in 604; the bishops being allowed to make use of the royal posts for the journey, as in the Roman Empire;[314] while orders were given that they should freely elect a proper person, with an eye only to his fitness for the post.

The bishops assembled to perform their office accordingly. Sabr-Ishu's wish in the matter was known, for lie had hoped to see a monk named Barkhoshaba take his place; but nobody seems to have supported that candidate in the council, and his name was tacitly dropped.[315] Chosroes, too, did not think that his orders for a free election precluded him from making suggestions as to the choice of a *melet-bashi;* and if he did not issue a formal *conge d'elire,* he at least let it be clearly known that he wished for the election of Gregory, formerly Bishop of Nisibis, the man in whose deposition by Sabr-Ishu he had at least acquiesced,[316] but whose worth he had apparently come to realize since. The bishops, however, were very unwilling to choose this man, perhaps because they feared his zeal; and another powerful influence was exercised against him, viz. that of Shirin, the King's Christian wife. She had her own candidate, another Gregory, a man of Kashkar and a professor at Seleucia, who had formerly been her steward; and further, she seems to have had a personal dislike for Gregory of Nisibis.[317] Here, then, the bishops saw their opportunity. Though every one knew as a matter of fact which Gregory the king had intended, yet apparently lie had not expressed his mandate so clearly that it was impossible to confuse the two men with any show of plausibility; and they hoped no doubt that if they avoided electing the man they dreaded, yet Shirin's influence would bear them harmless if they put her favourite in his place. Therefore, Gregory of Seleucia was elected, consecrated, and sent to do homage as Catholicos in the royal diwan; though it must have been with some nervousness that he came before the Shah-in-Shah. Chosroes was both angry and surprised. "This the patriarch!" he exclaimed. "This is not the man whom I nominated." Such explanations as were possible were given--to the effect that if they had confused two namesakes they were very sorry; but that the man was patriarch now, and that to undo what had been solemnly and regularly done was impossible, "so what can we do?" Further, that if this Gregory was not the King's nominee, he was the Queen's. Ultimately Chosroes accepted the *fait accompli*, but with a very bad grace. "Patriarch he is and patriarch lie shall be--but never again do I allow another election." Gregory himself was heavily fined; and all Christians suffered--as men do in oriental lands--from the feeling that got abroad that they were somehow "under the wrath of the Government." Eastern minor officials are very quick to recognize and act on any opportunity of doing a little safe squeezing on their own account that may thus be opened to them!

The patriarch personally (as is generally the case, when the prelate *is* not of very high character) was able to make good terms for himself; and got on comfortably, when once he had paid the fine exacted.[318] His imposing presence and ingratiating address, which had served him well with Shirin, commended him to Chosroes now; and after the first period of tension, he got on fairly well with the King. His consecration council, apparently, had been held before the difficulty came to a head, and thus it does not reflect this particular trouble.[319] Its canons-in addition to the usual confession of faith and canonization of Theodore--show that the Msaliani, as stated above, were a scandal and a nuisance; and further, that the relations of the authorities to the Monophysite section were becoming very severely strained. Qashas of this school still used the ordinary services (which by now were becoming stereotyped in form, though the absence of any printing press kept them more or less changeable until the nineteenth century); but they omitted certain anthems from the Liturgy, and from the Sunday version of the Daily Office, in which our Lord was spoken of as "the first-fruits of our nature." A Monophysite, of course, could hardly use such a phrase; and anything that can be described as "tampering with the services is extremely irritating to the Assyrian to this day.

It was, in fact, becoming Impossible for the Monophysite section to remain even outwardly attached to the Dyophysite Church, and the formal recognition of them as a separate *melet* could not be long delayed. Yet the authorities of the dominant Church were not at all willing that Christians who were not their subjects should have leave to exist in the "Eastern Empire"; a state of mind that we still find existing at the present day.[320]

Very soon Gregory showed that though he might ingratiate himself with the Shah-in-Shah, he was nevertheless a very bad ruler of the Church. His avarice and oppression became a scandal even to Magians,[321] and accusations against him poured in to the King. This habit of exposing the shame of Christianity to its enemies, and the constant appeal to the "unbeliever" against fellow Christians, is one of the most regrettable traits of Eastern Church life, and is one that has not grown less marked during the centuries. Among the petitions for the removal of Gregory appeared a caricature illustrating his greed. The patriarch was represented as feeling a (presumably-tithe) hen, to see whether she was fat enough for his consumption; while all around the bishops of the Church were depicted, "in attitudes that it would not be decent to describe."[322] The anecdote, *valeat quantum*, is evidence also that the seventh-century patriarchs--or one of them, at all events--were in the habit of eating flesh-meat, an indulgence not permitted at present!

All petitions for Gregory's removal were useless. Chosroes was not likely to go out of his way, when already annoyed at the fact of his election, to relieve unsatisfactory *rayats* from the consequences of their own disobedience. "It serves them right," was his not unnatural attitude; and the Church was left to suffer under the patriarch that they had forced upon the King, till his death relieved them of his presence. This was not long delayed; Gregory's patriarchate only lasting from 604-608; and as soon as his death occurred, the King confiscated to his own use the hoards that he had wrung from the Christians.[323]

On the death of their oppressor the Assyrians made the usual request for leave to elect a new holder of the office, but were met with a sharp refusal. Chosroes had not forgotten what had happened when Sabr-Ishu died; and though he perhaps might not have been implacable, or might have hoped that the experience of the results of their own choosing might make the *rayats*more obedient to a hint from him this time, there was an influence by his side that was bitterly hostile to the Dyophysite Church. This was his doctor, Gabriel of Singar, a man known usually by his official title of "Drustbedh." He was a strong Monophysite in creed, but is said by Assyrian writers to have only become so when Sabr-Ishu put him under censure for bigamy,[324] and refused, as almost his last act, to restore him to communion even at the request of the King. Speaking generally, accusations against an opponent's morals are too thoroughly "common form" in the East to be taken very seriously either by parties to the dispute, or by the historian; but it is likely enough (whatever his morals or immorals may have been) that some personal quarrel had made Gabriel change sides, and "go over to the opposition." In such a case, the party that wins a convert worth having does not always scrutinize too closely his reasons for doing what is so indisputably "the right thing," and conversions of the kind are not unknown to this day, either in England or Assyria.

Whatever his reasons, Gabriel used all his influence with the King against the granting of the permission to elect, and used it successfully. The vacancy thus caused lasted for twenty years (608-628), until, in fact, the death of Chosroes II.

The vacancy meant infinite disorder and inconvenience. Without a patriarch no metropolitans or bishops could be validly consecrated; for in theory, each of these ought to be "confirmed" at Seleucia, before exercising his office. In the East also all the important business of a subject *melet* passes through its patriarch's hands, in that he is the recognized intermediary between his people and the Government. To lose the patriarch is to lose at once the main embodiment of unity, and the most important safeguard against official oppression. The Eastern, too, depends on authority; and a prolonged vacancy in the patriarchate means to him, in the religious sphere, all that a prolonged vacancy in the Papacy would mean to a devout Roman Catholic; with this addition--that he is deprived also of the principal security of his civil life.

Of course, a "stop-gap" of some sort had to be provided; though probably nothing was done at first, as all would wait on time and chance, oriental fashion, and hope that in one way~ or another the difficulty would be removed. Ultimately, two men came to act as "vekils" of the non-existent patriarch, the more important of the two being Babai the Great, abbot of the monastery of Mount Izla, who was nominated inspector-general of the monasteries of the three northern provinces by the Metropolitans of Nisibis, B. Garmai, and Adiabene.[325] This office gave a good reason for itinerating, even if it had been easy for the most suspicious official to check the pilgrimages of a wandering monk; and Babai, though not a bishop, acted as patriarch in all ecclesiastical matters as far as authority went, though of course he could not ordain or consecrate, and was absolutely unrecognized by the Government.

Possibly it was not unprofitable that the Church should be taught that the exercise of spiritual authority did not depend on the possession of a firman from the King.

In the south, Aba, Archdeacon of Seleucia, did much the same work; for which he was qualified by the fact of his previous office, which had made him a sort of *oculus patriarchae*. In theory, the Bishop of Kashkar had the right to act as holder of the office during any vacancy to the Catholicate,[326] but in this particular case nobody seems to have thought of relying upon him.

Meantime the great Roman war of Chosroes was in full progress; and the Persians were marching from victory to victory in that astonishing series of triumphs which so nearly brought the Empire of Constantinople to an end. Already in 608, Daras, Edessa, Hierapolis, had all fallen. In 609, the loss of

Erzerum (Theodosiopolis) opened the road from Persian Armenia into Pontus; and a year later Antioch had fallen, while Persian cavalry were raiding right up to Chalcedon and the Bosphorus. All power seemed to have gone from the empire. Not only was it the case that the invaded provinces (which were largely Monophysite) had no loyalty for a Chalcedonian; but the ruffian Phocas apparently devoted all his energy to the discovery of plots, and had none to spare for opposing the enemies of his country; and probably no one had much desire to do anything under his leadership. In 610 he was got rid of, Heraclius taking his place; but the war, of course, did not come to an end; though it was probably about this time that Chosroes abandoned the transparent fiction that he was fighting in the cause of the boy Emperor Theodosius. His invasion, too, was no mere raid, like those of so many of his predecessors. If his grandfather had carried off the inhabitants of the provinces, he would have the provinces themselves; and the fact that he built himself a great and most magnificent palace in his new dominions[327] shows how little intention he had of ever abandoning them.

The years 611 and 612 saw a pause in the military operations. The Roman Empire was helpless; and Heraclius (who seems to have accumulated energy for the doing of great deeds during long periods of inertia) was for the time content with having destroyed Phocas, and did nothing against the Persians. On the Persian side the reasons for inactivity are unknown; but the period saw a curious episode in the history of the two rival schools of Christianity in the country.

In the year 612, after four years of vacancy, a fresh effort was made to get leave for the election of a Catholicos. Chosroes was apparently not unfavourable to the idea; for the absence of any official head of the *melet* had its inconveniences from the Government point of view, and it seemed not improbable that the request would be granted. The Monophysites, however, who of course had profited largely by the confusion among their rivals (though it is to be noted that their strength lay rather among the monks than the clergy or laity), set on foot a rival intrigue, of which Gabriel the Drustbedh and Shirin (who appears to have been now completely under his influence) were the chiefs. The object was[328] to get the petition for the granting of a patriarch duly conceded; but to get the appointment put into the hands of Gabriel. It was a bold bid for the capture of the hierarchy; for of course Gabriel's nominee would have been a staunch Monophysite, and during his term of office men of that colour only would have been promoted. The Church would have been made Monophysite (outwardly at any rate) for the time being, in much the same fashion as portions of it have been made Roman Catholic in a later age by the giving of bishops and clergy of the complexion desired to a laity that was ignorant and had only an instinctive attachment to the faith of their fathers.

The project became known, and the whole Church was horror-struck at the prospect. Petitions were sent in to the court, declaring that the course proposed would bring trouble and confusion in every province of the empire (as indeed would probably have been the case), and begging to be allowed a man, if not of their own choice, at least of their own Church. It was in the north, under Babai's influence and leadership, that the agitation was strongest; or at least we have more information on the point as far as that district is concerned; and here it was decided to send a deputation of bishops to the court, to press the matter. The men chosen were the metropolitans of Adiabene and B. Garmai, Jonadab and Shubkha l'Maran; and at their request the Rabban Giwergis, the convert from Magianism and opponent of Khenana, was associated with them, both as a theologian and as a man of experience in the ways of courts. On their arrival at court,[329] Christian habitues of the capital gave a most discouraging account of the prospects. "The horn of the heretics was exalted," and it would be wiser to let the request for a Catholicos drop, and to wait for better times. This course, under the influence of Giwergis, the deputation refused to adopt-and rightly, for to withdraw then would have been to give up the matter; and to acquiesce (or at least to be understood as acquiescing) in the appointment of a nominee of Gabriel's, who would have been consecrated by Monophysite bishops.

Accordingly, their petition for leave to proceed to an election was duly sent in, by the hand of a courtier of the name of Farukan; but was met with the reply, "Before allowing you to make any choice, we must see whether your faith is the correct Christianity or no." The idea of a public discussion, before either the King himself or his representative, was started somehow (our two authorities differ as to the original author of it) and was taken up by the King with an oriental's interest in religious problems. The two claimants to the name of Christian should argue their case before him. Both sides prepared for the struggle, neither realizing in the very least, as far as we can see, that they were presenting perhaps the most melancholy and unedifying spectacle to the whole mournful history of oriental Christianity. Two varieties of Christians, disputing publicly about the sublimest mysteries of their common faith, not for truth's sake but frankly for controversial victory. The umpire a Zoroastrian, who despised both *melets* about equally (regarding both as the allies of his enemy), and who was no doubt delighted to get the two objectionable parties together, and to set them fighting. The prize, that the Christian victor should have the right to set that pagan power persecuting and oppressing the Christian vanquished. Is any feature lacking to complete the justification for the sneering amusement with which every enemy of the Cross there present must have regarded the scene? Thackeray has imagined the one complete parallel to the situation that we can remember--the scene in "Vanity Fair" where the infidel Lord Steyne sets his son's tutor and his wife's confessor to argue against one another after dinner for his amusement.

Further, though we know of no other case in which Christian shame was thus paraded (though an instance or two might be found in India), a bitterer sting is given to the story by the reflection that this was no passing episode, however disgraceful, but was the epitome of the history of oriental Christianity. Mussulman rule exists by Christian divisions; and every Moslem knows it, and knows too that he need not fear for its continuance. If the Crescent has displaced the Cross on St. Sophia and many another noble fane, it was because the supporters of the holier emblem deserved nothing else; and the Crescent will not be removed until that lesson has been thoroughly learned.

The two sets of representatives (the Dyophysite party consisting of the men named above) met at the appointed place.[330] Jonadab and Giwergis handed in a confession of faith drawn up by the latter, which still remains. It is remarkable as being the first official occasion of the employment of the present Christological formula, which the Church in question uses to this day, acknowledging in our Lord "two natures, two *qnumi* and one *parsopa*." Coupled with the confession was a reiteration of the request for the election of a patriarch; and-one notes with regret-an expression of hope that, now that the Shah-in-Shah had subdued the whole Roman Empire, he would impose the confession of this faith on all his new subjects![331] If the Church of "the East" has not disgraced her history by "acts of faith" like those that we associate with Smithfield and like places, one must own that she has been saved that shame by her lack of power to persecute, rather than by any lack of will to do so!

The confession was countered by the presentation of three questions, suggested apparently by the King, and all three of them showing an entire lack of any real grasp of the theological questions at issue--a defect which is also apparent in the answers given to them from the Dyophysite side. Thus, it was asked--

I. Is the Blessed Virgin Mary "Mother of God"[332] or "Mother of Man"?

The two terms, it will be seen, were regarded as mutually exclusive.

II. Which is the elder party, and which separated from which?

Again, the thought of there being a common stock, from which both had separated, was a thing that neither could admit. The ignoring, by both parties, of the existence of "Chalcedonianism," is one of the noteworthy features of the wrangle.

III. Were there any, before the days of Nestorius, who taught "two natures and two *qnumi*"?

The thought of the possible rise of new controversies was, to all seeming, strange to both again.

Consideration of the theological question we reserve for another chapter, only remarking that in this dispute we have exemplifed to the full the method of controversy we have referred to above; viz. the absence of any effort to enter into the position of an opponent, and to do justice to the elements of truth that it contains. The opponent has to be proved wrong; usually by the use of *a reductio ad absurdum* line of argument--eminently calculated to annoy by its injustice. He is to be treated as an enemy; not as an estranged friend who may be won back. Similarly, neither side has any doubt whatever as to the applicability of logic to the question, or of the adequacy of human terms to express superhuman mysteries.

Of course, on these terms, no agreement was reached. And, equally of course, each set of disputants was convinced that their opponents had been pulverized, and only wondered at the failure of those opponents to see the same. Thus there ended an exhibition deplorable in itself; but important in the history of the Assyrian Church, in that it marks, not indeed their separation from the Church of Constantinople (that question, as we have seen, did not arise in any formal way), but the adoption of a terminology different from both the "Jacobite" and "Melkite" usages. The official use of the familiar catchword "two qnumi and one parsopa," the official repudiation of the term "Yaldath Alaha" (the nearest Syriac rendering of Theotokos), and the official acceptance of the term "Nestorian" as a term descriptive of the Assyrian Church, all date from this gathering. The sense in which the terms were accepted or rejected is a matter which must receive separate discussion. But, historically, we may date the formal separation of the Assyrian Church from both the other great theological divisions of eastern Christianity, as commencing from the year 612; so far, that is, as a process so gradual and informal can be attached to any date at all.

It would be more true to say that we can see that the process has begun at the time of Dad-Ishu's council in 424; and that we can see that it is complete by 640, when Sahdona was excommunicated. We have endeavoured to trace the various changes of relative position, and to emphasize the utter impossibility of fitting the relations of the two independent bodies into any cut-and-dried theory of ecclesiastical. correctness in the previous chapters.

The very late date of the completion of the process must be noted. It was not consummated, it will be observed, until the period of the great Mussulman conquests. And it is largely the existence of political and physical obstacles created thereby, that has made the closing of the breach impossible.

The conference ended, and the disputants separated; but no answer was given either way to the petition for a patriarch, and the matter remained in suspense. Perhaps Chosroes had had his amusement in the theological prize-fight that had been exhibited before him, and that was all that he wanted. More probably, he was really in doubt as to what to do-willing enough to give pleasure to his two favourites, Shirin and Gabriel; but yet realizing that to do so would mean a disturbance on which he had not quite calculated. Thus both parties were kept dangling about the court for some months, until in fact the approach of the summer heats brought the usual migration to "the hills."

That, under these circumstances, trouble should arise between the two was inevitable; but it was not until the court had reached B. Lapat that it came to a head. Near that city was one of the three monasteries that Chosroes had built to please Shirin-that of Mar Sergius.[333] Hitherto it had been in Dyophysite hands (this is one of several pieces of evidence that Shirin had been only gradually won over, probably by Gabriel, to favour the opposite party); and now Gabriel proposed to turn out its occupants, and to put it into the hands of his own supporters. Naturally the "Nestorian" bishops objected to this, and a crowd gathered about the monastery which defeated the intention of the Drustbedh. In his anger at the disappointment, he appealed to the King--accusing the bishop, Shubkha 1'Maran, of intending violence, and laying information against Giwergis, as an "apostate from Magianism." This last accusation was, of course, a deadly weapon in the hands of any one who could bring himself to use it; for supposing its truth (and in this case it was undeniable), it meant death to its object. Conversions might be winked at; but the Magians were only too glad of an opportunity to put the law in force in any conspicuous case. Gabriel must have known this well enough, and therefore cannot be acquitted of compassing the murder of his most formidable opponent. The only extenuating circumstance we are aware of, is this: the Drustbedh must have known all along that this weapon was ready to his hand, for Giwergis was a well-known man in the Church; and yet he had refrained from availing himself of it. The deed may have been done in a moment of anger-passion roused by the dispute over the monastery-but it remains one more instance of the fatal readiness of the oriental to grasp at any means of gratifying the immediate personal spite.

Giwergis was arrested, accused, and at once admitted the fact. "I was converted from blasphemy to Christianity in your sixth year."[334] He was flung into prison; and a panic naturally spread among the Dyophysites, thus deprived of their protagonist. They scattered; and there was no more talk of permission for the election of a patriarch, for the bishops were glad enough to save themselves; and a panic, reflected in contemporary letters, spread through the Church.

As a matter of fact, their defeat was not as complete as they feared. If they had failed utterly to get a patriarch of their own, they had at least defeated the daring attempt of the Monophysites to capture the hierarchy by the appointment of a man of their school. Chosroes seems to have come to the conclusion that the resentment at such a scheme in the *melet* was too real and general to make the thing worth while; so that the desire of his favourites must go ungratified. Probably the whole affair appeared to him in no more serious a light. The Monophysites did not press their demand; and the Dyophysites, fearing that the arrest of Giwergis was but the prelude to a general persecution, were content to "lie low" under Babai and Aba, and to wait for the passing of the storm. A metropolitan, Samuel by name, was consecrated for the Monophysites,[335] who were thenceforward practically organized as a distinct *melet* in the kingdom.

Giwergis, whose arrest had caused the panic, remained in prison for fifteen months; so that anywhere but in the Cast, one would have judged his case forgotten, and his person fairly safe. A Rabban by profession, he could "do his Rabbanutha" as well in prison as anywhere else. Then, again in eastern fashion, he was suddenly remembered-brought to trial-and given his choice between apostasy and martyrdom. Choosing the latter, he was sentenced to "crucifixion,"[336] a penalty which he underwent in the suburbs of Seleucia-Ctesiphon.

Meantime, the war with Rome went on, and the series of Persian triumphs received no check. Palestine and Jerusalem were conquered; and the Cross, proudest trophy of all, was carried to Persia and presented to Shirin. Egypt was overrun-the Monophysite population offering no resistance to invaders who at least were not Chalcedonians-and a Persian army was encamped for years at Chalcedon itself. Chosroes had attained the great ambition of all his house. The Empire of the Achaemenids was his in all its old extent. But it must be owned that no witch's power ever stopped at running water more abruptly than did that of the Persian at the salt river of the Bosphorus. The greatest prize of all, though in his sight for years, was never in his grasp.

Heraclius offered almost any concessions as the price of peace; and it would seem to have been the contemptuous reply sent to him ("Let him resign his throne and turn Zoroastrian") that roused him at last by its sting from his lethargy. After an attempt at flight, he prepared and delivered his wonderful counterstroke. For six years (622-628) the armies of the combatants marched to and fro across Persia and Asia Minor, a period of "Alarums and Excursions" in which there is no Church history to record, till all the world was utterly weary of war. Chosroes alone continued obstinate; refusing all terms of peace, and ordering the execution of his best general for the crime of failing to command victory. At last, his subjects turned on him; and the simultaneous rebellion of that general, Shahr-barz, at Chalcedon, and of the King's own son Kobad (or Siroes), at Seleucia, suddenly brought the fighting to a conclusion. Heraclius, so long the protagonist in the war, became a mere spectator of the revolutions of his opponents.

In the conspiracy of Kobad against his father, the principal agent was a Christian, Shamta, the son of Yazdin;[337] a man who had private cause for enmity against Chosroes, in that the King had reduced his house to penury, by the confiscation of the property of his father. That father had been "farmer-general" of the taxes of the kingdom, and in his business had amassed, of course, a huge fortune.[338] This the Shah-in-Shah seized at Yazdin's death; and Shamta, in revenge, was easily led to join in the plot of the crown prince. He it was who secured the person of Chosroes when the time came for action. The King was, of course, soon put to death--"two kings in a land are impossible," was the significant advice given to Kobad by the nobles[339]--and the most brilliant of the Sassanids, whose greatness and whose fall are both so striking, died as fallen princes die. The prisons of princes are not far from their graves, particularly in the East. The last words attributed to him--"the reign of a parricide will be short--"found a grim fulfilment in the early death of his undutiful son.

Shamta rose to honour, for the moment, for his services; but eastern kings know better than to trust regicides, even if they profit by them, and he soon vanished from the scene. In his hour of power, however, he did a service for his Church, obtaining the new king's sanction for the election of a patriarch at last. All the college voted unanimously for Babai, the unofficial Catholicos, who had borne the burden and heat of the day, but he declined the honour, and retired to his cell at Mount Izla.[340]

The fathers then elected Ishu-yahb II, of Gedala, who no doubt found full occupation at first in re-organizing the Church, shaken by the long years of confusion.

The Jacobites had also to organize themselves[341] now on a footing of clear and acknowledged separation from the main body of the Church in Persia. Samuel the metropolitan was seemingly dead; but the patriarch of Antioch (Athanasius the camel driver) sent a successor to the East, and the *melet* was arranged in twelve bishoprics (the number shows that numerically the sect was not so very important), which acknowledged the jurisdiction of the metropolitans of Mar Mattai and Tagrit, both of whom were, and are, subordinate to the Jacobite patriarch of Antioch. Both "Nestorian" and "Jacobite" Churches were content to recognize in theory, and in practice to ignore, the existence of the other; and what both desired was a period of quiet after the generation of strife, political and ecclesiastical, from which they had just emerged.

Chapter Thirteen - Official Christology of the Assyrian Church

THE subject of this chapter is a matter which is of necessity both tangled and thorny; but the object which we put before ourselves in writing it admits of fairly simple statement. This is, first, to ascertain what was the official teaching of the Assyrian Church on one particular doctrinal point, from the time of their acceptance of the Nicene Creed in 410 until the definite crystallization of their present formula in 612; secondly, to determine, if possible, in what sense they intended the technical terms then adopted to be used.

The doctrinal point in question is, of course, their Christology='their conceptions of the relations between the divine and the human in Christ; and we have to study the development of the formula in which they express their ideas and its meaning.

Practically, the question begins with their acceptance of the Nicene Creed in 410; and their acceptance with it of the results of western philosophical thought on the great problem up to the date of Nicaea. We may regret that it was impossible that an eastern Christianity could not be left to work at, and express its feelings about these subjects, in its own way. Had such a thing been possible, Christianity might in due time have been presented--*e.g.* to

Brahminical and Buddhist thinkers--without the western trappings of which we cannot free it even in thought, and which do apparently constitute an obstacle to those thinkers. They are no more an "encumbrance" to us than is his power-driven lathe, with all its gear of belts and "chucks," an encumbrance to an English mechanic. Yet that admirable machine is a very real nuisance to a workman who, squatting on the ground, works a primitive lathe with "bow and string." Similarly, the framework of western thought is an encumbrance to minds cast in a different mould from ours. An oriental can learn to use an English lathe, of course; but he does not turn out with it work of English quality--nor would the Englishman, with oriental tools.

Thus for the Assyrians, the fact that they could not be left to work out their own theological salvation under the God who worked in them no less than in St. Athanasius and St. Basil was a misfortune. They never really grasped the theological philosophy of the West; and one of the causes of the separation was really this--that an oriental doing his theological thinking in Greek terms is David in Saul's armour. Saul's armour may be very good for Saul, but other weapons serve another better. The attempt was made to transfer Greek thought to minds of Semitic and oriental cast; and "thoughts," says Bishop Westcott, "cannot be transferred, they must be appropriated." Still the Greek terms became the medium in which, for better or worse, the Assyrian Church had to work after 410.

Previously the only expression of their Christology that we have is that expressed in the homilies of Afraat; and this ought to be taken as the expression of an influence tending to modify what was subsequently accepted, rather than as an official Confession. The Christology of this writer is very undeveloped; and (as stated above) is. a strong testimony to the absolute remoteness of the Assyrian Church from all the quarrels of Nicaea. Afraat's Christ is described as hardly more than the "man approved of God"--which St. Luke once described Him as being; to be "adored" as we "adore" kings, and to be God as Moses was "a god" unto Pharaoh.[342]

Elsewhere, it is true, the writer uses language expressing a far higher idea; and which goes to show that his previous description-true as far as it went-no more expressed his entire thought of Christ than does the quotation given express the entire thought of the evangelist. "God and His Christ, though they are one, yet dwell in many men; and in their reality are in heaven."[343] a If Some of Afraat's words suggest Christ as mere man, we may reply with Browning--

"Could mere man do this? Yet this, Christ saith, He lived and died to do. Call Christ then the illimitable God."

Still, whatever Afraat's conception in his hours of insight, it is undeniable that the thought of a merely human Christ, which could be drawn from his works, might readily produce what we know as "Nestorianism," when contrasted with developed Trinitarian doctrine-a doctrine which was not presented to the "easterns" till it was developed. Thinking of Christ as a supremely great human teacher, they might think of the Incarnation as a mere association with Him of what they had recently learnt to call the Second Person of the Trinity. Thus there was in the East a soil in which Nestorianism might easily spring up, and in which it probably did often spring up; just as both it and Monophysitism have often done, in truth, in lands where their catch-words are strenuously denied.

We give the creed found in Afraat, which is most probably the original baptismal creed of the Assyrian Church.

I believe in God Almighty, Maker of heaven and earth and all things therein; who made Adam in His image, gave the Old Testament to Moses, sent the Spirit on the prophets, and sent Christ into the world. And 1 believe in the resurrection of the dead, and the sacrament of baptism.[344]

It is, however, with the acceptance of the Nicene Creed that we really approach to a "Christological question."

In 410, as stated, this document was first put in its original form before the Church, and was accepted *ex animo*. A confession which they hold to be the "Creed of the 318," and which is doctrinally identical with it, is their confession to-day. In all the strife of intervening ages they have always held that they continued loyal to the confession they had always been taught, and that if any changing had been done others had done it. The belief is at least a testimony to their hearty acceptance of the new creed.[345]

In accepting it the Church took for the first time into regular use a term that bulks largely in her history, the word "Qnuma." This occurs to Afraat and Ephraim, but it now first becomes official; and it is noteworthy that it was adopted in a sense that the West was then abandoning. In the translation of the Nicene Creed Qnuma stands for , which is there (as is well known) equivalent to . Already, however, in the West this word was coming to mean (in common use) "person," not "substance" or "subsistence"; and seventy years later the "East" had so far followed suit that the Assyrian Church was speaking of "three Qnumi" in the Trinity. The older usage, however, so far persisted as to be still in official use in 585;[346] and thus an important technical term, while in use both in East and Nest, was developing in both, but was not developing on the same lines-a fact that was to be fruitful of misunderstanding.

Time passed; the Christological controversy definitely extended itself into the "East," and several official Confessions composed in the glare of it were put forward. Bar-soma's is the first of these in date, but its repudiation and destruction have spared us the problem of determining on its character; and the first of its kind to survive is that put forward by Acacius in 486. We append it here, and take the opportunity of repeating our opinion concerning it--viz. that though it is pronouncedly "Dyophysite," and composed (probably with design) in terms that a "Nestorian" could accept, it is to itself orthodox, and it was judged so to be by Constantinopolitan prelates of the day. The strongest point against it appears to be that its writer (alone among the series of writers who composed this collection of formal documents) uses the term "Parsopa" in another passage in the sense of "appearance."

Confession of Acacius, 486. *S. O.*, 54, 302.

The faith of us all should be, in one confession of one divine Nature in three perfect Qnumi; one true and eternal Trinity of Father, Son, and Holy Spirit; the confession by which heathenism is conquered 'and Judaism is rebuked. Further, concerning the 'Incarnation'[347] of Christ, our faith ought to be in the confession of two natures of Godhead and Manhood; and let no one of us venture to introduce mixture, confusion or commixture into the diversities of these two Natures, seeing that the Godhead remains unchanged in its own characteristics, and the Humanity in its own; and we join the diversities of the two Natures in one majesty and adoration, because of the perfect and inseparable [348] that existed between the Godhead and Manhood.

If any one thinks, or teaches others, that suffering or change can attach themselves to the Godhead of the Lord, or if he does not keep to the confession of perfect God and perfect Man in the unity of the Person (Parsopa) of our redeemer, let him be anathema.

After the time of Acacius there is no official Confession published for seventy years. This period, however, or at least the early part of it, is the time when Narses flourished; and we therefore give a series of extracts from the writings of that important theologian, premising, however, that his homilies--be they good or evil-are not an official Confession of his Church, any more than (for instance) those of Latimer or Ridley are of the Church of England.

MIMRA X. 91.

One is the Word, begotten of the Father, without beginning, And one the Manhood, of Adam's humanity.

Two in Nature, "essential being" and humanity complete, One Son of God in honour and power.

The Son of God is one in Person,[349] though not so in Nature, Essential being abides, and man is man, and the two are one.

Hidden is the mystery of one Person, of essential being and

MIMRA X. 145.

The power that framed man chose one man from among men,

And gave Him power to reconcile all with all.

MIMRA X. 267.

Said Cyril, "Why does he not call Mary 'Mother of the Godhead '?"

She who bore essential being in fleshly wise, in that He became flesh.

MIMRA X. 414.

Blame the evangelists, if blame you must,

For their books express the distinction of the Word and the Body.

Nay, even our Lord lies under their rebuke,

Who showed in His body the print of nails and smiting spear.

He and His disciples made the distinction manifest, Declaring the nature of essential being, and the nature of man.

They separated them, that their order might be clear, They gathered them, in the unity of the Person.

The Evangelists proclaim one Person, of the Word and the Body.

MIMRA x. 437.

The Photinians declare the divine Three to be one Person.

MIMRA XL. 17.

When then was come the fulness of appointed time, God sent His Son, to come and renew our creation He came to us mortals, to renew the image defaced, And of our fallen nature made Him a temple and dwelt therein.

*****

Heretics say: "the Word was, changed, and became flesh as it is written; He did not take a body from Mary, but His Qnuma became flesh."

It was not that the Word was changed, and became flesh in His Qnuma,

But the Word clad Himself with flesh, that in it He might set us mortals free.

It was not that the Word was changed, but that He took manhood;

The manhood underwent birth, growth, thirst, hunger, and death in due time.

*****

Let not the reader think, in reading "Man," That I mean two Sons, for the Son is one indeed, Equal to the Father, who in His love to us took perfect manhood

And made it one thing in lordship and power with Himself. From the time that the Spirit formed Him in the womb He is Lord and Heir and Ruler, in height and depth alike.

MIMAA LXX. 189.

The Word wove the mantle of flesh, to conceal in it His greatness,

And to show to men in manhood the image of the greatness,

*****

His will limited itself in it, but His nature was not limited by it,

He was completely in it by will, by nature in it and everywhere.

This became the Maker, that He should not be limited by His work,

For His body was His own work, in which He willed to dwell.

Without limitation of His nature, He dwelt in it fully by His will.

But it may be that disputants strive with words, as is their wont,

"How say you that created and Creator are one Person?" I say that the temple is created, that the Word wrought for His abode,

The only-begotten is Creator, who willed to dwell in His own work.

As Soul and Body together are called one Person, The Soul the immortal nature, the Body the mortal, and they are called one Person, these distinct two;

So with the Word, essential being, and the body and nature of man,

The one created, the other Creator, they are one in union. The soul is enclosed in the body, yet is its activity without the body;

The body is in one place, the motions of the soul are unconfined;
So the Word. dwelt in the body, and was in the height and depth,
His manhood was limited, His Godhead was everywhere. The Soul suffers not in the body, when its limbs are scourged,
And the Godhead suffered not, when that body suffered, in which it dwelt.

If the soul suffers not, which is created, like the body, How should Godhead suffer, that is by nature impassible? The soul suffers with the body, in love and not by nature, And the sufferings of the body are by figure attributed to the soul.

We believe these extracts to be fairly representative of the teaching of this writer. That passages *of* them are what we mean by Nestorian--or at least are very capable of bearing that interpretation--is an undeniable fact; and if it be asserted that the whole mind of the writer should be interpreted by them we do not see how to disprove the charge.

Personally, however, we prefer to take a more charitable line, and to interpret the bad by the good, rather than *vice versa;* to accept as expressing the writer's intention his own exposition of the figure contained in the *Quicunque vult*--"as the reasonable *soul* and flesh is one man, so God and Man is one Christ."

Narses was, of course, a controversialist. He conceived that an important side of the truth (the absolute reality of the humanity of our Lord) was denied; and lie was probably right in that belief. If he used unfortunate expressions, and overstated the truth he meant to guard (as in some cases he certainly did), we need not defend him; and, after all, he is one writer, not the Church. One thing we may point out in fairness. We do not think that any expressions we have found in Narses are more emphatically "Nestorian" (or at least what would be called so in any other writer) than those in the *De Incarnatione* of St. Athanasius of Alexandria.[350]

Further, it may be well for us to remember that in his insistence on the need of emphasizing the absolute reality of the humanity of Christ, Narses was fighting no imaginary danger. He was in controversy with men who denied the humanity in terms; and asserted one nature, and that a Divine one. If the mistaken reverence which prompted the Monophysite idea, with its tendency to deny the true humanity of our Lord, was verbally defeated at Chalcedon, yet that thought in a measure *victores captivos cepit.* Both in East and West, as we use the terms, the conception of Christ as Alaster and Exemplar faded away more and more before the conception of Him as God and judge; while the natural craving of humanity for a divine Friend-a craving which Christ came to satisfy led to the practical substitution of another figure for His in that capacity. We may add that owing to this current of thought another side of divine truth has remained unexplored as yet--viz. that expressed in the tremendous words of St. Athanasius, "He became Man, that we might become God."

Of course it cannot be asserted that Assyrian theologians ever progressed on the path they had open before them; but we, too, must admit that in the West we have not given its due proportion (in fact, not in word) to the truth they have so steadfastly asserted, and which gave them their strength -the truth, that is, of the absolute reality of the humanity of Christ.

If, as some hold, we are working our way towards a better synthesis of theological truths than we have yet attained, in the new lights on man and matter which science has revealed, we may yet come to feel that we owe Assyrians a debt for the testimony that they have borne.

After Acacius, the next authoritative exposition is that of Mar Elba (*S. O.*, 541, 551). This, however, is an explanation of the Creed for unlearned men only, and is too lengthy to transcribe. It is emphatic on the point that Christ is God and Man, and that He is One. But, save that it speaks of the Qnumi of the Trinity, it uses no technical terms. The worst that can be said of it is that it is somewhat indefinite on the point under dispute.

We may now pass on to the series of official Confessions, which, following one another in quick succession, lead us to the crucial year 612. Those. that is to say, of Joseph, Ezekiel, Ishu-yabh, Sabr-Ishu and Gregory.

Joseph, 554, *S. O.*, 98, 335.

Before all else, we guard our Confession of the two natures of Christ, that is to say, of His Godhead and His Manhood; we guard the characteristics of the natures, and we repudiate the existence in them of any kind of confusion, disturbance, change or mutation; we guard, too, the number of three Qnumi in the Trinity, and we confess, in one true and unspeakable Unity, one true Son of one God, the Father of truth.

If any one thinks or says that there are two Christs or two Sons, or in any wise or for any reason, introduces a" Quaternity," we have anathematized and do anathematize him.

Ezekiel, 576. *S. O.*, 113, 372.

God ** in the last days *** spoke to us in His Son, Jesus Christ our Lord, in Whom were revealed afresh the glorious Qnumi of the Father, and of Himself, and of the Holy Spirit. ** He was abased of His own free will for the redemption of our nature, that had grown old and worn in the works of sin; and He tool: it, inseparably, a perfect temple, to be the dwelling-place of His Godhead, of Mary the Holy Virgin.

He was conceived and born of her by the power of the highest, Christ incarnate, to be acknowledged and confessed in two natures, God and Man, one Son. In Hint the old age of our nature was renewed, and the debt of our race paid, in the robe of His manhood, by His acceptance of suffering and the death of the Cross.

Ishu-yahb, 585. *S. O.*, 194, 453.

The same Christianity teaches us, by the Holy Spirit, through the Apostle, of the revelation of God the Word, and of His dispensation in the body, and of His incarnation, that came to pass for us men and for our salvation, and for the renewal and reformation of all creation. Because of the great love with which He loved us, He departed from the bosom of the Father, of His own free will, not of necessity; and came into the world and was in the world; and as it is written, that which was invisible was manifested is the flesh. "The Word became flesh, and dwelt among us." He became, but was not changed; He who is in the form of God emptied Himself, and took the form of a servant; He took, but did not increase Himself, for both in the "becoming" and in the "taking" His essence remained without change, and without increase. Jesus Christ the Son of God, God the Word, Light of Light, came down and was incarnate and was made man, "economically" without transference or change. Jesus Christ our Lord, God, He who was begotten of the Father before all worlds in His Godhead, was in the last days born in the flesh of Mary; ever Virgin, the same, but not in the same. The Word became flesh in inseparable unity, and dwelt among us. **** Jesus Christ, the Son of God, God above all, begotten in His Godhead eternally of the Father, without Mother, He the same but not in the same, was born in His *manhood* of a mother without Father, in the last days. He suffered in the flesh, was crucified, died and was buried, under Pontius Pilate, and rose from the dead the third day. Christ, the Son of God, suffered in flesh, the same. In the nature of His Godhead, Christ the Son of God is above suffering; Jesus Christ is both passible and impassible, the Creator of the world, and the endurer of suffering. He who was rich, for our sakes became poor; God the Word endured the humiliation of suffering, in the temple of His body, "economically," in the lofty and inseparable union, *though* in the nature of His Godhead He did not suffer.

Sabr-Ishu, 596. *S. O.*, 198, 458.

We believe firmly, according to the letter and spirit of the scriptures, and the traditions of the Holy Fathers, in one Lord Jesus Christ, the only begotten Son of God, Who before the foundation of the world was begotten in His Godhead spiritually, without mother, and in the last days was born of the 14oly Virgin in fleshly wise, without union. with man, by the power of the Holy Ghost. In His Godhead, He is eternal, and in His Manhood, of Mary one true

Son of God. He in the nature of His manhood, endured for our sake suffering and death, and by the power of His Godhead, He raised up His body uncorrupt on the third day, and has promised us resurrection from the dead, ascension into heaven, and life of the world to come that passeth not away.

Gregory, 605. *S. O.*, 209, 473.

One eternal nature, recognized in three Qnumi, which, by means of the first-fruits of our nature, wrought the deliverance and renewal of our race, for the "form of God." according to the word of the apostle, took the "form of servant," and in Him was completed and consummated the exalted dispensation of our redemption. He who was the form of God in the form of servant is the one Son, Jesus Christ our Lord, by whom all things were made, perfect God and perfect Man, perfect God in the nature of His Godhead, perfect man in the nature of His manhood, Godhead and manhood keeping their characteristics, and being united in the true unity of the one Person of the Son Christ. The Godhead perfected the Manhood by suffering, as it is written, but neither suffering change, nor mutation, in any wise touched the Godhead.

Assembly of Bishops, 612. *S. O.*, 565, 582.

Thus for us men and for our salvation, the Son of God, the Word, came into the world without removing from His Father, and was in the world, that yet was made by His hands. And, because it was not possible f6r created natures to see the glorious nature of the Godhead, He formed for Himself, in wondrous wise, a temple from the very nature of the race of Adam, from the Virgin Mary. That temple was fashioned without human intercourse in the order of nature, and He clothed Himself with it, and united Himself with it, and in it revealed Himself to the world. ** Because of the wonderful connection and inseparable union that there was, from the first moment of conception, between the human nature that was assumed, and God the Word that assumed it, we are taught henceforward to recognize one Person of our Lord Jesus Christ, the Son of God, begotten of His Father in the nature of His Godhead without beginning, before the world was, and born of the holy Virgin, the daughter of David, in the nature of His manhood, in these last days.
****

Of the one nature it is written that "He took," and of the other that "it was taken." Thus, it is impossible to confuse the characteristics of the natures, for it is not possible that the Taker should be the Taken, or that that which was taken should be the taker. It is possible that God the Word should be manifested in the flesh that He put on, and that His human nature should be visible to the world in the order of Manhood, one Son of God in inseparable union. This we have learnt and hold.

It is not possible that Godhead should be converted into Manhood, or Manhood into Godhead, for essential being is not capable of change or suffering; and if Godhead be changed, it is not a revelation, but an alteration of Godhead; and if Manhood be taken out of its nature, it is not the redemption, but the destruction of Manhood. That is why we believe with our heart and confess with our lips One Lord Jesus Christ, the Son of God, whose Godhead was not concealed, neither was His Manhood spirited away, but Who is perfect God and perfect Man.

When we call Christ "perfect God," we do not mean the Trinity, but one of the Qnumi of the Trinity, God the Word. And when we call Christ perfect Klan, we do not mean all men, but that one "Qnuma" that was visibly taken for our salvation into unity with God the Word. Thus our Lord Jesus Christ, begotten in His Godhead eternally of the Father, was in the last days born in His manhood of the Holy Virgin.
****

And we are taught clearly that His Manhood ascended into heaven, and that the Qnuma of His Manhood was not dissolved or changed, but that it abides in inseparable unity with His Godhead, in the supreme glory; and in it He will appear, in His last manifestation from heaven, to shame those that crucified Him, and to the glory of those that believe in Him.

A study of this series of official Confessions, issued by the Assyrian Church up to the year 612, shows that the adoption of the Christological formula in present use dates from that Year. Of this series, the strictest theologian could Hardly say of the worst that it is worse than indefinite; while from that they range to one (that of Ishu-yabh) which is orthodox and Catholic, even on the delicate point of the "Communicatio Idiomatum."

In 612, however, a new formula is adopted, "two natures (kiani), two Qnumi, and one Parsopa in Christ"; and in the light of this change, and the simultaneous repudiation of a title of the Blessed Virgin which all the rest of the Church declares to be hers of right, a defender of the Assyrian Church must be prepared to answer the question, "In what sense was the new form adopted, and the term Yaldath Alaha rejected?"

The first term of the formula, "two kiani," need not detain us. The word is the equivalent of or "nature," and, of course, any one who regards the Council of Chalcedon as having any authority would insist on the phrase as necessary.

The term "Parsopa" ܦܪܨܘܦܐ, requires a little examination.

The author of the Appendix to Bethune-Baker's *Nestorius and His Teaching,* on the Syriac theological terms declares that in the New Testament and in older writers this term has always the meaning of "face" or "appearance"; and in later writers comes to acquire the force of "person."

As far as the New Testament is concerned, this is not quite correct. The word is found, so far as we are aware, about forty times therein;[351] but though it is translated "face" on most occasions, it is usually "face" in the sense of "real presence," and hence is much nearer to "person" than to "appearance."

Typical texts are, "Their angels behold the *face* of My Father"; "The light of the knowledge of the glory of God, in the *face* of Jesus Christ" (a text, by the way, which gives the Assyrians some right to claim scriptural authority for their use, for the text will certainly bear the sense of "person"); "To appear before the *face* of God for us." While in one case the word means "person," in the sense of representative--"For your sakes forgave I it, in the *person* of Christ." We shall have to notice this curious use of the word elsewhere.

As regards its theological force, a study of the great series of councils which form the *Synodicon Orientale* brings some interesting facts to light. First, with the one exception of the Council of Acacius (486), referred to above, the term is not used at all of our Lord until quite late in the history-- until, in fact, Ishu-yahb employs it in 585. After 612 it is used regularly. A whole series of patriarchs, Aba, Joseph, Ezekiel, Sabr-Ishu, and Ishu-yahb in the exposition quoted, speak of our Lord as "One," "one Son," and the like, but use no technical term for the union.

Second, during this period the term "Parsopa" itself is used regularly and frequently in the Synodicon, in different contexts; and it invariably has the full sense of "person"--a human individual.

In the whole of this great collection of official documents, extending over 250 years, and the work of fourteen different writers, the word is used forty-six times. It is used in every council except the first two and the last. On twelve occasions it is used in that theological sense whose force is under discussion. Once it means "appearance" (in the Council of Acacius, as stated); and on all of the remaining thirty-three occasions[352] it means clearly and unmistakably "person." Such contexts as "the person chosen for patriarch," the "persons who brought in duality," "choose a fit and proper person," are the usual position in which it appears; though in four cases it is used in the sense of "personal representative" or "vekil," as in 2 Cor. ii. 10.

The inference appears to be plain. So long as might be, the Assyrian Church avoided the use of any technical term for that which no words can describe. When forced by controversy- to use one, they adopted the word to which a century of habitual and official use had given the full meaning of "person."

Similarly, Narses, as we have seen, and Babai more regularly, employ this word to express the "Persons" of the Holy Trinity. The use of the last writer is particularly important, seeing that he, if he did not preside at the gathering where the term was first used officially, was practically the patriarch of the Church at the time. Of course Babai, as a general thing, uses the term "Qnuma" where we should speak of the "Persons" of the Trinity; and we must return later to the question of what that word means to him. He uses "Parsopa," however, in that sense eleven times,[353] which is ample to show that it will fully bear the meaning.

Further, in writers not primarily theological, like Ishu-yahb III and Thomas of Marga,[354] "person" is the ordinary, though not the invariable, meaning of the word.

Surely we may say that the evidence is very strong that in the seventh century "Person" was the ordinary force of the word "Parsopa"; and that very clear proof must be brought that it was then adopted for theological use in another sense before an independent Church be condemned for so adopting it.

We can now turn to discuss the theological meaning of the other term in question, Qnuma. Usually it is assumed that this means "person"; particularly as it is the general representative of, and is used regularly (as we have seen) where we speak of the "Persons" of the Trinity. It is not unfair, perhaps, to say that because this has been assumed, it has been taken for granted that "Parsopa" must mean something less, like "appearance."[355]

As, however, we have shown that the ordinary interpretation of "Parsopa" in official use in the seventh century was "Person," the presumption is really the other way-that "Qnuma" is not "Person," but something else, consistent with its ordinary "Trinitarian" use. We have now to see what that something else maybe. Before approaching the question, however, we should like to enter a caveat against the general impression that because "Qnuma" is the general representation of "Hypostasis," it therefore responds to every shift of meaning in the tangled history of that perplexing word. The one word is not a translation of the other by any means, as "kiana," for instance; may be said to be of . The relation of the two words may best be expressed by the figure of two circles which cut one another but have different centres. More or less of the two fields included in the two circumferences coincide, but by no means the whole. vado1ravts is the inward reality which underlies the outward appearance; the word looks, as it were, from outward to inward. "Qnuma" is the specialization of that which is common to many; it looks from the abstract to the concrete.

Bethune-Baker's Appendix points out that, in general use, "Qnuma" means "self"; and would be represented in Greek by , or some one of its compounds. With this we fully agree; and where it appears in the New Testament the word does, as a rule, translate that pronoun,[356] though, of course, it is not by any means its exclusive rendering. In non-theological writers, such as Ishu-yahb in his letters, or the "Acta Sanctorum," would be almost invariably the Greek rendering of it. The same Appendix points out that in Ephraim the word means "subsistence" or "reality"; and that Babai defines it as being "the specialization of ," "the set of natural characteristics," as they exist in the individual.[357] It is obvious that these three senses, "self," "reality," and "set of attributes," melt very readily into one another.

Still the question must be faced, even if these are the original senses, What is its force in the Christological controversy? Particularly in the light of the fact that, if it be not "person," it is at least used where we use that word.

Here we may refer to two contemporary authorities-Babai, the man who was practically patriarch of the Church at the time when the phrase "two Qnumi" was adopted, and who, either then or a little later, explained his own tenets in an elaborate treatise; and Ishu-yahb, afterwards third patriarch of that name, and in 612 Bishop of Mosul.

Babai we have referred to above; and it is obvious that if the term "Qnuma" be kept to its meaning of "set of natural characteristics," nobody who accepts the Tome of Leo as of authority could deny "two 'Qnumi' in Christ." Of course writers do not always keep to that use, nor does Babai himself always do so; but in his formula, as given, we have the explanation of the term given by the theologian more responsible than any other for its introduction. The inference that it was adopted in his sense seems almost irresistible.

Another point may be brought forward to show in what sense Babai used the word. This writer is very fond of quoting Hebrews i. 3,, where (as is well known) is equivalent to , and is rendered in the Pshitta by "Ithutha," "essence." In his work he quotes this passage eleven times--six times correctly, five times with the substitution of "Qnumaö for "Ithutha." It would thus seem that to the writer who introduced "two Qnumi," "Qnuma" and "Ithutha" were almost synonyms, and may be rendered respectively "subsistence" and "essence."[358]

From Babai we turn to Ishu-yahb; but as we have to deal with this writer in the next chapter, we may be content here with one brief quotation, sufficient to show in what sense that writer accepted "Qnuma" theologically.

"'Qnuma' has the meaning of naturehood, ܟܝܢܘܬܐ, kianutha, and that meaning only. It stands steadfast in the simple expression of that essential meaning, and all that we mean by 'naturehood' is demonstrably included in it. It does not admit of subtraction from, or addition to its meaning."[359]

To these two writers, then-the two writers of eminence in the Assyrian Church at the time in question--"Qnuma" most certainly, if words mean anything at all, meant something different from what we mean by "person"--something much more like what we mean by "subsistence," "mode of being," "set of characteristics." Thus we see how they can speak of three "Qnumi" in the Trinity, and two "Qnumi" in Christ; of three "Parsopi" in the Trinity, and one "Parsopa" in Christ.

Of course the phrase has its dangers. It is orthodox or not according to the intent of the user; and can be misinterpreted, as can most other phrases; the "one nature incarnate" of St. Cyril is a case very much in point. There is an interpretation of "two Qnumi" which is as Nestorian as words can well be. "Take its ordinary sense of . No Catholic would deny, we imagine, and many Monophysites would admit, that Christ is, which would in Syriac be, ܐܠܗܐ ܒܩܢܘܡܗ ܘܒܪܢܫܐ ܒܩܢܘܡܗ, alaha b'qnumeh o'barnasha b'qnumeh, yet there is an interpretation of two that is Nestorian enough.

That, in adopting this formula, the Assyrian Church adopted a formula verbally different from that of the Greeks is clear enough. That in clinging to it they intentionally clung to something different from the Greek use is clear also. Did they, in so doing, intend to deny what the Greeks intended to affirm-namely, the true Divinity, the true Humanity, and the true Personal Unity of the God-Man? This we do not believe to have been the case. We know by their own statements that they did not understand what the Greeks affirmed, and in their attacks upon them fought a shadow of their own creation; and we believe that under and by means of their different expressions each party asserted a doctrine identical with Catholic truth, even though neither would believe it of the other.

We have now done what we set out to do. We have shown how and when the Assyrian Church adopted her Christological formula; and what the technical words of it meant to those under whose influence it was adopted. That others, both before and after, may have used them in a less desirable sense may be true enough, but is nothing to the purpose. Have writers to the Church of England never read a Calvinist sense into Catholic formulae; and do we consider the Church of England bound by that which every one of her sons has written?

When the formulae used by an independent, auto-cephalous Church will bear a Catholic sense; and when there is no convincing evidence that it was imposed in another sense; surely that independent Church has the right to use it. In this case all the evidence available tends to shoe= that the Church adopted the formula in a sense (to use no stronger expression) that a Catholic could accept. Is not this sufficient to secure that *unitatem in necessariis* outside whose bounds we of the Church of England allow to others that *libertatem* that we use so amply ourselves?

There is, however, another point of theological importance which was first raised officially in 612, and which must be discussed before the question is quitted--viz. the rejection by the Assyrian Church of the term "Yaldath Alaha,".

Up to the date mentioned the Church had, as far as we know, taken no official attitude towards this term. Narses had discussed and rejected it, as being nothing but "Mother of the Godhead"; and at the 612 gathering it was more or less definitely repudiated, the general feeling concerning it being (and remaining to this day) practically that expressed by Narses.

In discussing the question we must point out that "Yaldath Alaha" is no satisfactory rendering of the Greek word, though admittedly the best available. Most Western thinkers would admit, we believe, a difference of *nuance* between "Deipara" or and "Mater Dei," even if their theological intent be proved identical; and some who disliked the last term would have no objection to the first two. The term "Yaldath Alaha," however, is harder for an Assyrian than is "Mater Deiö for an Englishman; for it suggests almost inevitably "Alater Deitatis," and even "Mater Trinitatis," seeing that "Alaha" is the name common to all three Persons of the Holy Trinity.

The fact that this objection is sometimes urged captiously ought not to blind us to the truth that it is really felt by one who does his thinking in Syriac. Nothing is harder than to realize all that a word one knows in an acquired language may suggest to one to whom the language is his mother tongue.

Further, if "Yaldath Alaha" has to an Assyrian an objectionable ring that has not to the Western, his term "Mother of Christ" has a far higher force than the Greek . "Christ" to him (though his word "Mshikha" is etymologically identical with the Greek) is the word which stands, not for the Messiah-King of prophecy, but for the union of the two natures-the God-Alan. Babai is never weary of asserting this fact.

It would be rash to assert that "Yaldath Mshikha" to an Assyrian implies all that does to a Western; but at least they are far nearer to one another than European thought would lead one to expect. Thus when the term "Mother of God" was put before them in 612, their answer to the Monophysites was, "why not 'Mother of Christ'? 'Yaldath Alaha' and 'Yaldath Barnasha' ('Mother of God' and 'Mother of the Man or Manhood') are alike objectionable; for the first omits, and may be taken as denying, the humanity; and the second fails adequately to recognize the divinity of our Redeemer. If one be admitted, the other ought to be admitted too; but why not be content with the term that expresses both natures?"[360] Some of their arguments have a captious and unpleasant ring, as, for instance--"Christ, *qua* God, existed from all eternity; Christ, *qua* Man, took being of Mary; why refuse to call her the Mother of that which took being of her, and insist on calling her Mother of that which did not so take being?" Or again, and worse--" You only insist on calling the Virgin 'Mother of God' in our desire to attribute suffering to the Divinity."

Still it is important to notice that Babai, in his treatise, expressly and repeatedly admits the lawfulness of the term if it be properly guarded, and we transcribe one of these, passages.

Babai, "De Unione," Mimra VII, Head xxii. p. 242. (See also p. 236.) It is just and right and proper that Mary should be called "Mother of Christ," for that is the name that shows that there was one Person of unity, who in His human nature was of her nature, and in His Godhead, not of her nature. But seeing that from the first moment of the conception of the Manhood of our Lord, that He took from her, God the Word dwelt in it temple-wise and unitedly, and made it with him one Son eternally, we do say that she was thus "Mother of God" and "Mother of the Manhood." Mother of the Manhood by nature; Mother of God, in that He was united to His manhood from the first moment of its conception; and it is His temple eternally, and He is God and Man unitedly, one Son, one Christ.

It will be noted that this writer accepts the word in a force identical, and in terms practically identical, with those of the Concordat between Cyril and John of Antioch, made in 433 (the Epistle "Laetantur Coeli")-a document which Cyril accepted as being, for him, equivalent to the acceptance of the Council of Ephesus. Perhaps the coincidence is designed, but more probably Babai is simply using "Antiochene" phraseology.

Is a Concordat, the second which this document has effected, possible upon these lines? Given, a Church which accepts the Councils of Nicaea and Constantinople, which has not accepted Ephesus, but which does consider that it has accepted Chalcedon. It stands suspected of heresy for its non-acceptance of the third council of that series, which (whatever better-informed men may say) it does not regard as included in the fourth.

Can more be asked from it in fairness than the acceptance of the document which the protagonist of- Ephesus-disregarding its formal decree regarded as the embodiment of all that he contended for there?

This document has all the weight that the authority of a general council can give it. It was composed to deal with the very question at issue. It has nevertheless never been fought over. But (lamentably rare distinction among the great documents that are Church standards of truth and sound theology) it has always been a medium of peace.

Note I - On the Creed as Used by the Assyrian Church

THE present Creed of the Assyrian Church, while doctrinally identical with that of Nicaea accepted by the Church in 410, is by no means the same verbally as that document. Those who use it, however, are as a rule ignorant of this fact, and the development of the present form presents a rather difficult question.

This Creed is far nearer to the Creed of Constantinople than to that of Nicaea; but differs from it, not merely in the transposition of several clauses, but also in the addition of two new clauses, one of which at any rate is, we believe, peculiar to itself.

We believe, however, that it was developed from the Nicaeno-Constantinopolitan creed that we use to-day-though the introduction of this version of the Creed into Persia is as mysterious as the introduction of it into Asia 'Minor-arid that the alterations for the most part came from verbal repetition. The date of its becoming fixed in its present form is uncertain; but the Book- o f the Sunhadus, in giving the Creed, quotes neither the present nor the original form, but a version quoted as if in common use in the Council of Ishu-yahb in 585. It does this without apparent knowledge that its version is at all different from that in daily use; and the fact would seem to imply that the present form of the Creed is later than the compilation of the *Sunhadus* in the thirteenth century. One must own, however, that this conclusion is very doubtful. We give the three versions in "synoptic" form, as this method illustrates (what we believe to be the fact) that It "Ishu-yahb's Creed" constitutes an intermediate stage in the development of the present document from the Constantinopolitan.

CONSTANTINOPOLITAN CREED	CREED OF ISHO-YAHB	PRESENT-DAY CREED
I believe in one God the Father Almighty, maker of heaven and earth, and of all things visible and invisible. And in one Lord Jesus Christ, the only-begotten Son of God, begotten of his Father before all worlds, God of God, Light of Light, very God of very God, begotten, not made, being of one substance	We believe in one God the Father Almighty, maker of all things, visible and invisible; And in one Lord Jesus Christ, the only-begotten Son of God, First-born of all Creation, by whom the worlds were framed, and all things created,	We believe in one God, the Father Almighty, maker of all things, visible and invisible; And in one Lord Jesus Christ, the only-begotten Son of God, First-born of all Creation, begotten of his Father before all worlds,

with the Father, by whom all things were made; Who for us men, and for our Salvation, came down from Heaven, and was Incarnate by the Holy Ghost of the Virgin Mary, and was made Man, and was crucified also for us, under Pontius Pilate. He suffered, and was buried, and the third day He rose again according to the scriptures, and ascended into Heaven and sitteth on the right hand of the Father, and shah come again with glory to judge both the quick and the dead, whose kingdom shall have no end. And I believe in the Holy Ghost, the Lord and giver of life, who proceedeth from the Father and the Son, who with the Father and the Son together is worshipped and glorified, who spake by the prophets; and I believe one Catholic and Apostolic Church, I acknowledge one Baptism for the remission of sins,	begotten of his Father before all worlds, and not made, Light of Light, very God of very God, being of one substance with the Father, Who for us men, and for our Salvation, came down from Heaven, and was Incarnate by the Holy Ghost, of the Virgin Mary, and was made Man, and was crucified also for us, under Pontius Pilate. He suffered, and died and was buried, and the third day He rose according to the scriptures, and ascended into Heaven and sitteth on the right hand of the Father, and shall come with glory to judge both the quick and the dead, whose kingdom shall have no end. And in one Holy Spirit, the Lord, and giver of life,	and not made, very God of very God, being of one substance with the Father, by whom the worlds were framed and all things created; Who for us men, and for our Salvation, came down from Heaven, and was Incarnate by the Holy Ghost, and was made Man, and was conceived and born of the Virgin Mary, and suffered and was crucified under Pontius Pilate, and was buried and the third day He rose, as it was written, and ascended into Heaven and sitteth on the right hand of the. Father, and shall come again to Judge both the quick and the dead. And in one Holy Spirit, the Spirit of Truth who proceedeth from

and I look for the resurrection	who proceedeth from the	the Father,
of the dead,	Father,	the Spirit that giveth life;
and the life of the world	who with the Father and	and in one Holy, Apostolic
to come.	the Son is worshipped,	and Catholic Church;
	who spake by the prophets	and we acknowledge one
	and apostles	Baptism for the remission
	and in one Holy, Catholic	of sin,
	and Apostolic Church,	and in the resurrection of
	and one Baptism for the	the body
	remission of sins,	and the life eternal.
	and in the resurrection of	
	the dead,	
	and the life of the world	
	to come.	
	And those who my "there	
	was, when he was not,"	
	or "before he was begotten,	
	he was not, or that	
	"he was made of nothing,"	
	or that he was of different	
	qnuma or essence, or think	
	that the Son of God was	
	subject to change or to	
	alteration, these does the	
	holy and apostolic church	
	anathematize.	

Putting merely verbal changes and transpositions on one side, the peculiar features of the present Assyrian Creed lie in (a) the omission of the clauses, "Whose Kingdom shall have no end," and "Who with the Father and the Son together is worshipped and glorified, Who spake by the prophets."

This omission is a distinct loss to the fulness of the Creed, but has no doctrinal significance. No member of the Assyrian Church would dream of denying the doctrine of the omitted clauses.

(b) On the other hand, Assyrians insert in the Creed two other clauses. First, they declare that the only begotten Son is "the first-born of all creation" (Col. i. 15); and next, they insert words to emphasize the doctrine that He who was "Very God of Very God, of one substance with the Father," was "conceived and born of the Virgin Mary." In other words, those who are accused of Nestorianism have been at some pains to alter the wording of their Creed in an anti-Nestorian direction. It is odd, and (as we hold) significant, that both the national Churches that stand accused of heresy (Armenian[361] and the Assyrian), should. have introduced into their versions of the Creed clauses clean contrary to the particular heresies of which they are suspected.

Note II - The Assyrian Church and the Council of Chalcedon

IN the preceding chapter we have studied the technical terms of Assyrian Christology, and have proved (as we trust) that to those who adopted the terms "one Parsopa" meant "one Person," and not "one appearance"; and "two Qnumi" "two subsistences" (or some analogous word), and not "two Persons," in our Lord. Further, we have seen that those responsible for the refusal to use the name "Yaldath Alaha" declared themselves willing to accept it in the only sense in which "Chalcedonians" imposed it.

We must now consider the attitude adopted by the Assyrian Church towards the Council of Chalcedon-that gathering which spoke what most English Churchmen to-day would consider the decisive, if not the last, word in the Christological controversy.

The general belief on this point has hitherto been that, in rejecting the Council of Ephesus, the Church of Assyria rejected all subsequent councils; and thus went openly and avowedly into heresy, either in the time of Barsoma, or before it. Previous chapters have shown, we trust, that this simple and clear-cut belief (though it would simplify matters if it were true) has nothing to do with the facts. It is very difficult to say whether the Church of Assyria and the "Orthodox" were or were not out of communion with one another until a date subsequent to 640; and if (as logically would seem to be the case) you cannot reject anything till you have been asked to accept it, the said Church can hardly be said to have even rejected Ephesus as yet. Concerning Chalcedon, Monsigneur Chabot (in his edition of the *Synodicon Orientale*) expressly mentions that council in the list of western councils received by the Assyrian Church; adding that the "Tome of Leo" was also received by them, as a separate document of synodical authority, and as an orthodox exposition of the faith.[362] This editor does not print the Syriac versions of either document in his book, or for that matter any other of the several "western" synods referred to; for the sufficient reason that they are known and accessible to all students and that his great work was already rather bulky.

The announcement came as a surprise to all who had judged the Assyrian Church heretical; for obviously a Church that accepts Chalcedon and Leo's Tome occupies a very different position towards Nestorianism to one that, rejecting Ephesus, rejects all subsequent councils. It is at least a possible position that acceptance of Chalcedon implies acceptance of Ephesus; and certainly a Church that regards the "Definitio" of Chalcedon, and the Tome, as of authority, is not what we mean by "Nestorian." So great was the surprise that some held that they must have accepted the council "by mistake," though the chances of their accepting, in error, two separate documents of practically similar force may be described as infinitesimal.

The writer has been at some pains to examine this point, and now gives the results of his investigation.

In the manuscript of the *Synodicon Orientale* at Mosul (the text from which other copies have been taken) the "Definitio" of Chalcedon is undoubtedly included; and when compared line by line with the Greek text it is seen to be, as a whole, fairly and accurately rendered. There are, however, one or two alterations of words.[363] Thus where the "blessed Cyril" is referred to, "accursed" is substituted, with a magnificent disregard of the effect on the sense of the passage; and the phrase "to rebuke the folly of Nestorius" is omitted. This we consider to be, in all probability, the "emendation" of a later copyist. One cannot conceive of sane men admitting the paragraph if it stood originally as it stands at present. Thus it is made to run--

"Concerning those who dare to corrupt the mystery of the dispensation, and to say that that which was born of the Virgin was a mere man, the Synod accepts the Synodical letters of the 'accursed' Cyril, he who was the 'evil' shepherd of Alexandria, that he wrote 'evilly' to the 'holy' Nestorius, and to the head of the 'Easterns'" (to rebuke the folly of Nestorius and) "to give in God-fearing zeal an exposition of the Faith to those who desire knowledge. With these letters it joins, as is proper, the letter of the holy and blessed Leo."

The Definitio proper is also fairly translated, except that the Greek "Theotokos" is rendered by the periphrasis, "Mother of Christ, who is both God and Man," and for the "one Hypostasis" they substitute "two Qnumi." Of these renderings, the first seems to us adequate, in light of the fact that "Yaldath Alaha" conveys an idea different to that of "Theotokos," and the latter we suspect of being another later corruption, in light of the fact that the phrase was not adopted for at least two generations after the acceptance of the council. Its force we discuss elsewhere.

Thus the Definitio is made to run--

"Joining ourselves therefore to the holy Fathers, we all confess alike and with one accord-one and the same Son, our Lord Jesus Christ, perfect in His Godhead,. and, the same, perfect in His Manhood, of reasonable soul and body. Of one nature with His Father in His Godhead, and, the same, of one nature with us in His Manhood, in all thins save sin; begotten of the Father before the worlds in His Godhead, and born in these last days, the same, for us men and for our salvation, of Mary the Virgin, Mother of Christ. God and Man; One and the same Christ, Son, God, Lord Only-begotten; to be acknowledged in two natures without confusion, without change, without mixture, without separation; the distinction of the two natures being by no means done away by the union, but the individuality of either of the two natures being rather preserved, and running together in one Person and two Qnumi; not to be divided or separated into two Sons, but there being one and the same only-begotten Son, our Lord Jesus Christ."

The manuscript has suffered in places, and we have not the means of comparing the Syriac with the Greek and Latin throughout (*i. e.*; in the text of the Imperial decree, and in the patristic testimonies, appended to the "Tome of Leo"), but we believe that there is no other omission or alteration of any doctrinal significance. In particular, the translation of the "Tome of Leo" is complete and accurate.

The date of the acceptance of this council by the Assyrian Church cannot be determined at present. It was certainly accomplished previous to 540, when the council is referred to by Mar Aba, and presumably, subsequent to the arising of the Christological controversy in Persia, in the year 480. It is possible that it was introduced by Bar-soma, the only Assyrian, so far as we know, who was in any way directly concerned in its acts--but that is a conjecture merely.

Here we may leave the matter. The views of the Assyrian Church upon the character of Cyril are not matters of faith, even if the emendation referred to be not the work of an unauthorized copyist. Doctrinally, the Council of Chalcedon was accepted by the Assyrian Church, and inserted in their collection of councils, standing there exactly on the same footing as any one of their own gatherings. To all learned theologians of the Anglican Church we would put this question--

The official teaching of this Church lies before you. judged by these documents (and we have no right to judge her by others) is the Church that uses them guilty of what we call Nestorianism?

Chapter Fourteen - Last Efforts at Reconciliation-- Embassy of Ishl-Yahb and the Sahdona Episode

AT the end of that struggle of giants, the Romano-Persian war of 602-628, Heraclius set himself to a task far more difficult than even that of conquering Chosroes; namely, the task of putting an end to the religious quarrels that distracted, and to a great extent paralyzed, the whole Roman Empire. There is little doubt that in doing this the object of the Emperor was largely political. No doubt he was a religious man personally; and probably, too, he took an interest, as everybody then did, in the game of theological strife. It was, however, as Emperor, rather than as governor of the Church, that he strove to find a formula which, by reconciling the Monophysites to the Council of Chalcedon, might render the inhabitants of Syria and Egypt once more loyal subjects of the throne of Constantinople.

This effort to make a peace which nobody but the servants of the State desired, only added one more to the contending ecclesiastical factions in the empire; and enabled one more unrecognized nation (the Maronites) to find a theological "point d'appui" for its national life. Outside the empire, however, though the actual effort made by Heraclius seems to have passed quite unnoticed,[364] the general peace-making intentions of the Emperor did produce a curious episode in the history of the Church of Persia. It is true that he completely failed to draw back into union a body that had drifted into separation; but the effort, and the partial response to it, throw light on the internal, condition of the Church in question.

The Romano-Persian war came to a natural end with the death of Chosroes in 628; but owing to the revolutions that followed in Persia, no formal treaty of peace was drawn up till the reign of Queen Buran (or Burandocht) in 630. When the formal embassy was sent for the purpose from Persia to Antioch, its members were as usual mostly Christian bishops. Ishuyahb II, the then patriarch, a man of Gedala,[365] was at its head; and with him were the metropolitans of Nisibis, Arbela, and Karka d'B. Slok; and two bishopsùIshu-yahb of Mosul, afterwards the third patriarch of that name, and one Sahdona of Ariun in Garmistan, a man who had already made a name for himself as scholar, ascetic and author.

The patriarch, like so many of the bishops of his Church, was a scholar of Nisibis, where he had been a pupil of Khenana, and had been one of the 300 students that left the college[366] when the great professor was expelled. He may have imbibed his theological views from his tutor; but, if so, they do not seem to have interfered with his promotion in the Church. According to one account he was a married man.[367]

The diplomatic business of the embassy was soon finished. Both sides desired peace, being in fact fairly "fought to a stand-still"; and all that had to be done was to ratify the agreement already practically arrived at, and to accept the status quo *ante betlum* as an arrangement which both parties probably expected would last for generations.

After, or during, the diplomatic negotiations, Heraclius raised the question of the theological status of the Persian Church. Nearly 200 years had elapsed since the "Easterns" had had any direct dealings with the "Westerns," and much water had run under the bridges in the interval. There was a general feeling, no doubt, on either side, that the other was heretical; but it is certain that the "Easterns" did not know what the "Westerns" taught, and probable that the "Westerns" were no better informed in their turn. Heraclius asked the patriarch for a Confession of the faith of his Church. Ishu-yahb gave it; declaring his belief in a Christ who, as Perfect Man, was consubstantial with us; - and who, as Perfect God, was consubstantial with the Father, in one "Personalitas."[368] This was accepted as orthodox (indeed the keenest controversialist could hardly say that it was worse than indefinite), and the Eastern was allowed on several occasions to celebrate the Mysteries before the Emperor.

On his return home, however, probably with good hope that he had brought about the end of two long quarrels, secular and religious, Ishu-yahb found his conduct challenged by his own suffragans. One of these probably was his colleague and namesake Ishu-yahb of Mosul, and the party was certainly headed by another important prelate, Bar-soma of Susa or Karka De Lidan. "You must have anathematized the three fathers, Theodore, Diodore and Nestorius, and have accepted the term Galdath Alcha () or those Greeks would never have allowed you to approach their altars." The position taken up by this zealot is noteworthy, as showing on what points the Easterns conceived the admitted separation to have taken place. The technical term "two qnumi" is not mentioned; and indeed it had at the time scarcely made its way to universal acceptance among Assyrian writers.[369] The "names" and the word Galdath Alcha were the real crux; and the first apparently the more important.

Ishu-yahb defended himself, and indeed there is no evidence that he had ever in fact been asked to make the concessions condemned. The controversy was stopped by royal order; but its arising showed the real difficulty in the way of re-union, namely, the suspicion felt by each party towards the other, and the conviction that whatever "those others" did or said was bound to be wrong. Such a moral atmosphere as this, persisting as it does in a measure to this day, is a more formidable obstacle to any real union than any number of differing theological formulae.

While the patriarch was settling the affairs of Church and State at Antioch, his companions, who were quartered in a monastery at Apamaea, had (of course, being orientals) started a warm discussion on matters theological with their Chalcedonian hosts. The battle ended naturally (according to the Eastern account) in an utter rout for the "Westerns." One of the men of the East at any rate, Ishu-yahb of Mosul, was not likely to be affected by any arguments; for his letters remain to us, and in the numerous controversies of which they give a picture, the writer shows a most conspicuous inability to enter into any other side of any question at issue than his own. When the diplomatic work was done the embassy returned home, triumphantly convinced as regarded most of them, of the truth of their own opinions, and by no means empty-handed.

The Emperor would, of course, give rich gifts to the ambassadors; and with good reason if (as is stated in one account) it was by their hands that the "True Cross"[370] (captured in 614, when Jerusalem fell before Chosroes) was restored. They had also secured, however, in less honourable fashion, something that was no doubt more valuable to them than any imperial gift. Ishu-yahb of Mosul had been shown in Antioch a reliquary containing some "of the bones of the blessed Apostles." This he piously and, prayerfully contrived to steal, and presented to his favourite monastery of Bait 'Abi[371] near Mosul.

The chronicler, of course, records the fact with devout exultation, and one notices with interest this early instance of the conviction, later so universal, that relics are "fair game"-things that the most honourable and conscientious of men may blamelessly annex.

One of the party, however, left Antioch by no means so satisfied with the controversial victory as his fellows. This was Sahdona of Ariun, whose "perversion" was soon to cause so much confusion to his Church. He had; contrary to the advice of his colleagues, vaingloriously attempted to dispute with the abbot of the monastery where they had lodged; and this aged man, by "art-magic and sorcery," as Ishu-yahb held, "corrupted his mind from the true faith." As, however, Sahdona had opened the discussion, not by denouncing his opponent's heresy as he should have done, but by kneeling and asking for the old abbot's blessing, it is perhaps not surprising that they ended by coming to an agreement. Sahdona, too, does not seem to have been led to the conviction that the "Church of the Easterns" was wrong, and that of Constantinople right;[372] but to the belief that the doctrines that both held were essentially identical, and only verbally different.

Thus on his return to his diocese he soon began to proclaim that the "one qnuma" (Hypostasis) of the Westerns, in the sense in which they used the term, was practically identical with the "one Parsopa" of the Easterns, as used by them. He can hardy have denied that each word was patient of interpretations that could not possibly be got within the limits of the other; but he did assert that the theological sense of one word, as used by one party, was identical with the theological sense of the other word, as used by the other. The writer believes that this view of Sahdona's was absolutely correct as regards the general use of the terms, though it might be possible to find individuals who used either term in different senses. Still, however right, it was not for that reason welcome to men accustomed to look on Westerns as heretics, and on themselves as the elect and correct people. They wanted controversial victory, not reconciliation; and they were no more willing to revise their views of an opponent's teaching, and of the limits of loyalty to their own Church, than was the average Anglican dignitary of the middle of the nineteenth century. Ishu-yahb of Mosul, Sahdona's companion in the embassy, and previously his friend in the college of Nisibis and the monastery of Bait 'Abi, took the field against him now. This man was now Metropolitan of Arbela, and at a provincial council at which the Bishop of Ariun (who was not one of his suffragans) happened to be present, he expostulated with him very warmly, and so far succeeded in his aim that Sahdona agreed to retract certain obnoxious. passages in a book that he had written to explain his views.[373]

The dispute, however, very soon broke out again, and we find Ishu-yahb writing to Sahdona, denying vehemently the possibility of identifying "Parsopa" and "qnuma" in any shade of meaning that either would admit?[374]

"When you use a word," writes Ishu-yahb, you cannot make it mean just what you want it to, and these two terms have special meanings of their own. * * * Parsopa, I grant, can be interpreted in various ways, but Qnuma is a word of one interpretation only, namely 'naturehood' (kianutha), and it sticks to the simple expression of its essential meaning. You say Parsopa and Qnuma are synonyms. Much more so are Qnuma and Kiana, and this idea of yours thrusts you straight into the pit of (Monophysite) heresy. *** The Greek equivalent of Qnuma is Hypostasis, and that means, 'Stability,' 'Position,' 'Substance' (Quyama) ܩܘܝܡܐ."

Ishu-yahb would have found it difficult to maintain his position that Qnuma is like a coin, of unchangeable value, but the importance of his letter lies in two directions. It shows in what sense one prominent theologian at the time accepted the term "two Qnumi in Christ," and it shows what he conceived himself to be denying when he denounced the Western "one Hypostasis."

If Qnuma means "naturehood" and can mean nothing else, then to assert "two Qnumi" is not to assert "two Persons"; and if Ishu-yahb conceived Hypostasis to mean substance, then in denying one Hypostasis he was not denying the doctrine of, e. g., the Council of Chalcedon, but a caricature of it that existed only in his own mind. That he should have thus caricatured it was pardonable enough. The Easterns were still conceiving of the Greek term Hypostasis as used at Nicaea, and as they had themselves accepted it in 410. They did not realize that the term had since been employed in a new, and it must be owned in an artificial sense. The dispute was essentially a misunderstanding, as far as doctrine was involved in it; and the separation that followed was based thereon. An Athanasius might perhaps have healed it, as we know he did heal a similar dispute; but Sahdona had not the calibre to fill that majestic role, and even the "royal-hearted" might have failed where neither party desired a reconciliation.

The dispute came before the Catholicos, who was now not Ishu-yahb of Gedala, whose views were practically those of Sahdona, but Mar Imeh. Ishu-yahb of Mosul carried his point in the council, proclaiming, with a confident ignorance that touches the sublime,[375] "Now, when every province of the Roman Empire confesses with one accord the duality of the Qnumi in Christ, exiles every Bishop that does not confess this, and anathematizes the name of the accursed Cyril, is it the time for us to fall away from the Faith?" Sahdona was excommunicated; and, leaving the East, was received as a confessor in the West (or the Roman Empire), where he became Bishop of Edessa, and wrote works on asceticism, in which he confesses "two natures, one Qnuma, and one Parsopa in the Christ." Before very long, however, the man who had been expelled from "the East" as a practical Monophysite, was expelled from the "West" also, as a practical Nestorian. For a moment it seemed possible that he might be restored to his old see; but the project came to nothing. Anathematized by all parties, the peacemaker ended his days in a hermit's cell.

His own age saw in him only a man whom no party in the world could trust. We may see in him a man for whom the world was too hard; of whom, perhaps, it was not worthy. The end of his noble attempt to bring about a premature reconciliation stands as a warning to those who strive to do that which he failed to do-to tell them that though they may hope by God's blessing for better success, they need not hope for more of this world's praise.

In giving the story of Sahdona's ill-starred effort at peacemaking, we have somewhat anticipated the order of events. Ishu-yahb II, with whom the Bishop of Ariun visited Roman territory, was patriarch 628-644; and though the Sahdona controversy (unfortunately perhaps) did not come to a head in his day, his time of office did not lack great political events. During that period there occurred the collapse of the great Persian Empire, and the substitution for it of the rule of the Khalifs.

Kobad-Siroes, who acceded 628, did not live long, as had been foretold in his dying father's curse. He died of plague within the year; and his one son (almost the only male Sassanid surviving, after the massacre of the royal house of which his father had been guilty) was an infant. This gave an opportunity to the ambitious General Shahrbarz, who determined to play the role that Bahram had essayed a generation previously; he seized the throne, and the boy-king (Ardashir III) disappeared. But the national instinct against any ruler who was not of the royal house, was still too strong for the usurper to be able to maintain himself. Shahr-barz perished in a mutiny of his own troops within a month; and the people, as male Sassanids had failed, called upon a daughter of the house to occupy the throne. Buran, who thus became queen-regnant (a most unusual thing in the East) made peace with Rome as stated above; but her reign, too, endured for a few months only, and her death heralded a period of utter confusion. Pretender after pretender rose, ruled for an hour, and vanished before his successor; till at last all wearied of anarchy, and called for a king of the old house. Such an one was found, a lad of the name of Yezdegerd, hardly fifteen years old, and apparently of no very strong character. He was not of the direct line, but was near enough to it to satisfy men who were crying out for a ruler with some show of title; and he became, in 632, the last of the line of Sassanid kings.

The question if this lad could have restored and reorganized the kingdom of his ancestors was never to be fairly tried. That outburst of volcano-like energy, which the Khalifs who followed Mahommed in Mecca were able to call out and direct, was in its full strength just then, and the lava-streams were pouring out both to the north and east of their crater. In 633 the tributary kingdom of Khirta was attacked and conquered; and though the wave of conquest was checked for the moment, yet 636 saw the great battle of Cadesia; and by 640 the kingdom that looked back to Cyrus as its founder was a thing of the past. Yezdegerd, a fugitive King, maintained a shadow of royalty for a few years longer at Merv, but that little State only endured until the Arabs were ready to annex it.

During the same years other armies were pouring out against the Romans, in obedience to that strange impulse which was to carry the Arabs so far and so fast, and then suddenly to carry them no. further. Syria, Palestine, Egypt were lost to Constantinople one after the other; the Monophysites preferring the Saracens to the Chalcedonians, much as at Constantinople men of a later age were to cry, "Better the Turks than the Latins." The Roman Empire shrank till its boundary extended no further than the range of Taurus; but the provinces that had become Chalcedonian in faith resisted the invader.

Jacobite and "Nestorian" (for as they had now accepted the label which others affixed to them, we perhaps may use it too) found themselves under one Government, and each proceeded to make terms with it as best they could.

Ishu-yahb was the negotiator in the case of the Assyrian Church; and neither. that body nor the Jacobite had any difficulty in securing the recognition of their *melet* status, and they obtained much the same terms. Neither, of course, was likely to be content, if the other wore either lighter or heavier chains than themselves!

In each case the right to exist on payment of tribute, the right to keep their churches but not to build new ones, and the exemption from military service; were cheerfully conceded; and the two settled down into that comfortable neutrality, and ignoring of one another's existence, which describes their mutual relationship to this day. Assyrian tradition declares that special privileges were given to their Church and to their patriarch, by a firman from the prophet himself; and a document, purporting to be the grant in question, was actually preserved until the middle of the nineteenth century, when Kurdish hatred of Christians overcame all their reverence for the prophet, and the grant perished in the "Massacres of Bedr Khan Beg." It is an undoubted fact that the patriarchal house, as such, is regarded with a respect among Moslems, which they do not show to other Christian bishops;[376] but the claim to a special position is one that can hardly be substantiated under present conditions.

Here a new chapter opens in the history of the Assyrian Church, and one that demands separate treatment. Their history was far from ended, for they still had great triumphs to win, they still had their greatest suffering's to undergo;. but they had now definitely settled into the position-political and theological--that they occupy to this day. That is to say, they were now a melet in the great Mussulman State, definitely separated from the Church of Constantinople, as well as from that of Antioch and contented so to be.

The two bodies had drifted apart; and though we hold our conviction that the theological dispute was a misunderstanding, and one capable of settlement, in the right circumstances, and by the right men, neither necessary was forthcoming. "Thus they continued on their separate way, each forgetting how near the other had once been. For practical purposes they even forgot each other's existence, though travellers like Marco Polo might mention the discovery of Nestorian Churches as interesting facts. Each branch of the Church Catholic, busied with its own problems, and cut off by circumstances from all others, ignored those others almost completely; and in the thirteenth century a "Nestorian" archdeacon, whom circumstances brought to Rome (and to the presence, in France, of our Edward I) found himself hailed there almost as a visitor from another planet.[377]

Since then the world has grown smaller. Western and Eastern Christians have come to realize the existence each of the other, and to realize, too, that they must take such existence into account. What the future may hold we know not; but if National Churches as such have any part at all to play in Catholic Christendom, their relations to one another must be important; and the attitude of the youngest, and for. the moment the most vigorous, of those bodies to her elder sisters, is now recognized as a thing that must be considered and determined. The Assyrian Church has been preserved through trials and sufferings such as no Western body has ever been called upon to endure; and independent and national still, it holds fast its allegiance to "the holder of the throne of Mar Adai," the representative of the Catholicos-patriarch of Seleucia-Ctesiphon. Now, a new life is springing up in all the "East"; a life nobly embodied in those who rule the kingdom of which Assyrians are the subjects. What work has God in the future for those whom He surely has not preserved in the past without an object; and who in that past, with all their faults and failings, have served Him so loyally and so well?

"O Lord, we beseech Thee let Thy continual pity cleanse and defend this Church; and whereas it cannot continue in safety without Thy succour, preserve it evermore by Thy help and goodness, through Jesus Christ our Lord. Amen."

Footnotes

¹ With two exceptions, "Ishu" is the same name as "Jesus," but where it appears in compounds like "Sabr-Ishu" ("Hope-in-Jesus") I have kept the Syriac lettering. Also the name "Shimun" is, for reasons known to every friend of the Church, too familiar to be represented by "Simon."

² The sculptures from this palace are in the R6nig Friedrich Museum, Berlin.

³ Mshikha-Zca. *Life of Khiran*.

⁴ Armenia, of course, owed much to Cappadocian help in later days, and became a sort of adopted daughter of Caesarea. Christianity, however, existed in the land before the conversion of the King by Gregory the Illuminator, and Armenian. writers declare that it owed its existence to Edessene- teachers, and principally to Thaddeus the Apostle. They also declare that Osrh6ene was a tributary state of the "Armenian Empire," but the ecclesiastical tradition may be better founded than the political.

⁵ *Acta S. Maris*, 32. Ed. Abbeloos.

⁶ B.-H., A.D. 266-330. Mari Ibn Sulieman (Liber Turris), A.D. 247_326 (1). Papa's latter-day successors are consecrated in their "teens," but even these do not attain to such magnificently lengthy tenures.

⁷ Sources Syriaques, vol. i., Msiha-Zkha, texte de traduction. A. Mingana, Mosul, Life of Pqida.

⁸ Samson, successor of Pqida, died "seven years after the victory of Trajan," i.e. A.D. 123. This was nine years after the death of Pqida, whose episcopate lasted ten years. Pqida was therefore consecrate A.D. 104.

⁹ See *History of parka d'B. Slok, Bedi.*, ii. 512.

¹⁰ St. Thomas is called the "rounder" by Bar-Hebraeus, but is represented as a bird of passage only. The work is done by Adai, and his disciples Agai and Mari. B.-H., i.

¹¹ Acta S. Maris, 19, ch. viii; 32, ch. xi; 33, ch. xii. Note.-Labourt (p. 14) and Duval (Litterature syraque, p. 118) both criticize the *Acta S. Maris*, on the ground that they represent the hero as contending with the worship of sacred trees and springs; not with Magianism or starworship, as ought to have been the case had they given a reliable picture of Mesopotamian life at their supposed date. This is true; but it should be noted that the author represents the nature-worship as existing in provinces like Adiabene and Garmistan, where, according to Mshikha-Zca, it was very strong at the time, and where fire-worship was never a national cult. There are no references to it in the chapters that deal with Seleucia and Khuzistan. As in the district named the worship of trees and springs is not extinct to this day, centuries of Christian and Mussulman teaching notwithstanding (the writer knows two sacred springs, and sacred trees by the dozen, in the country in question), it is reasonable to conclude that it was more conspicuous in early centuries.

The almost total absence of any mention of fire-worship is a difficulty that cuts both ways. That a sixth-century writer in Persia should not have known of the cult is inconceivable-as well could a Hindu Christian be ignorant of the existence of Brahmanism-so the omission must be designed. Possibly, the writer did not care to speak of a campaign against the State faith, for fear of consequences. A Syriac biographer of to-day, for instance, would hardly venture to boast of his hero as making converts from Islam.

[12] *Melet ("Millet") is the technical word in Turkey for a Christian subject nation, organized, as they always are, in a Church, and dealing with the Government through its religious head. It suits the condition of the Church in Zoroastrian Persia so perfectly that we must use the word, particularly as no Western nation possesses the name or the thing. A rayat, or subject, is a member of such a melet.*

[13] Many of these magical formulae are current among Assyrians of today, and these are often essentially the same as those on the most ancient Babylonian tablets. A substratum of the oldest faith of the country has survived the changes of 7000 years.

[14] M.-Z., Life of Samson.

[15] M.-Z., *Life of Isaac.*

[16] M.-Z., *Life of Noah.*

[17] M.-Z., *Lives of Pqida, Isaac.*

[18] Bedjan, ii. 184

[19] M.-Z.

[20] M.-Z., *Life of Isaac.*

[21] M.-Z., *Life of Abel.*

[22] Mar Augin of Egypt, the friend of James of Nisibis, is stated to have been the first to bring the monastic life to the East, and he certainly did not arrive before the year 300. Bedj. i. 424 (*Life of Mar Shalitha*).

[23] Chabot, *Syn. Orientale,* p. 34, 273; M.Z., *Life of Khiran.*

[24] M.-Z., *Life* of *Khiran.*

[25] The "tels" so common, e.g. round Mosul, are very different things from the "ash-mounds" of Azerbaijan.

[26] Acta Maris, ch. viii, 19.

[27] M.-Z., Lives of Shakhluta and of *Akha d'abuh'.*

[28] This bishop is said (Liber Turris) to have been given his strange name, meaning "brother of *his* father," from his personal resemblance to that relative. M.-Z. declares, with much greater probability, that it was applied to him from the fact that he was born of one of the incestuous marriages common among Zoroastrians. He was of that faith by birth; and served as a soldier in Sapor's great invasion of Roman territory that followed the capture of Valerian in 258.

[29] We incline to date the composition of this document as between the years 424 and 530, *i.e.* to place it after the Council of Dad-Ishu, seeing that it seems reminiscent of some of the language there used; and previous to the time of Mar Aba, seeing that the. arrangements described in it for the election of a patriarch do not agree with those pre. scribed by that prelate. If this be correct, the document would roughly coincide in date with the separation of the "Nestorian" or "Dyophysite" Church of the Persian Empire from the West; a date in itself not unlikely for its composition. In this case the fact that the tradition is common to both Dyophysites and Monophysites, and so is probably older in date than their separation one from the other, would be explained.

[30] Chabot, Synadicon Orientale, pp. 46-49, 289-291.

[31] The author rather imprudently gives us some synchronisms, and gets sadly confused therein; making his imaginary Bishop Jacob (172-190) contemporary not only with Commodus, but with Ardashir I of Persia (acceded 225), and with Porphyry (born-232). Of course, the existence of four patriarchates m the year 19o is itself unhistorical.

[32] M.-Z., *Life of Akha d'abuh'.*

[33] We follow M.-Z. in preference to Bar-Hebraeus, who says that Papa Avas consecrated by the Bishop of Prat d'Maishan or Bassora. That see, how-

ever, was in existence at the time, M.-Z, *Life of Khiran.*

[34] *Acta S. Maris,* 32.

[35] The Episcopate of Akha d'abuh' lasted 273-291 (M.-Z.). There is no evidence where the consecration should be placed, inside those limits.

[36] Rawlinson, *Seventh Oriental Empire,* ch. iv.

[37] In Syriac, Qardu, Bait Zabdai, and Arzun. The others are, Bait Rakhimi (Rehimene), and Bait Moksai (Moxcene). Arzun and B. Moksai still retain their ancient names. Qardu is jezire, and B. Zabdai Fundik.

[38] If we identify Papa, as seems least difficult on the whole, with the oppressive Bishop of Aphraat's Fourteenth Minim, he was also a man of very fine presence. In any case, a man who held his bishopric for more than three times the ordinary period, must have had some unusual physical qualities. Bar-Hebraeus calls him learned in Syriac. One must own that we do not know in what Syriac books he could have been learned (except the Diatessaron), at a period when even Aphraat was still unwritten.

[39] M.-Z., *Life of Shri'a.*

[40] The life of Mar Mari does make the claim, but it *is* significant that Seleucia was regarded as the throne of Shimun the Martyr, not of Mari the Apostle.

[41] It may be noted that this influence, which always tends to give some one head (whether lie be called patriarch or not) to the Church *of* a subject *Melet,* tends also to make it independent of any extra-national authority. The non-Christian ruler does not like his subjects to carry appeals, even on purely ecclesiastical points, out of his dominions. Hence the favour of the Mussulman or Zoroastrian ruler is always thrown on the side of the native Church, as against that subject to any patriarch or pope outside the kingdom;--provided, of course, that the non-Christian ruler is strong enough to keep the foreigner out of his dominions.

[42] M.-Z., *Life of Shri'a.*

[43] *Syn. Or.,* 46, 289.

[44] Or Sabba'e.

[45] *Life of Miles,* Bedj., ii. 267.

[46] The date, hitherto a matter of doubt, is practically settled by M.-Z. *(Life of Shri'a).* The council met during the episcopate of Shri'a, Bishop of Arbela 291-317. Papa, after the council, appealed to S'ada of Edessa, who was consecrated 313. The period 313-317, therefore, must have seen the assembling of the council.

[47] Ammonius must be a slip for Ammon, pupil of Anthony.

[48] The above is taken mainly from the *Life of Mar Miles* (Bed'. ii. 260). This document is marked by a tone much opposed to the Catholicos, but the main incidents, and notably the "Speak, Gospel, speak" episode, which struck the imagination of all parties, are corroborated by other writers. See council of Dad-Ishu, Synodicon Orientale.

[49] *Life of Miles,* Bedj., ii. 264.

[50] M.-Z., *Life of Shri'a.*

[51] B.-H. says, also to Ephraim Syrus, but that saint was then about ten years old. The existing correspondence of Papa with these bishops is apocryphal. See Labourt, p. 83, note 2.

[52] See note 50.

[53] M.-Z., *Life of Shri'a.* I incline to think that this more nearly represents what happened. With M. Labourt, I hold that the acts of the Council of Dad-Ishu ought not to be trusted too absolutely, in that they have gone through a process of doctoring themselves; and in any case, the historical statements about Papa are the reported speech of

a member of the council only, not its formal declaration.

[54] The statement in the *Life of Miles,* that Papa survived his stroke of paralysis twelve years, has the ring of truth about it, as stated, though Bar-Hebraeus has doubts on the matter.

[55] M.-Z., *Life of Shri'a;* Bedj., ii. 180.

[56] Afrant, Mimra i. Labourt, p. 32 *et seq.*

[57] e.g. those of Nisibis. B. Zabdai, etc.

[58] A John "of Persia" occurs in some lists of Nicene signatories, but this is probably a mis-reading for Perrha. Persia was never the name of a see in the Assyrian Church, though the province of "Fars" formed the jurisdiction of a metropolitan in later days. The legend referred to by Bar. Hebraeus (*Primates Orientis, Vita Papae*), that either Papa. or Shimun attended Nicaen, we reject without hesitation as the figment of a latter day, when Assyrians had come to believe that "so great a throne as ours must have had a representative at so great a council." See Labourt, p. 32, note.

[59] It must not be forgotten that, as we hope to show later, there is a second and important motive, for these schisms in the Church; viz. the desire to find expression in the religious sphere, for nationality.

[60] Labourt, p. 48. Afraat, Mimra, xii.

[61] Theodoret, Eccl. Hist., i. 25.

[62] Labourt; p. 50.

[63] It was on this occasion that the besieged city %vas preserved by the moral influence of St. James, its bishop, and also by the "miraculous" swarms of flies that his prayers sent against the besiegers (Theodoret, ii. 30). The influence of the great bishop did much towards keeping up the courage of the defenders, we may well believe. As to the flies, still less need we question the reality of the swarms. Sapor tried to flood the city; therefore his huge force was camping in a swamp, during a Mesopotamian summer!

[64] Bedj., ii. 134.

[65] Bedj., ii. 154.

[66] Specially Bright, *Age of Fathers, I. A.*

[67] Acts of Aqib-shima, Bedj., ii. 351. The list of accusations is said to be taken from a royal Firman. Whether that is so or not, they give at least the popular feeling.

[68] Westcott, *Gospel of Life,* ch. v. 3.

[69] It is worth noting that in the matter of food (the one point on which there is clear scriptural direction to the contrary!) the Christians do seem to have given way. Their modern descendants regard certain animals, e.g. the hare and the pig, as unfit for human consumption.

[70] Sometimes they were employed, but there were probably few Christians among the" Azadan," the free tenants in chief who furnished the cavalry of the Sassanid feudal army the "infantry" were undisciplined peasants.

[71] Bedi., ii. 241.

[72] Bedj., ii. 245. Obviously "Rabbans" and "Rabbanyati" also wore some sort of distinctive dress. See Bedj., ii. 233.

[73] ii. 246.

[74] The organization of society under the Sassanids was broadly feudal; so that there was nothing strange in the Agha, or Seigneur, executing justice, high, middle and low.

[75] M.-Z., *Life of John.*

[76] *Ibid.*

[77] B.-H., *Primates Orientis, Shah-dost.*

[78] The Agha was Hormizd of Raziqai. Miles had wandered far, but the homing instinct of his people brought him home to die (Bedj., ii. 271).

[79] To convert pagans proper to Christianity was blameless, and even laudable; though proselytizing from Zoroastrians was punishable with death, even in a time of peace. At the present day,

Christian teachers are free to convert, *e.g.* Yezidis, if they can; and fanatical Mussulmans have been known to offer to spare disciples of that strange faith, even in time of massacre, if they will consent to turn "Mussulman or Christian."

[80] This is mentioned as quite an unusual thing. Apparently the Manichees, if (as stated) they helped to rouse Sapor to persecution, drew down vengeance also on themselves. Sassanian officials had not the experience which enables the Ottoman to distinguish between different kinds of Christian, one of whom you may kill when you must not touch another!

[81] This act of the Manichees forms an interesting comment on a recent Hulsean lecture. "Take from the Christian Church," says Dr. Figgis, "the mysterious birth and the availing death, the empty tomb, and the sacramental presence, and see what you have left. Would it be very much to live by? Would it be anything at all to die for?" It was precisely those four points that the Manichees (no doubt in the name of a so-called deeper mystery) cut out of their Christianity.

[82] They would probably be forced to marry Zoroastrians; and a wife whose faith was not that of her husband was unthinkable. The same offer was hardly ever made to monks; probably because the Zoroastrian, like many orientals today, simply did not believe in the existence of male celibacy (Bedj., ii. 233, 308).

[83] Bedj., ii. 291.

[84] The idea was, that the bodies would be used for magic, and the fear had this much of justification, that dust soaked with a martyr's blood, or from his grave, was (and is) regarded as a remedy for most diseases. The substance is called "Khenana," "Grace" or "Mercy."

[85] Bedj., iv. 137.

[86] Bedj., ii. 316.

[87] Acts of Aqib-shima.

[88] Bedj., ii. 233. Martha, as usual, was offered life and freedom, by the Mobed who tried her, if she would consent to marry. She explained that she was sorry, but that she was betrothed to "Ishu" (*i.e.* Jesus,--the name is still a very common one), and enjoyed the confusion of the Mobed, who asked after the family and village of the supposed Bridegroom, and declared that he would send for Him. Later, the fearless girl indulged in some similar sparring with the executioner!

[89] This must have been the convert's baptismal name. Bedj., iv. 133. M.-Z., Life of *Maran-zca*.

[90] There were also an immense number of unrecorded sufferers.

[91] He had been appointed by the council, and the act of an oecumenical council can hardly be irregular!

[92] It is not meant, of course, that this rivalry between two great sees was the only, or primary, cause of their quarrels; only that it was a factor in it, and one that ought not to be forgotten. No doubt Timothy, Theophilus and Dioscuros were no less convinced than was Cyril that their zeal in the conflict was purely zeal for God and Truth.

[93] See Rawlinson, *Seventh Oriental Empire*, ch. xi.-xii.; Lynch, Armenia, i. pp. 277-315.

[94] Let us in fairness admit, however, that as yet no foreigner has even attempted to govern the country respectably!

[95] Or Norseses.

[96] Bar-Hebraeus and Amr, in the *Liber Turris*. See also *Elia of Nisibis* (Ass.).

[97] B.-H., p. 42 note, and additional note, p. 81.

[98] Tabari, p. 71, Ed. Noldeke.

[99] M.-Z., *Life of Shubkha 1'Ishu*.

¹⁰⁰ The name is that of the planet Mars, according to both B.-H. and modern Assyrians. The connection between the planet, the month July-August (Tamuz), and the Babylonian sun-god, is outside our present field.

¹⁰¹ A. and S., Liber Turris.

¹⁰² B.-H., p. 42. It is quite possible that the historian may have mistakenly attributed the thought of his own age to an earlier one. Still the conception referred to is certainly one of the innate stock ideas of the oriental Christian today.

¹⁰³ B.-H:, p. 42.

¹⁰⁴ B.-H. declares that the synod, by advice of Marutha (who may or may not have been present at it) accepted the resignation, and that Qaiuma retired to a hermit's cell. Both agree that he practically withdrew from office.

¹⁰⁵ *De Bello Persico,* i. 2. There may have been no formal act. Perhaps Arcadius only commended his successor to the care of his "brother," and received such a reply as "he shall be to me as my own son."

¹⁰⁶ Yezdegerd knew his countrymen! One might not ask, but would always suspect some such bargain to be behind any such request.

¹⁰⁷ Socr., vu. 8. No doubt the historian repeats what was common talk in Church circles in Constantinople; and which he, a lad of twelve at the time, might remember.

¹⁰⁸ Amr, Assem., iii. 363. The Assyrian "Sunhadus" declares he was present at Nicaea also; but this is a manifest blunder, due to his having brought the canons of Nicaea to Seleucia in 410.

¹⁰⁹ So says Amr. His whole account, however, is too confused to be much relied on. For instance, he declares that A4arutha after this gathering, reported the devotion and orthodoxy of the Assyrian Church to the Council of Constantinople.

¹¹⁰ Socr., vi. 15. The only definite act recorded as his, however, is that he trod so emphatically on the (presumably gouty) toe of Cyrinus of Chalcedon, as to incapacitate that determined enemy of St. Chrysostom from attendance at the council.

¹¹¹ Amr, Liber Turris. A few centuries later Eastern Christians had certainly a practical monopoly of medical practice under the Khalifate; and to this day, Mahommedan doctors are few in number and primitive in practice.

There does not seem any reason to doubt the story that Marutha was a doctor; and, if it be admitted, this prelate may fairly be claimed as the first historic instance of the medical missionary.

¹¹² For the rest of this chapter, see *Synodicon Orientale* Council of Isaac.

¹¹³ The seat of the holder of the office has changed repeatedly in the course of ages, from Seleucia-Ctesiphon to Baghdad, Mosul, Maragha on Lake Urmi, and, for the last century or so, to Qudshanis in Kurdistan.

¹¹⁴ The word is used in the acts of Shimun and his two successors (Bedi., ii. 134, 276, 296). Previously, there was hardly opportunity for official use.

¹¹⁵ See *Dict. Christian Antiquities,* and *Procopius De Bello Persico,* ii. 25. It is noteworthy that Assyrian writers also use the term for the prelate when we should certainly call "Patriarch" of Antioch. Chabot, *Syn. Or.,* 18, 255. An expert in hierarchical precedence may say what the difference between Catholicos and patriarch ought to be, but to a Persian in the early fifth century, they were practically interchangeable terms.

[116] See Ass., iii. 59, note 4. It will be seen that the theory first broached by Assemani, and accepted by others (E. C:. Neale, but not by Labourt), that Seleucia was a metropolitan in the Antiochene patriarchate till the Nestorian controversy, is rendered untenable by the evidence of the *Synodicon* and Mshikha-Zca.

[117] Assem., iii. 51-58. The so-called "letter of the patriarchs" is a very late composition. See p. 41.

[118] It will be remembered that Papa, when condemned by the council, did not appeal to Antioch, but to Edessa and Nisibis.

[119] The maxim of a later age, "imperium sine Patriarcha non staret," may not commend itself to the purist, but it represents one of those facts that are apt to deal rather discourteously with a purist's theories. Nationality is bound to express itself in, the religious sphere; and the lesson is writ large on Church history, that the refusal of its legitimate expression to this natural human instinct leads to disaster. From the days of Jacobites and Nestorians in Syria, to those of Vlachs and Exarchists in the Balkans today, the story has been the same.

[120] Chabot, *Synodicon Orientale*, 49, 293.

[121] Anything west of Constantinople was as thoroughly beyond the purview of Assyrians as they were beyond the purview of writers in Italy, Gaul or Africa.

[122] *Syn. Or.*, 20, 258.

[123] "Forty days in seven weeks," showing that Lent was kept originally according to the modern Western rule. Modern Assyrians keep a Lent of fifty days, and include Sundays in it.

[124] As Marutha was at Constantinople; this fact is noteworthy.

[125] Bar Ithutha.

[126] Bar Kiana.

[127] Qnuma.

[128] Ithutha.

[129] Qnuma.

[130] The council had to determine whether Bait Lapat or Karka d'Lidan (Susa), (both of which were royal residences), should be metropolitan; and decided in favour of the former. Further, *it* had to say which of four, or more, claimant to these two sees was in the right. For the time all the *soi-disant* bishops were suspended; but as one of them, Agapitus of B. Lapat, appears fourteen years later as a warm supporter of Seleucian supremacy, it would seem that a *modus vivendi* was reached. The condemnation of a bishop of the Bahrein Islands in the Persian Gulf shows how far the Church had extended (p. 273, 34).

[131] *Synodicon Orientale*, 43, 285.

[132] A Kurd is a Mussulman, but no fanatic, though sometimes represented as such. He is not very zealous in any direction, except that of plundering his neighbour's goods; and is not specially efficient, even as a brigand.
A sept of Heriki, wildest of nomad Kurds, still carry with them as a tribal palladium a relic that purports to be the head of Mar Gewergis, a Christian martyr. It is the last relic of the Christianity of their ancestors.
It is worth mentioning that the Catholicos Yahb-Alaha had a tent-church (Bedj., iv. 256), which may have been for the benefit of nomad Christians, Arab or Kurd. Its existence, however, may only mean that then, as now, all who could afford it camped outside the towns, in gardens, during the summer heats.

[133] *Syn. Or.*, 43, 285.

[134] Bedj., ii. 2o6, 208, 281. Bar-shbia means "son of captivity."

135 Bedj., ii. 316. This captivity was settled in Huzistan, and may possibly be the captivity of Belashpar referred to. Even if Demetrius of B. Lapat be legendary the growth of the legend is evidence of the existence of "Roman captivities."

136 If the fact of violent transportation be condoned, captives were generally well treated in their new homes, and even their supposed whims consulted. Thus, Chosroes I built his "New Antioch" exactly on the lines of the city on the Orontes; and the shah who' transported the Armenians to Ispahan was anxious to bring the Cathedral of Etchmiadzin with them--and would have done it, but for his captives' petition!

137 *Syn. Or.*, 276, note.

138 Amr, Assemani, iii. 368.

139 Liber Turris.

140 Liber Turris. Socrates (vil. 8) also mentions the miracle, but refers it to Abda.

141 *Bedj.,* iv. 170

142 *Syn. Or.*, 49, 293.

143 This actually occurred during the twentieth century, but was equally possible during the fifth.

144 *"Pand," i.e. an expedient, clever and usually shady. The two go together.*

145 *Syn. Or.*, 37, 276; 43, 284.

146 Bedj., iv. 171-2.

147 Bedj., iv. 170-180: Acts of Narses.

148 Bedi., iv. 250; Theodoret, v. 39. Seleucia-Ctesiphon was an "urban district" rather than a city, in which separate towns existed. One of these, Dastagerd, had a separate bishop in 424 (*Syn. Or.*, 44, 287). Probably this fact explains the existence of a bishop in the capital, who was not the Catholicos.

149 The Syriac acts, which are far fuller and more reliable, fail us here.

150 Tabari, p. 95.

151 Theod., v. 39; Bedj., ii. 539-558; iv. 189, 253.

152 It must be remembered that they were not alone in this trait. St. Cyprian records that African confessors could not communicate together when in prison for their common faith. The fact really shows oriental acceptance of violence, rather than oriental quarrelsomeness. An occasional massacre stands on much the same footing in their minds as an occasional invasion or flood.

153 Liber Turris, Amr, Assem., iii. 376.

154 Bar-Hebraeus, p. 54. B.-H., ordinarily tolerant, can no more do justice to a Nestorian than can a Protestant to the Scarlet Woman.

155 Amr, Assem., iii. 214. It is possible that we have another martial prelate here!

156 *Syn. Or.*, 45, 288.

157 Amr, Assem., ii. 214.

158 *i.e*, to Judi Dagh, near the modern Jezireh, a mountain which local tradition identifies with the Ararat on which the Ark rested. Here St. James of Nisibis had a hermitage, and here there exist still the remains of a monastery, which we may probably identify with that of the "Ark" to which Dad-lshu retired.

159 We follow the acts of the Council of Dad-Ishu (*Syn. Or.*, 43, 285; 53, 298), though, as stated above, with some doubt as to their absolute authenticity.

160 See p. 29.

161 *Syn. Or.*, 51, 296.

162 The "war" seems to have been no more than a military demonstration, intended to prevent the building of fortresses, contrary to treaty, on the Roman side of the frontier. It succeeded in its object.

163 For instance, the "Orthodox" said to the "Nestorian," "You call the B.V.M. 'Mother of Christ.' You must mean by that, 'Mother of a mere Man.'"

"We mean nothing of the kind," said the "Nestorian" to the "Orthodox," 'but you call her 'Mother of God,' and that can only mean, 'Mother of the God-head.'" Both were quite logical, particularly when the varying nuances of the technical words in the different languages used are remembered, and both were wrong.

[164] For the thought expressed in this paragraph, the writer must express his indebtedness to a friend, the Rev. O. H. Parry.

[165] M.-Z., pp. 144-145. Is it possible that Assyrians confounded in their minds the first council of Ephesus with the second, the Latrocinium?

[166] M.-Z., p. 144. Life of Rkhima.

[167] Assem., i. 445; Chabot, De S. Isaaci vita, etc., ch. i.

[168] Bedj., ii. 559.

[169] Bedj., ii. 519, and, *passim*, 518-531. Certain officials are ordered "to deal with" the Christians of Karka. The order reads like one of a series issued to governors at large, but M.-Z., though he knows of the persecution (p. 147), does not refer to it as extending into Adiabene.

[170] The writer believes the existing building, a church of unusual design, to be at least built on the lines of the original. Memory of other sites referred to in the History of Karka (Bedj., ii. 510-531) has perished; the Christian community of Kirkuk (as Karka is now called) having been almost exterminated by plague about 100 years ago.

[171] The Acts put the Bishop of Arbela among the victims. This is contradicted by M.-Z.

[172] The act may be paralleled elsewhere, but the fact does not imply "borrowing" but simply that human beings under similar conditions tend to act similarly.

[173] Bedj., ii. 528.

[174] Bedj., ii. 531; M.-Z., p. 147. Ilul is September (old style).

[175] Bedj., ii. 583-603. Some of the peculiar tortures inflicted on Anahid and other confessors were, until very lately, still in practical use in the country.

[176] See Rawlinson, *Seventh Monarchy*, ch. xv.

[177] To call Armenians a nation of cowards is a gross injustice; but as soldiers they have never produced anything higher than good "generals of division" like Loris Melikoti, and artisan leaders.

[178] *Syn Or.*, p. 6. See chap. xiii. note 2.

[179] M.-Z., p. 147.

[180] Rawlinson, *Seventh Monarchy*, ch. xvi. Peace had been made with the Turks, and it was to be cemented by a royal marriage. Piroz substituted a slave for the princess, and (the real crime to oriental thinkers) was detected.

[181] B.-H. and Liber Turris. The former says that he was imprisoned after consecration, and released "when peace was made with Rome." We have no information of any war, and the statement reads like a confusion of his career with that of his predecessor.

[182] One may accept fully the doctrinal statement endorsed by the first Council of Ephesus, and yet feel that the contrast between it and the second is not so marked as to make it obvious why the members of the first form a gathering of inspired fathers, and of the second, a "gang of brigands."

[183] *i.e.* with the abandonment of Arianism by the Lombards, *temp.* Gregory the Great.

[184] *i.e.* "King's man," from *melka*, king.

[185] One must use this improper term for what was properly called "the Orient." One has to use the term "western" in two different senses, for the folk about Antioch and the folk about Rome.

It is too much to have the same difficulty with the word "eastern."

[186] A convenient term for those who held the doctrine of the "two natures" in some form: the alternative terms "Orthodox" and "Nestorian" both beg the question of the status of those so labelled.

[187] Shimun of Bait. Arsham. Assemani, i. 351.

[188] Labourt, p. 133.

[189] Shimun of B. Arsham confuses this expulsion of Barsoma and his companions with the general dispersion of the school, thirty years later. There can be no doubt that Bar-soma was Bishop of Nisibis long before the latter event occurred.

[190] Liber Turris, Life of Babowai. M.-Z., Life of Abushta, p. 147. Bar-soma, Letter 2 (*Syn. Or.*, 526, 532).

[191] To the Bishopric of B. Lapat. *Syn. Or.*, 83, 300; Assem., i. 352.

[192] Assem. declares Shimun to have been orthodox, but a man who accepted the Henoticon and rejected Chalcedon can only have belonged to one party in sympathy.

[193] Bedj., ii. 631-634.

[194] Bar-soma, Letter 3. *Syn. Or.*, 528, 534; Bedj., ii. 631.

[195] The omission or insertion of one soundless consonant makes the difference of meaning ܪܫܝܬܐ, *rishaita*, for ܪܫܝܬܐ, *reshi'ta*. Incidentally, it is interesting to notice how many of the formalities of the Sassanids survive in their modern heirs, the Ottomans. The familiar phrase., "the sublime Porte," is only "the King's door"; Turkey is in all formal documents "the sublime Kingdom," all others being merely "princely." It even appears that the Mobed Mobedan had a position like that of the Sheik-ul-Islam, and could on cause shown issue a "fetva" declaring his King unfit to rule-unless the King anticipated the intention, and executed him

[196] Labourt, p. 136.

[197] Bar-Hebraeus does not seem to think this policy of blackmail at all discreditable to his heroes!

[198] B.-H., p. 71. As a matter of fact it was B. Lapat. It it said to have been held in the "house of Yazdin, the Taxfarmer." The only man of that description we know lived 150 years later, but the name is common.

[199] "Son of shoes" instead of "son of fast." The name given to Bar-soma by Bar-Hebraeus in derision.

[200] Adeney, *The Greek and Eastern Churches.*

[201] It is also quite true, that things do go more smoothly for the *melet,* if they do not outrage the prejudices of the dominant religion too openly; and the enforced celibacy of an order is not a thing that can be concealed. Thus, the Moslem of to-day thinks that a Christian who does not use pictures or images in his worship, is a decidedly less contemptible animal than one *who* does use them. It is, of course, quite easy to prove that this matter of devotion or discipline is a purely Christian affair, nothing to Magian or Moslem; but what profit to prove it, if your opponent of the dominant faith does not agree? He has a vast superiority to argument.

[202] This canon is only preserved to us through its having been quoted and adopted by a later council (Gregory, A.D. 605; *Syn. Or.*, 211, 475). It was of course annulled with the other canons when the council was repudiated; but the fact of the canonization of the then uncondemned Theodore, in 484, must be remembered when we come to discuss the attitude of the Assyrian Church toward the posthumous anathema, pronounced on him in 553.

203 *Syn. Or.*, 621.
204 Liber Turris. It is about the only reliable statement in that account.
205 Council of Acacius, Canons I and II.
206 *Syn. Or.*, 61, 308. Bar-soma, Letter i.
207 Bar-soma, Letter 2. *S.O.*, 526, 532.
208 This tribe at least, and very probably the Tu'ans also, still live in the district.
209 Letter 4.
210 Parsopa. For the force of this term in the councils, see chap. xiii.
211 The word *naqiputha* has a ring that is not quite pleasant, but is no more Nestorian than the, of the Council of Chalcedon.
212 *S. O.*, 528.
213 Otherwise Vagarshapat. It is the place now generally called Etchmiadzin, which was originally only the name of the great monastery.
214 Ass., ii. 266.
215 The question of Armenian "heresy" does not concern us. We may mention, however, that so severe a judge as J. M. Neale considers them to be "orthodox in intention"; and that they have introduced into their version of the Creed clauses emphasizing the reality and eternity of the Human nature of Christ, and therefore can hardly be "Monophysite" in the ordinary sense.
216 *Syn. Or.*, Council of Babai, 63, 312.
217 B.-H-, 76. In that case, he either did not go on the embassy referred to in the second letter of Bar-soma, or he went twice. Both explanations are possible. It is possible, too, that Acacius did not anathematize Bar-soma till the "West" insisted on it as a condition of Communion. In that case, one must feel some sympathy with Bar-soma in his retaliation, and admit that in this case he was not the aggressor. To us, what we have written above appears more probable.
218 B.-H., p. 78. "Killed with the keys of their cells," says the historian. If so, one would like to know how it was achieved, for the oriental key is not an iron bar that can be a weapon on emergency, but a notched slip of wood some eight inches long, and about as formidable as a paperknife.
219 Rawlinson, ch. xx; Tabari, p. 142-144.
220 Possibly the lost letters of Bar-soma may be rediscovered, as those of a later prelate have recently been. His comments on such a movement would provide most interesting reading.
221 Of course the technical term belongs to a later period; nor need we suppose that the quaint formality of the present age was followed then, and the question asked, "If Zeid, who is commander of the faithful, does such and such things, is it lawful to depose the said Zeid?"
222 *S. O.*, Council of Acacius.
223 Labourt, p. 158; B.-H., p. 86.
224 "Black Amida." This is still the Turkish name for Diarbekr, whose basalt walls are largely of Roman building. Kobad was so discouraged by the resistance of the town, that he offered to raise the siege, if a small ransom was paid, "to save his face." The overconfident garrison sent in a bill for the vegetables consumed during the siege, and the women mocked him from the ramparts. Kobad persevered and, shortly after, an unguarded tower gave him entry (*Zach. Mitylene*, vii. 4).
225 Liber Turris, Amr, Assem., iii. 614.
226 S. O., 339.
227 Bishoprics in the Assyrian Church to-day usually descend, by what is known as the "*natar-cursya* system," from uncle to nephew. The custom, of course, is uncanonical, and as completely opposed to primitive usage as is

nomination by a lay rime Ministet, or by an universal Pope! The first two habits at any rate can only be defended on the ground that they are the outcome of historical conditions, and in practice produce results that are not intolerable.

[228] Liber Turris.

[229] S. O., Mar Aba, de Dualitate.

[230] Liber Turris.

[231] B.-H., 88. Singar is at the present a Yezidi stronghold, but many of these men are descendants of Christians, and keep "Christian holy books" in their shrines, which, however, they allow no stranger to study.

[232] Belisarius fought that day behind the shelter of big "field entrenchments," and, when the Persian attack was repulsed, would not trust his troops to make any pursuit.

[233] In ferries on the Tigris a man who misses one crossing may often have to wait for three hours before the boat has been towed back to the crossing place against the rapid. current, has crossed again, and is ready for another trip. Of course, no big man is going to wait his turn, merely because a rayat was in the boat first!

[234] Marcionites were called Christians, and Christians, Mshikhai (Mshikha, or Messiah, being Syriac for Christ). Christians, as we see from other evidence, wore some distinctive dress, as they did until the present generation. It appears that Marcionites were a numerous sect in Persia at the time.

[235] Labourt suggests (p. 167) that the accession to power of the Monophysite Patriarch Anthimus (535) was the reason for Aba's departure. This is probable enough, though there is no evidence for it in the Biography, and I cannot identify the statement, attributed to Mari, that he was expelled for refusing to anathematize Theodore of Mopsuestia. Its the see-saw of ecclesiastical politics at Constantinople a man might readily find himself orthodox one week and heretical the next.

[236] S. O., Council of Aba, 546, 556.

[237] Mar Aba, de Recta Fide, S. O., 540, 550. See chap. xiii., "The Christology of the Assyrian Church."

[238] So much per acre of cultivated land, and so much per tree, with an additional poll-tax for Christians who did no military service. This system, taken over by the Arabs, is that of the Ottoman Empire to-day, though the late revolution had made Christians liable to service in the army.

[239] M. Chabot (S. O., 546, 566) dates this council during Aba's exile. In default of very clear evidence there does not seem any reason for removing it from a time and place when it could have been held easily, to one where it would have been difficult. The point is not important, but one does not differ readily from Monsignor Chabot.

[240] S. O., De Dualitate; Mar Aba, iv.

[241] Normally, all but the officiating clergy receive the Elements at the door leading from the sanctuary into the nave.

[242] De recta fide, S. O., 540, 550.

[243] S. O., 80, 332.

[244] Life, p. 226.

[245] S. O., 90, 345; Mar Aba, v.; De Regimine Ecclesim.

[246] S. O., 543, 553; Mar Aba, "Practica."

[247] IV Catholici (Bedjan). 347, 413, 395.

[248] IV Catholici, "Life of Mar Aba," 226.

[249] Life, p. 228.

[250] Life, p. 249.

[251] The delightful casualness of the oriental prison is hardly changed to this day, though indeed it is hardly more marked than it was, say, in Newgate in the eighteenth century. The writer has known a modern Vali say, in reply to a petition on behalf of an imprisoned

Qasha, "You may take him out any Sunday for service, if you will engage to bring him back safe!"

252 About the same time, the arrival of a Qasha of the Hephthalite Turks, who was to be consecrated bishop, gave Chosroes a new idea of the extent and influence of the Church in his dominions. The tribe in question lived somewhere on the river Oxus.

253 Liber Turris.
254 *S. O.*, 97. 354.
255 Liber Turris.
256 Ibid.
257 Liber Turris.
258 Bar-Hebraeus.
259 *S. O.*, 111, 368.
260 "Elias, Damasc.," Ass., iii. 434. Liber Turris.
261 Liber Turris.
262 Modern Assyrians trace back this observance to the fast of the Ninevites in the days of Jonah. Without accepting that identification, one may note that the Bautha fast and subsequent feast are observed not only by the Assyrians of modern days, but by the Yezidis (Devil-worshippers) also. This fact makes it appear probable that the fast of the sixth century has been "grafted on to" another and much older observance.
263 Liber Turris.
264 Tabari, p. 268.
265 Tabari, 268; Rawlinson, ch. xx.
266 Liber Turris, Amr, Ass., iii. 110. Assemani declares Ishu-yahb must have concealed heresy to be so accepted. His writings certainly conceal it very effectually.
267 *S. O.*, 133, 294; 192, 452.
268 See, on this point, the doctrines of the Assembly of Bishops, 612 (*S. O.*, 565, 582).
269 *S. O.*, Council of Ishu-yahb, Canon II.
270 Ass., iii. 444. Life of Sabr-Ishu (Bedj., *IV Cath.*), p. 303.

271 Guidi, Chron., p. 7. Liber Turris refers the incident to another war.
272 Life, p. 290.
273 Ibid., p. 300.
274 Guidi, pp. 11, 12.
275 The performance of animal sacrifices (a relic, no doubt, of paganism) still persists among Assyrians, but modern bishops make no special effort to check it. Any one that did would have his hands full.
276 For these sectaries, see next chapter.
277 Guidi, p. 12.
278 Guidi, p. 16.
279 Ibid., p. 16; Liber Turris.
280 Guidi, p. 18.
281 Zach., Mityl., vii. 7.
282 Joseph, Canon II, *S. O.*
283 *Forced labour on bridges, etc. This danger at least has passed; roads and bridges are not maintained (S. O., Joseph, xii.).*
284 This danger is really an argument, during the present distress, for the present odd hereditary system. It at least provides as good a chance of a good bishop as of a good King!
285 That they existed still, appears from Canons XI and XVII of Josephus.
286 *S. O.*, 79, 331.
287 *S. O.*, 87, 342.
288 *Thomas of Marga*, i. xxxv.
289 Life of Mar Giwergis (Bedj., *IV Cath.*), p. 452, 448.
290 Joseph., Can. XI; Ezekiel, Can. XXV, XXX; Ishu-yahb, Can. VI.
291 This ingenious expedient is now impossible; the authorities hinting that as "Simon Peter, son of Jonas, Fisherman of Capernaum, vilayet of Beyrout," and "Paul, tentmaker of Tarsus, vilayet of Adana," were now dead, and had apparently died intestate, their trust property reverted to the ministry of pious benefactions.

292 For a discussion of the whole question, see Budge, *Book of Governors*, "Excursus on Mesopotamian monasticism."
293 Budge, *T. of M.*, vol. i. p. cxxxiv.
294 *T. of M.*, Bk. I. ch. viii.
295 Chabot, *Isaac of Nineveh*. Only comparison of those two very different works, *Isaac of Nineveh and The Miracle of Purun Bhagat* (Second Jungle Book), will show how very much the Indian and the Mesopotamian ascetic have in common, under the differences of their faith.
296 Theodoret, viii. 10.
297 In one case at least, perhaps in others, "founder's kin" claimed a visitor's rights in the monastery (*T. of M.*, i. vii.-x.).
298 Sozomen, ii. 12.
299 Sozomen, ii. 12.
300 Assem., iv. 929.
301 Ibid., iv. 932.
302 Arab Nicene Canons, Assem., iv. 934.
303 Liber Turris: Life of Dinkha.
304 Ecole de Nisibe, histoire et statuts. Chabot.
305 There was one exception to this, and we must chronicle the most magnificent instance of the obstinately separate existence of a *melet* that one is likely to find. The village of San, the ancient Tanis, is inhabited by a people of a non-Egyptian type, who are, and always have been, "Melkite" or "Orthodox" in faith. Tanis was the capital of the Hyksos Kings of Egypt, and the people of that place have maintained a separate existence, and probably a separate religion, since the Hyksos were expelled, about 1500 B.C. See Pinches, *Old Testament in Light of Historic Records*, p. 266.
306 B.-H., 104.
307 B.-H., 100.
308 It was on this occasion that 2000 Christian maidens, hearing that they were to be presented to the Sultan of the Turks, unanimously drowned themselves (John of Ephesus, vi.).
309 *S. O.*, Councils of Ishu-yahb and Sabr-Ishu.
310 Assemani, iii. 81.
311 There is no reference to the matter in Ezekiel's Council in 576, but the battle was over, before the assembly of that of Ishu-yahb, in 585.
312 Life of Giwergis, IV Cath., p. 483.
313 *S. O.*, Ishu-yahb, Canon II. Theodore, who anticipated many of the conclusions of modern critics, had ascribed it to a non-Jewish author, probably an Edomite.
314 *S. O.*, 208, 471.
315 Liber Turris.
316 *T. of Marga*, i. xxxvi.
317 B.-H., 108. Liber Turris.
318 Amr. Assemani, ii. 451.
319 *S. O.*, 212, 476.
320 During the Macedonian disorders, the Orthodox Patriarch at Constantinople was convinced throughout that peace and order would be assured if only the Ottoman Government would enforce his spiritual authority over all "Exarchists," "Vlachs" and other separatist bodies in the provinces concerned.
321 B.-H., 108.
322 *Thomas of Marga*, i. xxv.
323 Assem., iii. 451.
324 Guidi, p. 13, 17.
325 *T. of M.*, I. Xxvii.
326 Council of Isaac, Canon XX.
327 At Mashita. See p. 20.
328 Life of Giwergis, p. 505.
329 Life of Giwergis, p. 513, IV Catholici.
330 Life, p. 516-520; *S. O.*, 565, 582.
331 *S. O.*, 567, 585.
332 The term is one which may be either "man" or "manhood."
333 Life, p. 520-500; Guidi, p. 22; Labourt, p. 228.

³³⁴ Life, p. 526. There must be an error here. Chosroes acceded 590, and Giwergis was certainly a Christian in the time of his predecessor. See p. 72. "The sixth year of your Father" may be the right reading.

³³⁵ B.-H., 112.

³³⁶ "Crucifixion" under the Sassanids did not imply what we understand by the term. The victim was hung up, usually by the hands, to a stake, and shot to death with arrows. It might, therefore, be a very speedy and merciful death.

³³⁷ T. of M., i. xxxv.

³³⁸ One thousand pieces of gold per day appears to have been the sum which the "farmer-general" contracted to pay to the Shah-in-Shah, I. c.

³³⁹ Tabari, p. 261.

³⁴⁰ Thomas of Margo, i. xxxv. Babai, one notes with some regret, seems to have afterwards been sorry for the act of self-abnegation. On returning to his cell he had a vision of an angel standing there, who said, "With your leave, I now depart from thee." "Who art thou?" said the abbot. "I am the angel of the Catholicate of the East," replied the vision; "while thou didst fill the office, I was charged to be with thee ever. Now that thou hast given it to another, suffer me to go to him." "Had I known that thou was with me, I had not refused the charge," said Babai; "now depart, and pray for me."

³⁴¹ B.-H., Life of Athanasius, iii. p. 132.

³⁴² Afraat, Mimra I.

³⁴³ Mimra, vi, II. The word for "reality" is qnuma.

³⁴⁴ It will be seen that the creed has the general features of the primitive baptismal creeds, viz. confession of Father, Son and Holy Spirit; and of the Resurrection and Baptism.

³⁴⁵ For a discussion of the question of the relations of the present-day creed with that of the council, see p. 93.

³⁴⁶ Council of Ishu-yahb, S. O., 136, 398.

³⁴⁷ Lit. "dispensation." Another instance of terms borrowed from the Greek.

³⁴⁸ Syr. ܢܩܝܦܘܬܐ, naqiputha.

³⁴⁹ So I render parsopa throughout, believing (as I shall show later) that I am doing only justice thereby. It will be seen that Narses uses the term of the Persons of the Trinity. "Essential being," as used by him, is equivalent to Godhead (ܐܠܗܘܬܐ, Ithutha), and qnuma is practically "substance."

³⁵⁰ Chaps. viii, ix. The historic statements made by Narses concerning Nestorius and Cyril do not concern us. Some are utterly mistaken, some half true.

³⁵¹ e.g. Matt. xviii. 10; 2 Cor, ii, 10, iv. 6; Heb. ix, 24; &c.

³⁵² Council of Dad-Ishu, 49. 20. Babai, 64. 24; 65. 5. Aba, 69. 19; 74. 23; 85. 10. Joseph, 98. 11, 18; 99. 32; 100. 3; 102. 33; 104. 26. Ezekiel, 124. 7, 10; 127. 5, 7; 129. 2. Ishu-yahb, 136. 4; 142. 16; 153. 12, 21; 155. 1; 161. 10; 175. 23; 195. 24. Sabr-Ishu, 200. 16; 201. 29. Gregory, 207. 21; 208. 18; 210. 5. Gewergis, 218. 11, 22; 219. 2, 26; 233. 6; 240. 21; 242. 6. Assembly of Bishops, 565. 17; 567. 13; 573. 17; 575. 18; 577. 18; 578. 14, 20.

³⁵³ To give references to a Syriac manuscript is difficult, for reference to the paging is useless. The uses in question will be found, however, in the "De Unione Mimra I," Head v, pp. 26, 31; II. vi. p. 59; II. vii. p. 45, 46; IV. xvii. p. 141; VI. xx. p. 177, 181, 183. The MS. referred to contains the book in 260 pages.

³⁵⁴ Ishu-yahb, Letters, ed. Duval, Corpus Scr. In Thomas of Marga, Book of Governors (ed. Budge), the word occurs thirteen times in Books I, II, III; 1 theological sense, 1 doubtful (Budge translates

"person"), 2 Face or appearance, 9 "person."

355 A conspicuous instance of this occurs in the *Book of Governors*, ii. vii. Dr. Budge renders ܬܪܝܢ ܟܝܢܝܢ ܐܘܬܪܝܢ ܩܢܘܡܝܢ ܒܚܕ ܦܪܨܘܦܐ, *Trein kianein otrein Qnumein b'Khad Parsopa d'Barutha*, as "Two natures and two Persons in one created form" Surely there is a slip here. ܒܪܘܬܐ, *Barutha*, is "sonship," not "Creation," ܒܪܝܘܬܐ, *Bariutha*, and the right rendering, in the light of this writer's habitual use of ܩܢܘܡܐ, *Parsopa*, is, "Two Natures, and two 'qnumi,' in one Person of Sonship."

356 "Qnuma" in New Test.: Rom. i. 27, ix. 3; 1 Cor. vi. ix. 27, xii. 25; Eph. ii. 15; Col. ii. 15; 1 Thess. iv. 9; Heb. i. 3; ix. 28, x. 1. Probably the list is not exhaustive. One curious use may be noted, Col. ii. 15, where "in His Qnuma" appears to refer (and certainly can be interpreted as referring) solely to the humanity of Christ.

357 Bethune-Baker, p. 228. Babai, Mimra, IV, Head xvii.

358 Babai, "De Unione," 1. -v. p. 30; II. vi. p. 33; II. vi. p. 44, II. vii. p. 46; II. viii. p. 61; III. ix. p. 75; III- ix. p. 77; VI: xx. p. 181; VI. xxi. p. 222; VI. xxi. p. 223; VII. xxii. P. 248.

359 Ishu-yahb, Letters 2, 6, p. 131, Duval. Quoted also by Budge; *Book of Governors*, II. cxxxix.

360 Council of Bps: *S. O.*, 576.

361 Armenians, who are accused of Monophysitism, declare in their creed that our Lord became "body, spirit, soul, and the whole complete being of man," and that" He ascended in His own body to heaven, * * * and shall come in His own body to judge."

362 *S. O.*, p. 6. See also pp. 545, 556.

363 This "tampering with documents" has its humorous side--for those who have personal knowledge of the modern Assyrian Church. The Greek and Latin texts used were those given by Heurtley.

364 The Assyrian Church, or at least some of its writers, does use the formula "one will" as applied to our Lord. I am not aware of any evidence, however, that connects this directly with the Ecthesis of Heraclius. Incidentally it may be observed that when a Church lays itself open to the charges of the two contradictory heresies of Nestorianism and Monophysitism, there is at least a case for supposing that it is, to intention, Orthodox; even if it be clumsy in expression.

365 *Thomas of Marga*, ii. iv.

366 Liber Turris.

367 B.-H., 116.

368 Liber Turris. The Arabic word used and translated as *a singular* is Shakhsiet, which has no etymological equivalent in Syriac. The writer cannot undertake to say how it stands to the terms *Parsopa* and *Qnuma*. Probably *Parsoputha* would be the nearest form.

369 As late 'as the ninth century, Theodore Bar Koni still regards the use of the term as indifferent. Since then, it has become the battle-cry of independence.

370 So Noldeke, Tabari, Geschichter, der Perser, 392. Probably, however, the relic had been surrendered previously. See Budge, T. of Marga, ii. 125, note.

371 *T. of Marga*, ii. iv.

372 I purposely abstain from using the term "Catholic"; partly as it is, under the circumstances, a question-begging epithet; partly because it is doubtful whether the "Emperor's Church" was at that moment technically Catholic, and not Monothelite.

373 Ishu-yahb, Letter 6, p. 123- Budge, *T. of Marga*, ii. 138-9.

[374] Ishu-yahb, Letter 7, p. 131.
[375] Ishu-yahb, Letter 30, p. 212. Budge, ii. 146.
[376] *e.g.* the strictest Mussulman will eat an animal slaughtered by one of the house in question, which he will often refuse to do normally. A similar firman of protection (or what is held to be such) is preserved at one particular "Nestorian" Church (Mar Zeia, Jilu), and has repeatedly saved that shrine from being plundered by the Kurds.
[377] See *History of Rabban Soma*, Bedj., *IV Catholici*, pp. 53-84. It is noteworthy that this wanderer, who presented a confession of faith similar to that used at present (two natures, two Qnumi, one Parsopa in Christ), was received as orthodox at Rome. It is a fine point, whether this proves the orthodoxy of the confession, or the ignorance of the Pope qua private doctor. See p. 60 of authority quoted.

www.ingramcontent.com/pod-product-compliance
Lightning Source LLC
LaVergne TN
LVHW011419080426
835512LV00005B/154